PRINCIPLED RESISTANCE

PRINCIPLED RESISTANCE

*How Teachers Resolve
Ethical Dilemmas*

Doris A. Santoro
Lizabeth Cain
Editors

HARVARD EDUCATION PRESS
CAMBRIDGE, MASSACHUSETTS

Paperback ISBN 978-1-68253-227-0
Library Edition ISBN 978-1-68253-228-7

Library of Congress Cataloging-in-Publication Data

Names: Santoro, Doris A., editor. | Cain, Lizabeth, editor.
Title: Principled resistance : how teachers resolve ethical dilemmas / Doris
    A. Santoro, Llizabeth Cain, editors.
Description: Cambridge, Massachusetts : Harvard Education Press, 2018. |
    Includes bibliographical references and index.
Identifiers: LCCN 2018022062| ISBN 9781682532270 (pbk.) | ISBN 9781682532287
    (library edition)
Subjects: LCSH: Teachers—Professional ethics. | Teaching—Moral and ethical
    aspects. | Education—Moral and ethical aspects. | Education—Philosophy.
Classification: LCC LB1779 .P55 2018 | DDC 371.102—dc23 LC record available
    at https://lccn.loc.gov/2018022062

Published by Harvard Education Press,
an imprint of the Harvard Education Publishing Group

Harvard Education Press
8 Story Street
Cambridge, MA 02138

Cover Design: Wilcox Design
Cover Image: *Indigo/Study in Blue No. 1* by Heather Chontos

The typefaces used in this book are Adobe Garamond Pro and Helvetica Neue.

Contents

INTRODUCTION

Doris A. Santoro and Lizabeth Cain

TEACHERS WHO WORK IN PUBLIC SCHOOLS face myriad demands for compliance from an array of powerful actors: school leaders, politicians, highly paid consultants, and textbook publishers, just to name a few. Within this context, teachers' resistance is often interpreted simply as insubordination or recalcitrance. However, teacher educators, educational researchers, policy makers, and school leaders miss valuable information about how to support and motivate teachers when they fail to differentiate the motivations that result in different forms of teacher resistance.

With this book, we argue that some forms of resistance should be characterized as principled resistance, and we provide a new framework for understanding three principles upon which such resistance may emerge.[1]

This volume brings together a range of senior scholars and activist teachers to explore the concept of principled resistance as a necessary and ethical response to mandates that conflict with their understandings about quality teaching and the role of education in a democracy. Each chapter describes one teacher or group of teachers who attempt to resolve ethical dilemmas that arise when their beliefs about the purposes, significance, and standards of their work are in conflict with the policies and practices they are expected to enact.

The multiple perspectives on principled resistance presented in this volume enable us to highlight a tradition of teachers striving to shape a more just and democratic society, through and beyond their schools and work lives. Historical chapters on principled resistance reveal teachers' long-standing roles in social progress through their interpretations of their professional responsibilities. First-person contemporary accounts of principled resistance enable current teachers, who face significant demands for compliance in instruction and curricula, to envision ways to protect the mission that drew them to and sustains them in their work. Research by teacher educators invites critical discussions about the purpose and principles that should guide the teaching profession today.

Three Categories of Principles

The chapters in this book are organized by three general categories of principles that may motivate teachers' principled resistance: pedagogical, professional, and democratic. Principled resistance is rarely guided by a single principle, but we make these distinctions to highlight the kinds of concerns that disrupt teachers' sense of good work. As a heuristic device, these categories reveal that principled resistance is an expression of teachers' understanding of professional ethics, not simply a reaction out of personal preference. No particular principle is more important than the others, but each principle enables us to ask specific kinds of ethical questions about the multidimensional work of teaching.

Teachers articulate *pedagogical principles* when they make claims about working with students and the curriculum. When faced with a dilemma, teachers refer to pedagogical principles in their responses to the following questions: What is the best way for me to teach this concept, skill, or topic? What is the best way for me to teach this student or this group of students? These kinds of principles usually articulate beliefs about teachers' responsibility to support students' well-being, academic engagement, and positive outcomes. They reference beliefs about best practices, child development, youth psychology, subject-specific norms, and assessments. Principled resistance in this category can take many forms, including altering prescribed teaching materials, refusing to engage in mandated practices, or taking steps to change the policies that affect teaching and learning.

When teachers make claims that they possess power, knowledge, and judgment unique to their role, they express *professional principles*. When faced with a dilemma, teachers articulate professional principles in their responses to the question, how should I act and be treated as a teacher? For instance, teachers who express concerns about how decisions are made in their schools may be signaling that the professionalism of teachers is being violated. Concerns about salary—whether teachers can earn a living wage, or the effects of merit pay—are an invocation of professional principles. Principled resistance based on professional principles may take the form of teachers demanding rights as members of a profession with special training, knowledge, and experience. Teachers also articulate professional principles when they make claims about what teaching is and is not that extend beyond their own classrooms; many professional principles can also refer to pedagogical principles. Principled resistance is a result of teachers who respect and value their special role as public servants expected to uphold education policies of various kinds. If teachers disregarded that dimension of their work, as common portrayals of teacher resistance suggest, no dilemma of professional principles would surface.

Teachers affirm *democratic principles* when they make claims about how teachers and public schools should function in a democratic society. When faced with a dilemma, teachers articulate democratic principles in responding to the following questions: How is this school preparing its students for democratic futures? How am I promoting and embodying democratic participation? These beliefs may focus on the school as a key institution in a democracy or the role of teachers as public figures in a democracy. Principled resistance in this category may be argued on the grounds of promoting civil rights, encouraging democratic participation, or modeling democratic behavior. It is always possible for pedagogical principles and professional principles to be intertwined with democratic principles. For instance, arguments for a more inclusive curriculum or culturally competent teaching are articulations of pedagogical principles that are informed by democratic principles.

Within each category, there is room for disagreement and debate about teachers' actions and responses based on the principles described above. Taking professional principles as an example, some groups of teachers may believe that merit pay is the proper recognition for educators who perform at higher levels than their colleagues. Others may argue that collegiality and collaboration are jeopardized by the focus on student outcomes based on standardized test scores underlying merit pay schemes. A principle does not settle the matter, but it provides an axis that makes one's claims and judgments comprehensible on ethical grounds.

The Nature of Resistance

Although theories of student and youth resistance have exercised substantial influence on the field of education, research on teacher resistance has been sparse.[2] Educational leadership research often approaches teacher resistance as an obstructionist tactic to be overcome.[3] This limited view of resistance restricts the knowledge that can be gained from analyzing principled resistance, as well as the range of productive responses to teachers' resistance. As the research on youth reveals, we can read teachers' acts of resistance as expressions of their agency and intelligence.[4]

Some studies have highlighted the possibility that teacher dissatisfaction and school reform may be fueled by conflicts between the values teachers bring to their work and the principles that inform schooling and school reform.[5] Teaching has long been known as a profession with a high rate of attrition, yet US figures far exceed those of other countries.[6] In 2011, only 44 percent of teachers reported that they were "very satisfied" with their jobs, the lowest percentage in over twenty years, down from 62 percent just three years prior.[7] Social networking and the rise of media platforms such as YouTube have allowed teachers to publicize their reasons for leaving the profession, and many of them describe tensions between their principles and the values that seem to be guiding changes at their schools.[8]

Resistance, principled or otherwise, is rarely the opening salvo in teachers' attempts to uphold their professional responsibilities. Many of these chapters illustrate that teachers often begin by fulfilling the expectations expressed by their school leaders in policies. Teachers first enact strategies of negotiation and creative accommodation if they find that following the policies or mandates harms students, subverts learning, damages the profession, or is antithetical to the democratic purpose of public schools. When teachers engage in principled resistance, their actions usually come after failed attempts at dialogue or negotiation to resolve the conflict.[9]

Principled resistance, therefore, is a professional strategy of last resort, and one that may entail serious risk. Principled resistance may jeopardize teachers' standing in the profession and their communities, and may also threaten their livelihoods. In making their professional commitments public, teachers may risk disparagement and conflict when others disagree with the principles that motivate their actions. Instances of principled resistance provide a unique opportunity to examine the core beliefs and commitments that teachers reveal through these resistant acts. As we will show in this volume, there is constancy in teachers' commitments to the well-being of their students, their profession, and the role of public schools in a democratic society. However, this constancy does not necessarily indicate consensus; these chapters illustrate that while principled resistance is often a collaborative action, the decision to undertake it can be contentious.

Teachers who engage in principled resistance are not acting alone, but in implied or actual solidarity with others through an appeal to ethics rooted in their practice. John Dewey explains, "What is learned and employed in an occupation having an aim and involving cooperation with others is moral knowledge, whether consciously so regarded or not. For it builds up a social interest and confers the intelligence needed to make that interest effective in practice."[10] The teaching profession, like many other forms of work and life, constitutes a community of practice in which a group of practitioners share a common vocabulary and set of experiences. The members of this community recognize and share many fundamental goals and tenets that guide the profession. Yet they also need to continuously participate in self-critical communities of practice.[11] Philosopher of education Thomas F. Green calls common understandings of what constitutes good work "craft conscience."[12] Shared orientations toward good work provide the principles by which teachers recognize and assess their own and their colleagues' actions.

Linda Darling-Hammond has argued, "It is unethical for a teacher to conform to prescribed practices that are ultimately harmful to children. Yet that is what teachers are required to do by policies that are pedagogically inappropriate to some or all of their students."[13] Principled resistance often points to a conflict between teachers who view themselves as professionals and those who would cast teachers as paid laborers. Barbara S. Stengel and Mary E. Casey explain that pedagogical responsibility entails judgment rooted in the thoughtful assessment and interpretation of policies and principles in particular situations: "[T]eaching is not merely a matter of adhering to prescribed strategies of instruction, nor is it merely enacting a predetermined philosophical vision in one's classroom, nor is it merely exemplifying a set of pedagogical virtues—though strategies, visions, and virtues are among the teacher's tools."[14] Pedagogical responsibility can be achieved only by granting teachers the moral and professional status to evaluate their work in light of their professional ideals or principles.

Teachers' acts of principled resistance illuminate how they understand the fundamental responsibilities of teachers and the teaching profession. By maintaining the boundaries of their professional responsibilities to students and society, teachers make schools stronger when they demand that education policies align with the ideals of the teaching profession. Teachers take significant risks when they engage in principled resistance, and because they occupy a unique, privileged position in the classrooms of the United States, it is incumbent upon members of the public to give teachers' acts and articulations of ethical concern full weight. As we face ongoing dilemmas in the reform of public schools, teachers' resistance must be consulted for the principles that could guide our future actions.

The dilemmas that may evoke principled resistance threaten teachers' understandings of good work—that is, they are dilemmas that invoke professional ethics. These dilemmas are in a class distinct from teaching's more quotidian tensions, which include how to meet the needs of individuals versus the needs of the whole class, how to teach students in the present for an unknown future, how to share knowledge while teaching students to be critical of knowledge, and how to care for and protect young people who are not one's own children. These dilemmas also raise ethical concerns, but on a different scale; asking these questions is part and parcel of good teaching. Our position is that principled resistance illustrates deeper and more troubling dilemmas rooted in the work of teaching that have the potential to threaten it as a profession; it is this destructive potential that teachers resist.

Although teaching is a value-laden profession where every choice made and action taken by teachers communicates a belief about what constitutes good teaching, teachers may give little conscious thought to the principles that guide their work. This indifference is not an indication that teachers are failing to take the proper philosophical attitude. Rather, as Dewey and other philosophers have argued, ethical deliberation is an exception to the rule. We are spurred into inquiry and reflection by tensions, dilemmas, and conflicts about what we are to do in a problematic situation.[15]

In times when we are torn between different courses of action, our principles, or guiding beliefs and core commitments, rise to the surface. Principles are not rules; they do not easily settle conflicts or make choices in moral situations straightforward. Dewey explains that "the object of moral principles is to supply standpoints and methods which will enable the individual to make for himself an analysis of the elements of good and evil in the particular situation in which he finds himself. No genuine moral principle prescribes a specific course of action."[16]

Principles provide us with an opportunity to assess our past and current actions in light of the ideals we hope to embody. Dewey argues that articulating principles enables thoughtful action. He writes, "The principle is not what justifies an activity, for the principle is but another name for the continuity of the activity."[17] Examining principled resistance enables us to see more than the obvious fact that teachers possess principles about their work. We can also gain insight into the kind of teaching and schooling, the activity and its purpose, that they are trying to sustain.

About This Book

This book focuses on teachers' principled resistance from the early twentieth century to the present. We selected contributors who could provide vivid examples of the pedagogical, professional, and democratic principles that may motivate teachers' principled resistance. Each author offers a distinct perspective: teachers who reflect on their acts of principled resistance; teacher educators who study teachers and support their professional growth; historians who demonstrate that a tradition of teachers' principled resistance has had a significant impact on American society, not only on schools and teaching.

Across the disciplinary perspectives of the contributors, each chapter in this volume exemplifies professional ethics in action. The authors uncover, render visible, and clarify the values that shape teachers' work in situations of ethical dilemmas. The authors in this volume enable us to demystify why and how teachers engage in principled resistance by showing the steps they take, in their reasoning and in their actions, to resist policies and mandates they are expected to enact.

Readers will have an opportunity to examine a variety of ways to engage in and analyze principled resistance. The chapters are grouped according to the type of principle invoked by the resistance, but each case provides opportunities to consider how pedagogical, professional, and democratic principles may work in concert or be in conflict with one another. We invite readers, teachers especially, to examine their reactions to the examples in this volume. Those reactions may yield important information about their own professional principles.

Chapters 1–4 focus on resistance rooted in pedagogical principles. In chapter 1, veteran Chicago public school teacher Michelle Strater Gunderson charts her individual resistance to the Common Core State Standards and how it became part of the collective resistance of the Chicago Teachers Union that emerged from pedagogical principles. The Chicago Teachers Union passed a resolution in opposition to the Common Core State Standards and launched a successful effort to bring it to the floor for debate at the annual convention of the American Federation of Teachers. This chapter provides insight into the strategies of a union local that used its collective power and influence to effect change in education policy and practice.

In chapter 2, teacher educator Clive Beck and his colleagues draw on a longitudinal study of early-career teachers to explore how and why teachers resist institutional and policy mandates. Their findings suggest that schools of education that teach critical, constructivist pedagogies may plant the seeds for principled resistance based on pedagogical principles. The authors recommend that teacher educators take responsibility for preparing their students to engage in principled resistance. The authors conclude that teacher resistance needs to be researched and documented by those less vulnerable than teachers (e.g., academics), thus informing teachers, teacher educators, and policy developers about its form, rationale, and impact.

Randy R. Miller, Sr. describes his principled resistance to no-excuses discipline in chapter 3. Comparing his tenure as a teacher in two Camden, New Jersey, charter schools, he highlights a moment when he could no longer uphold the no-excuses compliance expectations for students. Miller realized that principled resistance was necessary to fulfill his pedagogical commitments to critical thinking and meeting students' needs. Ultimately, he was compelled to ask himself who or what would define him as an educator. Miller writes this chapter as an invitation to teachers of color to examine the beliefs that guide their identities as educators. His response embodies the paradox of conscientious objectors; he refused to violate the way students would be treated in his teaching practice, but that led him to leave his teaching position, where had been committed to serving Black and Brown students well.

Chapter 4 offers another perspective from teacher educators. Alisun Thompson and Lucinda Pease-Alvarez describe a powerful collaboration between teachers resisting a compliance-based work environment and university-based collaborators and researchers. The authors portray teachers as agents of educational policy. They study a teacher collective in Northern California that has resisted policies of standardization aimed at requiring them to teach and assess students in ways that ignore students' instructional needs, interests, and experiences. As members of the collective, the authors use participatory and ethnographic approaches to describe how teacher resistance and agency are implicated in the educational policy-making process. The history of this organization will be instructive for those who want to create synergies between experienced teachers and university-based teacher educators.

Chapters 5–8 focus on professional principles. In chapter 5, Emma Long chronicles the history of the lengthy and successful strike of New Orleans public school teachers in 1990. This strike illustrates the solidarity between certified teachers and the paraprofessionals and clerical workers that make their work possible. It also highlights the teachers' commitment to professional recognition for their lowest-paid coworkers. The teachers' oral accounts of this strike indicate that they organized a campaign to unseat the school board based on strategies learned through their prior involvement in the civil rights movement. Long's chapter will be instructive to any teacher union planning to take a stand against its school board on matters of professional principles.

In chapter 6, Margaret Smith Crocco examines some of the dilemmas facing teacher education in three different states in which schooling and teacher preparation are being shaped by various neoliberal reforms, particularly privatization. In this chapter, she notes that teacher education appears caught between forces advancing greater professionalization through regulation (e.g., Council for the Accreditation of Educator Preparation) and those seemingly bent on de-professionalization (e.g., Teach for America and charter schools). She considers how to create hope and principled resistance in both teachers and teacher educators in the face of these challenges, especially through local alliances and online activism.

In chapter 7, Tom Meyer, Christine McCartney, and Jaqueline Hesse outline their process of helping teachers to articulate and make public their professional principles. The authors describe how they run a National Writing Project invitational institute that enables teachers to become more confident as they write for broader audiences and make their professional commitments known. Drawing on the writing of past participants, they show that workshops like these can develop teacher leadership that may include principled resistance.

In chapter 8, teacher Jocelyn Weeda analyzes her own act of principled resistance when she called upon families and their children to exercise their right to refuse high-stakes tests in her state. She describes how building and district administrators portrayed her principled resistance as an expression of personal beliefs, when she knew her motivations came from professional commitments. Weeda draws on her doctoral research in which she interviewed other teachers engaged in principled resistance. She found that their resistance emanated from a sense of professional responsibility. When she could not find community in her building or support from her administration, the alliances Weeda had developed on social media provided her with support and solidarity during a very difficult time in her career.

Democratic principles are the focus of chapters 9–12. In chapter 9, Lizabeth Cain recounts the experience of New York City teachers during the second Red Scare, using archival research of their personal and public correspondence as well as their formal teaching evaluations. They were accused of "insubordination and conduct unbecoming a teacher" for refusing to respond to questions implicating them and their colleagues as Communists. Aware of the political climate, the teachers knew their principled resistance would cost them their jobs, but they also believed they had an important role to play as educators in a democracy. These teachers were determined to use their positions to speak out against antidemocratic policies.

Karen Graves and Margaret A. Nash undertake historical research in chapter 10, which traces the history of the court battles of lesbian, gay, bisexual, and transgender (LGBT) teachers who demanded equal protection under the law. Since the Cold War, queer perceived/identified teachers in the United States have worked under strict public scrutiny. As the political terrain has shifted from gay purges to civil rights battles, LGBT teachers have adopted a number of strategies to maintain their jobs in elementary and secondary schools. In courtrooms stretching across the country, teachers and other school workers have taken public stands to challenge dismissals based on flawed claims of immorality, at great personal cost. At times these acts of principled resistance have resulted in legal steps toward equal employment protection for LGBT educators. They laid the foundation for the Supreme Court decision on gay marriage, even as the individuals named in the cases were not able to reclaim their own jobs.

Adah Ward Randolph and Dwan V. Robinson describe the life of Ethel T. Overby in chapter 11. Overby, an early twentieth-century African American teacher and school principal, spurred her community to resist injustice through her work in schools and other community organizations. Overby leveraged her education and leadership to challenge segregated schools and libraries, and to help Black citizens to overcome hurdles to accessing literacy and exercising their democratic right to vote. The authors highlight Overby's resistance and describe how her educational philosophy and practices fostered democratic change in Richmond, Virginia.

In chapter 12, teacher educators Jessica Hochman, Doris A. Santoro, and Stephen Houser note that teachers have been exhorted to turn to Twitter to connect their classrooms with the world, at the same time that others are warned to stay off social media to express professional concerns. The authors explore both the tweeting practices of teachers and the content of teachers' tweets. They show that Twitter offers a democratic space where teachers can use their voices to shape the discourse about teaching, find professional community, and support each other in acts of principled resistance. Their study shows that Twitter can be a site of principled resistance, where teachers are able to circumvent and challenge dominant narratives of teaching and education policy.

We conclude this volume with some provocations about principled resistance. What gives teachers the moral or political authority to make the decision to resist? How can they, and others, distinguish between principled resistance and justified civil disobedience, on the one hand, and antidemocratic, insubordinate rejections of democratically adopted policies, on the other? What are the limits of teachers' principled resistance, especially in the face of reforms financed by corporate entities with seemingly limitless budgets? What is the value of teachers' principled resistance if it might cost them their jobs? Most importantly, what responsibilities do we have to hear and heed the concerns of teachers, when they risk their jobs and reputations to bring attention to the erosion of schools as places where the highest principles of our society can take shape and expression?

PART ONE

Pedagogical Principles

CHAPTER ONE

THE CHICAGO TEACHERS UNION'S REJECTION OF THE COMMON CORE

A Case History of Teacher Resistance

Michelle Strater Gunderson

"LET'S MAKE THIS REALLY CLEAR. The Common Core standards were not created with teaching and learning in mind. They were created with testing in mind." These were the opening words to my speech before the American Federation of Teachers (AFT) during the Common Core debate at the 2014 national convention.

After careful analysis of the Common Core State Standards, the Chicago Teachers Union formed a national strategy to oppose the use of the standards in any form. This chapter is the narrative of my role in this decision and the careful and deliberate process that our union undertook to develop our strategy of principled resistance. It is an attempt to pull back the curtain for a moment and help others understand one distinct story of principled resistance. It is an account of personal awareness of pedagogy and policies linked to the

Common Core that I believed were harming children—they were a set of standards that I found developmentally inappropriate and rife with overtesting. From that viewpoint, I engaged with others to use the formal structures of our union to oppose Common Core on a national scale. As members of the Chicago Teachers Union, we opposed the Common Core because we believe that teachers and students should drive instruction and that decisions about teaching and learning should be made locally. We believe that teachers are professionals who hold pedagogical knowledge and knowledge of their individual students and that they can and should be trusted with instructional decision making.

The research questions that drive this chapter are as follows: How does an educator decide to take a principled stand against forces affecting her students, profession, and community? And how can union processes be used to amplify this stance to a larger level of resistance? This chapter also provides insight into how the Chicago Teachers Union uses its collective power and influence to effect change in education policy and practice. I hope this narrative can inform other forms of principled resistance and help others doing similar work.

This chapter is written in the first person. The resolution against the Common Core came from the committee that I chair, and I am considered its author (though union resolutions are a unique form of declarative writing that are written collectively). I wrote this chapter using my field notes, minutes from meetings, union documents, transcripts from video, analysis of the #AFT14 Twitter interactions, and interviews with key participants in the process. In the end, the manuscript for this chapter was reviewed by three members of the Chicago Teachers Union who were close to the process to evaluate for accuracy of events and clarity of interpretation. This was a highly personal journey for me as the driver of this work, yet I have made every effort to give a balanced view of the process. The resistance to the Common Core in Chicago was generated by classroom teachers fully immersed in the process and grounded in daily practice. This principled stand was not a top-down initiative of either our Chicago Teachers Union leadership or people who hold national acclaim as education leaders.

Building Personal Awareness

I have been an active member of the Chicago Teachers Union since 1993, when I began teaching in Chicago. My commitment and activity, however, had always been at the school level. I would work with our union delegate to make sure our school was a safe and healthy worksite and that our contract was upheld. It was not until the initial school closings in Chicago during 2010 that I became active as a leader. I kept running into the same people at community actions and meetings. They were members of a group called CORE (Caucus of Rank and File Educators). The members of CORE spoke at every gathering with passion and intellectual integrity. When I looked around to see who else was fighting school closings, it was clear that this group of educators and unionists knew how to organize and how to fight back against the systematic destruction of our school system. I soon aligned with this caucus and became a teacher leader within its ranks.

CORE is the driving caucus behind the leadership of the Chicago Teachers Union; that is, it currently drives the union's priorities and processes. Its bylaws reflect its core principles, including a commitment to a member-driven union; transparency and accountability for union processes; education for all, which involves partnerships with communities and parents; and defense of a publicly funded public education. CORE organized and mounted a strike in 2012 that mobilized close to 30,000 teachers. During this strike, we made it clear that our goals for education justice in Chicago went beyond bread-and-butter issues, such as pay and working conditions. We would fight for social justice issues, such as community services and counselors, and against the overtesting of students. After the strike was settled, our union local, through CORE's leadership, became a recognized leader in social justice unionism. Our next goal would be confronting national policies that we believed were harming our students and, in turn, educators. Those policies included the adoption and use of the Common Core State Standards and the subsequent testing that aligned with them.

Created in 2010, the Common Core State Standards (CCSS) were adopted by members of the College Board and the National Governors Association. The standards are not a national curriculum, but they were linked to waivers for No Child Left Behind and Race to the Top applications. Since they have been adopted by forty-six states, it could be argued that CCSS have become de facto national standards. The rationale behind CCSS is that they will lessen the disparities in educational experiences from state to state and that they will ensure a new rigor across the curriculum. The standards are linked to an ideology that American schools are falling behind in global competition. Arne Duncan, who was US Secretary of Education when the CCSS were promoted and adopted, said, "As the nation seeks to maintain our international competitiveness, ensure all students regardless of background have access to high quality education, and prepare all students for college, work and citizenship, these standards are an important foundation for our collective work."[1]

I teach in a neighborhood school that is part of the Chicago Public Schools. During the summer of 2012, I was hired by my school administration to write curriculum maps for our fourth-grade team that aligned to the Common Core. The work was actually quite easy. Most of what we were already doing in fourth grade clearly connected to the new standards. During this time I was reading and hearing opposition to the Common Core, but I really did not see what all the fuss was about. In a conversation I had with Kris Nielson, a blogger and critic of the CCSS, he said, "That is the problem with the Common Core. The standards are not universally horrid and some of them are deceptively good." He went on to explain that the entire process of the standards, testing, and evaluation were being used to transform our schools in ways he believed ate away at professional independence and personal relationships with children. At the time, I understood what he was saying, but his analysis did not reflect my lived experience as a teacher.

The following year changed my entire perspective. I was transferred from teaching fourth grade to first grade. It was during the course of planning inside of an early childhood program that it became apparent that the influence of the Common Core was having a direct negative impact on the teaching and learning in my classroom. The shift in reading instruction brought on by CCSS was swift and pervasive, and the requirements in early education seemed severe. Children in kindergarten are expected to read by the end of the year, and literacy in this grade is no longer considered adequate if teaching and learning are focused on letter and sound relationships. While working with the Common Core in my lesson planning, I could see that it was based on the end results of education, but it did not take into consideration the process needed to get there, nor did it consider the different rates and means by which young children attain reading proficiency.

At this juncture, I sought out reading and research on the Common Core, wondering whether other educators were having similar experiences. I found very little available in the academic literature that was critical of the standards. I was a doctoral student at Loyola University Chicago at that time, and the perspective offered in my coursework involved a considerable amount of

Common Core cheerleading. I found allies in the work of Nancy Carlsson-Paige from Lesley University, who was a senior advisor to the advocacy group Defending the Early Years, and in Anthony Cody, a blogger and author. Obviously, this was not a comprehensive review of the literature, but their work reflected what I was experiencing in the classroom.

Defending the Early Years is dedicated to ensuring appropriate practices for early childhood education and providing support for teachers who believe they need to resist reforms harmful to their students and their teaching practice. Carlsson-Paige and her colleagues make an argument for the developmental inappropriateness of the Common Core. The following syllogism resonated most strongly with me:

> For example, the average age that children start walking is 12 months. Some children being walking as early as 9 months and others not until 15 months—and all of this falls within a normal range. Early walkers are not better walkers than later walkers. A second example is that the average age at which children learn to read independently is 6.5 years. Some begin as early as 4 years and some not until age 7 or later—and all of this falls with the normal range.[2]

I have since joined the advisory board of Defending the Early Years as another alliance to support my principled resistance to the CCSS.

Cody's *Education Week* blog entry "Common Core Standards: Ten Colossal Errors" also shaped my personal understanding.[3] Cody argues that the Common Core is narrowly focused on the utilitarian philosophy of education as preparation for college and career. I consider myself a progressive educator with a strong philosophy of the purpose and promise of education. I view public education as a means for educating a populace of critical thinkers who will be able to shape a just and equitable society, and I believe that education can be a means to a good and purpose-filled life. This perspective entails more than the narrow focus on individual end-point outcomes. It had become clear that the very purpose and design of the Common Core was antithetical to what I believed as an educator, and I decided to take a principled stance.

Turning a Principled Stance into Collective Resistance

In 2013, the year following the Chicago Teachers Union strike, CORE conducted small book groups centered on Diane Ravitch's book *Reign of Error.*[4] CORE used one of its foundational principles, defense of publicly funded public education, to guide these conversations: "Whereas public education is under attack from a well-funded group of business interests, politicians, privatizers and enemies of publicly funded public education, CORE seeks to defend publicly funded public education as the last bastion of democratic expression and hope for students in all public schools across Chicago."[5]

With this strong framework as our guide and Ravitch's book as an anchor to our discussions, we began connecting our own classroom experiences to what we believed to be an attack on public education, and especially the education of the urban poor. I wrote a blog about the process, and I received some criticism that our choice of reading material was too one-sided. The complaint was that we were not being critical thinkers and impartially approaching the issue. This might seem a valid argument, but it was not the case. For an entire year we all underwent district-wide professional development that presented only a pro–Common Core stance. I spent hours poring over the standards in order to build curriculum maps, and I read dozens of articles promoting the Common Core.

Our choice of Ravitch's book was a way to broaden the stream of information from the one-sided perspective provided by our school district, not to narrow it.

Sitting in each other's living rooms, we recounted stories of students who were required to repeat entire grades because of seemingly arbitrary cut scores on tests aligned with the Common Core, teachers who were forced to teach from dull and narrow scripted curricula that were supposedly based on the standards. One early childhood teacher told the story of her principal entering the classroom for an informal evaluation. The teacher recounted that the children were actively playing at different centers throughout the room. These learning activities had been carefully planned and explicitly taught to the children so that the students could be self-directed. The activities included block play, a dramatic play area, small motor activities, and art exploration. The teacher was working with two children building sentences and taking them apart using their own dictated word cards. By any measure, this was the picture of a well-run and appropriate kindergarten. The principal turned to her and said, "I will come back when you are teaching." Later that week the teacher was told that if children were playing in the classroom, every activity must have a Common Core objective and that it would be required in writing.

Our collective understandings enabled us to realize that the CCSS undermined teacher expertise and led to disengagement that would further diminish student achievement and well-being. We asked teachers to think about the goals they had for students in their particular discipline and to keep in mind their philosophy of education while analyzing the standards. For my own practice, I looked at my philosophy of reading instruction. I believe in student self-selection of texts as motivational to student reading engagement. The Common Core practice of focusing on non-fiction work and the skill of "close reading"—the breaking down of small portions of text without the context of the whole work—were counter to my understanding of child development and reading processes. I also had grave concerns about the insistence that students work at "grade level" as stated in the standards. Our collective conclusion was that the CCSS were premised only on outcomes instead of on the interests and individual abilities of children; this ran totally against our principles as educators to meet students where they are. Furthermore, we determined that students *and* teachers were being evaluated in ways that did not accurately assess the quality of their learning or work. Through these conversations and book groups, we came to some collective conclusions about the current landscape. First, we were being asked to completely change entire curricula—things we knew well and taught well. Second, the curricula that the Chicago Public Schools provided us were scripted, test-based, and dull. And third, students and teachers were being evaluated on Common Core lessons and tests that had very little to do with what we considered authentic learning. One of our colleagues said, "It is as if they [the Chicago Schools] are making schools so boring that kids fail—and teachers fail."

We also realized it was not only the Department of Education and various corporate entities that were promoting the Common Core and the aligned tests; our parent union, the AFT, had spent time and energy promoting the Common Core standards as the answer to failing schools. The argument was that the Common Core itself was not flawed, but that teachers needed more training to deliver the instruction appropriately. Even our own union local had accepted grants to promote the Common Core through professional development and outreach. It was clear that we were up against a wide variety of stakeholders who did not see the problem as we did on the ground.

Union support at the local level was not universal. There were other union locals in the AFT that believed the Common Core should be rewritten. Some argued that implementation was the problem, and that the union should spend money on resources and training. Yet the educators in CORE looked at our experiences and how the Common Core was negatively affecting our students and our work. With a philosophical underpinning so drastically divergent from that of the Common Core, we did not have room for common ground with other locals who believed that the Common Core could be redeemed. We opposed the Common Core in any form or implementation. We harnessed our national union structure as the vehicle to oppose the standards we saw as harmful to students and their educations, standards that undermined the principles that guided our teaching.

Opposing the Common Core Through Union Work

We needed to follow official union processes in order to formally continue our local opposition. The first order of business was writing a resolution that outlined the current state of the problem and defined the actions that we believed the union must take. A union resolution is a very prescriptive and formal genre of writing. I gathered all the materials collected from the CORE group conversations and set to the task of writing the initial draft of the resolution. It then went through several revisions in the education committee I chair. Next, the resolution was brought before the Chicago Teachers Union executive board, and finally it passed unanimously at our House of Delegates with the mandate to send the resolution on to the 2014 AFT national convention. The statement by the Chicago Teachers Union at the end of our position paper sums up the thinking of the collective: "While Common Core Standards may appear to be benign or even helpful, they are part and parcel of the corporate reform strategy. Standards coupled with testing, and evaluation tied to student test scores, set the stage for greater control of what is taught in each classroom—destroying teacher discretion, and pressuring teachers to ignore the needs of the students in front of them by focusing on the fulfillment of requirements set by the school district."[6]

As union activists, we knew that there would be considerable objections from our national union, corporate education publishers, and individuals who are paid to promote and implement the Common Core. Yet we felt a moral obligation to our students, educators, and communities to engage in conversations that raised awareness and challenged presumptions about the Common Core. We printed three thousand copies of a position paper to distribute at the AFT national convention and made the paper available online. The opening paragraph succinctly addresses our reasons for this form of principled resistance:

> The Chicago Teachers Union is committed to helping members do their best work, and since the Common Core Standards (CCS) are required to be taught in Chicago public schools, the CTU supports teachers in this work through professional development. However, as educators, we are also obligated to question the true purpose of CCS, and expose flaws in the standards themselves, their developmental appropriateness, the testing requirements, uses of test results, equity of opportunity, their roll-out time frame, and their implementation.[7]

There is always quite a bit of show and drama at the national teacher union conventions. The Chicago Teachers Union was told ahead of time that the delegation led by the New York City school teachers was not going to allow our resolution out of committee, and that more than likely there would be limited debate on the floor. There is very little democratic process on the floor of the AFT conventions. Appointed leaders from New York control the microphones and the debate through overwhelming numbers and parliamentary procedure that is in their favor. The teachers from New York wanted their alternate resolution in support of reframing and adjusting the Common Core passed, and we learned they were ready to use their control of proceedings to squelch our opposition.

The Chicago Teachers Union decided that some flair and drama of our own was needed to get our point across. We printed large red circular stickers that said, "Ask me about the Common Core." I wore my stickers on both the front and back of my shirt, and I was approached often by those curious about our stance. We then asked our national allies to use social media to force a floor debate of the Common Core at the convention. Education activists all over the country advocated for a fair and open debate using their social media platforms. In the end, our actions were successful, and we were allowed to extend debate and actually hold a discussion on the floor for all the convened union members, a debate that was followed nationally through a live stream. We achieved our goal to lodge our concerns about the CCSS at the national convention.

We knew from the start that the AFT was not going to budge on their stance in support of the Common Core, but a precept of our principled resistance as unionists is that we get to decide what winning looks like. For us, winning meant being able to have an open conversation opposing the Common Core and the opportunity and ability to change hearts and minds.

Arguing Our Position at the National Convention

One of the positive outcomes of open debate was that we were able to address counterarguments. A large part of our strategy of principled resistance was writing a position paper that all of us could use to underpin our arguments, either in our interactions with individuals or in public debate. Principled resistance does not work unless teachers have clear belief systems and strong philosophies of teaching and learning. The most prevalent arguments against our opposition to the Common Core were that teachers must have standards in order to know what to teach, and that these standards elevate the teaching profession. Chicago teachers believe the reverse. We believe that teachers and students should drive instruction and that the decisions on teaching and learning should be made locally. As for the position that standards elevate the teaching profession, we believe that teachers are professionals who hold pedagogical knowledge of curriculum, child development, and their individual students. We believe that teachers can and should be trusted with instructional decision making.

Common Core supporters argue that it ensures consistency of materials and topics from school district to school district and classroom to classroom. During the AFT convention debate, Leroy T. Barr, from the New York City union local, said, "My son is in fourth grade. If I move from New York to California in November he should be able to pick up and move. I expect him to pick up exactly where he was."[8] This might seem logical, but if we believe that pacing of learning needs to be responsive, and that teachers should always take the interests of their students in mind, standards implemented nationwide are not a desirable way of driving instruction. I have taught for thirty years; no two years have ever been the same. Classrooms are dynamic spaces that are in a constant state of flux, and no school or system should be in lockstep with another, if we care about meeting students' needs and supporting their learning.

We were also able to argue against the insistence in CCSS of using "grade level" materials and content in all settings. Part of the reasoning behind the words "grade level" being specifically used in the standards is that some CCSS advocates believe that urban educators and special educators water down subject matter for their students, and that raising the bar is all that is needed to remedy the problem of perceived underachievement. During the AFT floor debate, Pia Payne-Shannon from Minneapolis said, "Allow me to bring my professional expertise into what I bring in front of my kids." Sarah Chambers, a special education teacher from Chicago, told of how one of her disabled students who was forced into taking a Common Core–aligned test at grade level had pulled out all of her eyelashes in anxiety. Because of the insistence on grade-level work and the testing that accompanies it, at the end of my speech on the AFT convention floor I said, "I cannot sit by and watch my first-grade students being labeled as failures before they have even started their schooling." When classroom teachers see harm being done to children, they can label it, refuse to sit on the sidelines, and take a principled stance against it.

Conclusion

The preparation necessary to appear on the floor of the AFT national convention sharpened our principled stance against the CCSS. Engaging at this level brought Chicago teachers together in a year's worth of discussions and writings. Working together also helped move our singular positions from the realm of deeply felt personal beliefs into a more defined principled resistance. We produced thoughtful and principled work and made it readily available to others, and we were able to address those that opposed our views in a public forum. An ancillary benefit of taking a principled stance collectively is that it builds relationships and understandings between the people working together.

Our successful effort to bring our opposition to the Common Core to the 2014 AFT national convention shows the importance of analyzing union structures and knowing how to work within them. The initial small team of unionists from CORE who joined me in realizing that the CCSS were unduly influencing our teaching and causing harm to our children knew that we had to follow established union protocol if we were going to take our stance to a larger audience. We worked through the committee system of the Chicago Teachers Union, approached the executive board for a recommendation, asked our House of Delegates (eight hundred teacher representatives from Chicago schools) to vote on our resolution, and then worked through national leaders to get our voices heard at our national convention. In the end, we were not able to push through our position at the convention, but the opportunity to present our views started a national conversation. In fact, an observer of the 2016 AFT convention said, "I noticed that opposition to Common Core was interlaced throughout many discussions—Chicago teachers were heard last time."

I began this chapter with my personal journey into this work. The act of teaching is highly moral and complex work, and a reflective practitioner must be conscious of the outside forces influencing classroom practice. I was faced with an ethical dilemma when I realized that Common Core standards and their subsequent testing regimes were harming the children in my care. I relied on the educators I work with in the Chicago Teachers Union to help me investigate issues that confront classroom teachers, to work with me in collectively developing a solid and principled argument, and to give me the support needed to carry the work forward.

When taking a stance to protect children and my profession, I expect the challenge and debate that comes with principled resistance. Some of it also comes at a personal price. There is powerful and influential money wrapped up into the implementation of the Common Core, and there is enormous profit to be gained. I was attacked publicly on social media and in print for my stance— often by people who were paid by foundations to do this work. Teachers who engage in principled resistance are often labeled as lazy or bad teachers. The objections to my work many times resulted in personal attacks on my character, but it would be wrong to consider this work martyrdom or as a superhero narrative. No one person should be given credit or personal acclaim for work that is done collectively. In addition, when you make a choice to take a principled stance and organize with others in resistance, they have a duty of care to protect and stand with you. None of this work should be done alone or in a silo. Education policy affects us all, and it is the responsibility of teachers and their allies to speak up when policies damage the profession and harm students. We believe the CCSS do both.

CHAPTER TWO

PRINCIPLED RESISTANCE TO SYSTEM MANDATES AMONG EARLY-CAREER TEACHERS

Clive Beck, Clare Kosnik, Judy Caulfield,
and Yiola Cleovoulou

I do not foresee dramatic changes in the basic structure of curriculum in America. We have to work within that basic structure. Sadly, I think we will go right on with English, mathematics, social studies, science, and foreign languages as the backbone of our curriculum. Indeed, if we continue in the direction we are now headed, the curriculum will become even more isolated from real life. . . . It is this tendency that we should resist, and effective resistance will require collaboration, critical thinking, and creativity.

— Nel Noddings, *Education and Democracy*

Introduction

Esteemed educational theorist Nel Noddings sees the present and likely the future approach to schooling in the United States as sad because its main focus is on teaching subject content "isolated from real life" issues. Her own position, as elaborated in her many books, is that schools should give a great deal of attention to teaching caring, values in general, and how to achieve happiness and well-being, as well as fostering subject knowledge.[1] She calls on educators to resist an overly subject-oriented approach to schooling.

But it is one thing for education *academics* to resist such schooling: they are expected and even paid to question how things are done and strive to develop better alternatives. What about ordinary school teachers who, as Noddings says, must work within that basic structure, maintaining good relations with everyone around them? What opportunity and responsibility do they have to resist the official curriculum and its underlying expectation of comprehensive "coverage"? This chapter tries to answer these questions, with special attention to early-career teachers and the pedagogical issues they face. Beginning teachers are sometimes referred to as the "shock troops" of educational change: coming with fresh ideas and youthful enthusiasm, they can transform schooling. But to what extent is this feasible or even appropriate?

This chapter draws on a number of sources, including the research literature and our discussions over the years with teacher candidates, teachers in the schools we visit, and teacher educators. However, the main source of ideas and information is a longitudinal study of forty-two teachers we have been following since they started teaching, twenty who began in 2004 and twenty-two who began in 2007.[2] Although the study is ongoing, this paper uses data from the period up to 2011–12, which were the first eight and five years, respectively, of teaching for the two cohorts. For present purposes, we consider these teachers as "early-career," even though many had assumed more veteran roles. A central concern of the chapter is to explore to what extent, in what ways, and for what reasons early-career teachers resist system mandates, which in turn will help us with our ultimate purpose of assessing the feasibility and appropriateness of teacher resistance.

Pedagogical Ideas and Values Underlying Teachers' Principled Resistance

Reframing Resistance

The word *resistance* tends to have negative connotations. It is often used in situations where resistance is seen as self-defeating or destructive—for example, where people resist dietary practices that are clearly beneficial, or where students are defiant and resist reasonable classroom norms. Referring to people as resistant is usually condemnatory, whereas calling them cooperative or accommodating tends to be positive. Here, however, we are using the terms resistance and resistant in a positive sense. It is principled resistance we are advocating, something we regard as crucial for the improvement of schooling.

Given the typically negative connotations of the term resistance, perhaps a different one would be better, such as *being creative* or *taking initiative*. But we believe resistance is a helpful term because it suggests that we in education have often been too passive and that the time has come to be more assertive. However, whatever word we use (and perhaps this should depend on the setting), it is essential to note that a balanced position is needed on this issue. Resistance is often appropriate—provided it is principled; but at other times being collaborative and accommodating may be more appropriate. (Of course, it may often be possible to be both, which again is a kind of balanced position.) A parallel may be seen with the word *critical*. It is possible to be too critical, always dwelling on the negatives of people and situations. However, the critical pedagogy movement in education has made major contributions to practice, and teachers should be introduced to critical approaches to literature, political systems, scientific theories, and so on (although the question of *how* critical we should be still needs attention).

In its negative sense, the term *resistant* is often applied to teachers. They are seen as resisting new pedagogical approaches, curriculum requirements, and professional development initiatives.[3] Our position is that this resistance is frequently reasonable, arising from legitimate concerns about what is important for students and whether the ideas and practices pressed on teachers by so-called experts are actually sound and feasible. Marilyn Cochran-Smith and Susan Lytle take exception to the common situation in which teachers "are expected to learn about their own profession not by studying their own experiences but by studying the findings of those who are not themselves school-based teachers."[4] In this chapter, we build a case in support of principled resistance by teachers, while qualifying and interpreting principled resistance in certain ways.

Critical, Constructivist Pedagogy and Resistance

A degree of principled resistance by teachers is in keeping with a critical approach to teaching, a position often proposed today. According to this position, it is essential that students be taught to be critical of accepted views, values, and practices in academia, society, and life. This has implications for teachers' resistance to system mandates. If they are to teach their students to think critically, then they must themselves think critically. When teachers do, they will inevitably see elements in the mandated curriculum, policies, and practices that should be resisted, on principle.

Similarly, some teacher resistance to system mandates is inherent in constructivism, again a widely advocated pedagogical approach. The central idea of constructivism is that, while teacher input is important, in the end students must construct their own views, reflective of their interests, needs, and life context. But if teachers are to consistently teach and model a constructivist approach, they too must construct their own views about the official curriculum and other mandates—leading teachers at times to resist these mandates. For example, inherent in constructivism is an emphasis on differentiated learning: individuals and subgroups must be strongly encouraged to construct their knowledge differently.[5] This requires that teachers resist to a significant degree the standardization prominent in current policies.[6]

Does this mean that teachers should just go their own way, ignoring the official curriculum and its underlying pedagogy? That is not our view. On the one hand, society and the school system would not allow it; and on the other, more positively, there is much value in traditional subject learning. The problem, as Noddings says, is not that we teach subjects in school but that we teach them "isolated from real life."[7] Deborah Meier makes a similar point: "I am not decrying a focus on facts, information, subject matter, or even memorization. . . . [But we must teach students] in ways that support the use of scientific thought in their own lives, as well as the capacity to hazard an opinion on matters of science that may pertain to political and moral priorities, and a healthy and knowing scepticism toward the misuse of scientific authority."[8] That is, teachers must as far as possible do both: teach subject content as well as ideas and attitudes relevant to everyday reality. And according to many researchers, it is quite feasible to do both; indeed, this is often a more effective way to teach subject content.[9]

Professionalism and Resistance

Again, a degree of principled resistance to the official curriculum and related pedagogical assumptions is inherent in a professional approach to teaching. Teachers are often described as professionals, and concern is expressed about the de-professionalization of teachers through detailed, top-down control.[10] Part of the idea here is that teachers do a better job if they are allowed to exercise judgment and make decisions. This is one reason why we call it principled resistance: its aim is to improve teaching. According to John Bransford, Linda Darling-Hammond, and Pamela LePage, teachers should be seen (and see themselves) as "adaptive experts" who "exercise trustworthy judgment based on a strong base of knowledge."[11] Apart from their general knowledge base, teachers have intimate knowledge of their students and the unfolding situation in their classrooms, which enables them to individualize student learning and take advantage of teachable moments as they occur.

Once again, this view of teachers pushes their role well beyond what is envisaged in most official curriculum documents. It is true that the introductions to curriculum documents often mention teacher decision making, individualization of instruction, inquiry learning, and so forth. But these messages are largely negated by the detailed listing of topics that follows, along with a system of standardized testing to check whether the topics have been covered. The assumption is that all these topics will be taught in roughly equal depth (partly so students will do well on the test); but this mandate is impossible to fulfill while also adapting the curriculum in such a way as to teach big ideas, address life issues, and attend to the individual needs and learning styles of students.

Resistance and Attending to Values and Students' Well-Being

Resistance to the official curriculum and its assumptions (notably, that teachers should cover all topics equally and do little else) often occurs in cases when teachers believe their students' personal development and well-being are at stake. Teachers who feel their students stand in need of "life learning" often modify their teaching to deal more fully with values and way-of-life matters. Similarly, teachers who see their students struggling or on the verge of dropping out of school—and seriously damaging their lives—often adjust the curriculum to make it more interesting and relevant. Many education theorists support an emphasis on values and well-being that goes significantly beyond the standard school curriculum.[12] Hazel Hagger and Donald McIntyre argue that, for most teachers, "their individual humanity and the totality of their human experience are essential resources on which they draw as classroom teachers."[13] Rose Ylimaki sees a need for teachers to draw on their "personal philosophies"; she is critical of scripted curriculum requirements that have little regard for "making the subject matter meaningful and relevant to children."[14]

Teachers' views about values and way-of-life matters influence their teaching in much same the way their views about academic subjects do. When they teach subjects, teachers are largely guided by the disciplinary understandings they have formed over the years. These influence the ideas they promote, what topics they emphasize, the examples they give, the questions they raise, and the assessments they make.[15] And the same is true—and must be true—in regard to values: teachers' understandings of what is valuable have a significant influence on students. This could be avoided to a degree if teachers gave up attempting to foster students' value development and well-being. But, as noted, many theorists argue this would greatly reduce the quality and effectiveness of their teaching.

Methodology: Studying Early-Career Teachers over Time

Research Approach

The main data source for this chapter was a longitudinal study of forty-two teachers, whom we interviewed and observed every year from the time they began teaching. In interviews, we asked a few ranking and rating questions, but most of our methodology was qualitative as defined by Sharan Merriam, Keith Punch, and Maggi Savin-Baden and Claire Howell Major.[16] In particular, we used a modified grounded theory approach. While we brought some ideas to the study, we did not build our research around a fixed theory but rather generated theory inductively from the data using a set of techniques and procedures for data collection and analysis.[17]

Participants

Early in the study, we had forty-five participants, of whom twenty-two began teaching in 2004 and twenty-three in 2007. However, two from the first cohort and one from the second left the study for unspecified reasons. As a result, we had a sample of forty-two by 2011–12, the final year reported here. Of the forty-two participants, thirty-eight were elementary and middle school teachers and four taught in junior high school settings; eight were visible minorities and five were male, roughly reflecting the proportions in these categories among new teachers from elementary to lower high school in the school districts represented. The participants were graduates of four schools of education in Canada and the United States. The sample consisted of all those 2004 and 2007 graduates who had a teaching position and accepted a general invitation to take part in the study. Throughout the study, most of the participants taught in relatively low socioeconomic status urban schools with racially and ethnically diverse student populations.

Data Gathering

We had a research team of fourteen, including the two principal investigators (Beck and Kosnik), who each followed eight participants. The rest of the team was made up of graduate students and recent graduates, each of whom followed one to three teachers. There were some changes in the team over the years, but, as with the teachers, the research team showed a high level of interest in and loyalty to the project, even though compensation was minimal. We had frequent team meetings to discuss relevant theoretical and methodological issues, agree on questions and codes, analyze the data, and discuss emerging findings. We interviewed and observed the participants annually, usually toward the end of school year. Each interview was approximately 60–75 minutes in length.

Findings: Principled Resistance Among the Teachers in Our Study

To varying degrees, all forty-two early-career teachers in our study resisted the official curriculum of their school system, system assumptions about pedagogy, explicit new "reform" initiatives, and system efforts to ensure teacher compliance. It seemed to us that in each case the resistance was largely principled, reflecting their concern both about the learning and general well-being of their students and their own need to survive and thrive in the profession and be there for their students. In what follows, we look at the types of resistance enacted and the reasons the teachers gave for their resistance. Much of the behavior we describe here would be regarded by some people, including some government and school district officials, as just sound and responsible teaching. However, the teachers themselves saw their actions as a type of resistance, requiring deliberate choice and including a definite element of risk.

We use pseudonyms when referring to particular participant comments and avoid any other potentially identifying information. This is in accord with the promise we made when asking for participants' consent in the study. However, we do mention the year of teaching they were in when they made the comments in question, in order to give a sense of how much experience they had when they arrived at a particular practice or viewpoint.

Types of Principled Resistance

Going well beyond mere subject teaching. All the teachers in our study took a broad approach to their role, strongly emphasizing practices such as caring for students, teaching values and way-of-life matters, building class community, and establishing positive teacher-student relationships. They implemented these practices despite being aware that their government and school district and the majority of the general public articulated an almost exclusive emphasis on subject teaching and test preparation. Moreover, they pursued these prac- tices as ends in themselves rather than just a way to maximize subject learning (although they were aware of the benefits in this regard). For example, Marisa commented in her third year, "What I want [my students] to remember from their experience [of school] is that they were welcomed, they felt safe, and they had fun; I want them to learn a lot, but I tell them all the time that I first of all want them to become cooperative, helpful human beings who get along with other people, know how to make friends and be a friend, and so on."

Linda, in her fifth year, said that two of the most important as- pects of her role were "caring for my students and having them feel part of the class community, and teaching them to be good citizens of the community and the world." Deirdre, in her fifth year, said, "When I was little I didn't really learn to read until second grade and everyone kept calling me stupid because English wasn't my first language . . . And I always told myself, one day I will become a teacher and I will never let this happen to a child. I will never let them suffer and cry every day on their way home as I did."

In the final interview of the study, we asked the teachers, "What are your three main goals for students?" Their responses illustrate their pedagogical principles (see table 2.1).

Of course, the teachers were concerned about their students' academic learning, as was clear from our interviews and classroom observations.

TABLE 2.1 Teachers' main goals for students (year 2011–12 interview)

Goal	Number of teachers mentioning goal in their top three
Social development	18
Love of learning	11
Development of self	11
Sense of community	10

Being selective in covering the official curriculum. Most of the teachers departed from the complete and even-handed coverage of the curriculum they knew to be the preferred official approach. Some admitted to leaving out certain topics entirely, although they usually hesitated before saying so on record. In his third year, David said, "You have to look at [the teacher's guide] and say okay, in reality, what can I do?" Also in her third year, Anita remarked, "We can't possibly cover all the content." In her seventh year, Marisa commented, "In order to find enough time, you have to judge what's important and weed out what's not, focusing on big ideas. For example, 'ancient civilizations' in social studies can take numerous different avenues and there's potentially so much to learn. But it's not so much about the specific content as the bigger ideas, like how they influenced our society."

Usually, however, the teachers said they cover everything but give much more emphasis to some topics than others. Sarah, in her fifth year, said that in math, "we spent a lot of time at the beginning of the year on patterning, number sense, and place value, because that's essential to understanding other things deeply; as a result we had less time for some other topics." In her fifth year, Kelly observed, "I like the idea of teaching around themes . . . so teachers can select what is applicable to the lives of their students. I don't think we should ever resort to a standardized, day-by-day script."

In her seventh year, Jeannie described how, in teaching about "pioneers" in social studies, she downplayed some of the traditional content, approaching the topic largely through a comparison with present-day experiences of immigration to which her students could readily relate. Vera, also in her seventh year, said, "[I]n my first couple of years I would always wonder: Am I doing this right? Is this going to meet the curriculum expectations? . . . But as I move along my concern is becoming, How can I ensure that the kids . . . are able to do the things they have to do, like read different types of materials independently, select appropriate texts on their own, tackle difficult words they come across, comprehend what they're reading? It's these big-picture ideas that I focus on."

Avoiding heavy emphasis on test preparation. To the extent possible, the teachers resisted spending a lot of time on direct test preparation, even though they felt pressure in this direction. In his second year, Paul was already critical of what he called a "bean counter" approach, "as opposed to seeing whether these kids are actually getting something out of their schooling, or . . . planning a writing assignment for struggling students, or whatever." Margaret, in her fourth year, commented: "I like the way our school prepared for the standardized test in third grade: we didn't even talk about it until the last month and then just devoted one period a day to test prep. . . . Tests aren't going away so we have to give students test-taking skills, but we shouldn't place too much emphasis on them."

Lucy, in her fifth year, said, "Basing my teaching on where the students are and where they need to be [according to the standards-based approach], I found I ended up teaching to the test; and the whole fun and love of learning went out the door. So I changed my process, and asked: What am I teaching? What skills need to be taught? How can I get that across in a way that they'll enjoy?"

At the end of her sixth year, Serena noted that she did some test preparation but only if it could be usefully integrated into her program; she did not do it just before the testing occurred. She observed, "There's constant pressure from the school board in relation to standardized test scores. It's hidden in a lot of other things like 'moderated marking' and 'critical pathways,' but higher test scores are the main goal."

Reasons Given by Teachers for Principled Resistance

We look now at the reasons the teachers gave for their resistance, reasons that in our view justify seeing their resistance as principled. In the previous section, we saw some of the reasons the teachers gave for resisting an almost exclusive focus on subject-content learning and a cover-and-test approach. First, they believed there are many other things students need to learn in school in addition to subject content. Second, they felt some curriculum topics are more important than others, depending on how useful they are in scaffolding learning or addressing big ideas and fundamental life concerns. And third, they believed standardized testing typically undermines learning in key areas by focusing on a narrow band of academic knowledge and diverting attention from fostering broader understanding.

Apart from the general subject content and testing emphasis, the teachers also resisted many specific government and school district initiatives that were presented as ways to maximize learning. They resisted these partly because they disagreed with the overly subject-heavy focus, as already discussed, but for other reasons as well: implementation of the initiative was not feasible; it represented poor pedagogy; its choice was politically motivated or simply arbitrary; and/or the professional development approach used to launch the initiative was ineffective. We will look briefly at each of these reasons.

Unworkable proposals. Some of the new pedagogies promoted at government or school district levels simply could not be implemented in the manner or to the degree envisaged. For example, the teachers were widely expected to implement "guided reading," an approach that involved dividing the class into small groups and having the teacher work with one group while the other students engaged in group activities. Many of the teachers said that, especially in their first few years, they could not ensure that the other groups would stay focused on their assigned tasks. Again, various detailed assessment methods promoted at a system level—for example, running records, diagnostic reading assessment—were found to be too time-consuming for implementation in a regular classroom: a modified form had to be created.

Poor pedagogy. Most of the teachers felt under system pressure to form reading groups based on tests of reading ability, and to have each group read leveled texts suited to their ability. However, most resisted this, feeling it highlighted ability differences in the class and restricted students' choice of reading materials. In general, there was concern about a system emphasis on small-group work. Most of the teachers found small groups only functioned well with certain topics and types of learning, and they moved to using a range of learning arrangements: whole class, centers, small groups, table groups, pairs, and individual work.

Politically motivated and arbitrary decisions. Many of the teachers were quite scathing about the processes whereby the "system," governments or school districts, arrived at new initiatives. Often, they saw the choice as political—the initiative was popular with the general public or served to give an appearance that things were under control. Or, they viewed the initiative as arbitrary and required without sound reasoning or purpose. In her eighth year,

Serena commented, "Probably my biggest change over the years is realizing how many new initiatives there are every year, and they don't necessarily jibe with the research but all of a sudden we're going to do this because the school district bought it, or a speaker came, or the principal got a deal, or whatever."

Paul, in his fifth year, said, "In school districts there are always these shiny objects, these new little programs with cute names that take up a lot of money and resources and distract everyone from the major issues." In her eighth year, Anna said, "The government initiatives keep changing . . . and they try to justify it by saying: 'Well, teaching is a lifelong learning process, you have to keep changing with the times.' But how can you develop a teaching strategy if every time you go there you feel, 'Wait a second, I should be doing something else.'"

Ineffectual professional development. The teachers often resisted system initiatives because the methods mandated to implement them were pedagogically inappropriate. For example, one major initiative across several school districts required groups of teachers to identify a particular problem (based on standardized test results), develop a common set of lessons to address it, and then all teach the same lessons using the same text. Many saw this as going against important principles of flexibility, individualization, and professional judgment in teaching. They went along with it only if their principal absolutely forced them to. In general, the professional development associated with system initiatives tended to be top-down, with insufficient regard for what teachers already knew. In his seventh year, John spoke about this problem: "There's a lot of PD lately around giving students descriptive feedback: giving more detail on what a student is doing well and what their next steps might be. However, I think I'm very good at that, I've always done it. . . . So while I get some benefit from the

PD, my problem is that it doesn't build enough on what teachers are already doing."

Conclusion

On the basis of this study and related research literature, we conclude that there is often a place for teachers' principled resistance to system mandates, whether to the almost exclusively subject-focused curriculum with its test-based accountability measures or to particular top-down system initiatives that constantly appear. The resistance we saw among the teachers in our study seemed to be reasonable, solidly based in notions of whole-child development, critical and constructivist pedagogy, and teacher professionalism. These are notions that are widely accepted by educational theorists. If such resistance is appropriate for early-career teachers, it would seem to be even more so for later-career teachers who have had more classroom experience and developed greater confidence in their abilities.

The types of principled resistance we witnessed included the following: going well beyond subject teaching into areas affecting students' personal and social development and general well-being; emphasizing certain topics more than others in the interests of scaffolding learning, exploring values, "big ideas," the "real world," and way-of-life matters; and avoiding an overly heavy emphasis on standardized testing. The reasons the teachers gave for resistance to particular system initiatives fell into several main categories: they were not feasible; they represented poor pedagogy; they were politically motivated or otherwise arbitrary; and the professional development activities used to implement them were ineffectual and wasted time that could have been used for teaching and learning purposes.

We regard the teachers' resistance as enormously important and as greatly enhancing the schooling their students receive. The teachers care deeply about their students' general well-being and are willing to take risks in promoting it, in the face of constant pressure to focus just on rote memorization of narrow subject content. Risks to the teachers include being viewed negatively by parents and school administrators. As a result, they may receive less desirable teaching assignments, have less respect and influence in the school, and even be removed from the school, depending on the terms of their tenure. Their resistant practices in going beyond transmission pedagogy may seem to be "creative" teaching that any good professional should engage in and that system authorities should accept. However, we have seen that teachers are acutely aware that such departures from traditional subject-focused teaching, though in the best interests of students, are *not* what most system authorities are currently looking for and attempting to enforce. Furthermore, resistant practices are not widely discussed and encouraged in preservice and in-service teacher education programs. The teachers in our study had to arrive at their acts of resistance largely on their own.

Of course, there are forms of teacher resistance that are unprincipled; for example, those arising from lack of concern for students or sheer laziness. More attention needs to be given to determining which forms of resistance are appropriate and which are not. However, in our view critics have often been too quick to condemn teachers as resistant in a negative sense, failing to explore the reasons behind their resistance. We hope our study will contribute to deeper exploration and a generally more positive view of many types of decisions that teachers make. Branding teachers as merely resistant can be an easy way to dismiss opposition to socalled "reform" measures that are in fact not in the best interests of students.

Given the apparent legitimacy and value of much teacher resistance, we believe principled resistance should be a major area of study in both preservice and in-service teacher education. There should be much discussion of reasons for it, when it is and is not appropriate, and strategies for exercising principled resistance without jeopardizing one's career. Attention also needs to be given to building teachers' confidence and sense of expertise at an earlier stage, so their legitimate resistance can begin during their preparation program and become strong even earlier in their teaching career. Furthermore, principled resistance by teachers should be researched and documented by those less vulnerable than teachers (notably academics), thus providing information to teachers, teacher educators, and policy developers about its nature, rationale, and impact. Finally, special "activist" roles and positions need to be developed that allow some teachers to move into explicit advocacy of resistant practices—rather than just talking about them in hushed tones with researchers pledged to anonymity.

CHAPTER THREE

RESISTING NO-EXCUSES CULTURE AS A BLACK MALE TEACHER

Valuing Critical Thinking and Relationships over Compliance

Randy R. Miller, Sr.

AS A TEACHER OF COLOR, particularly a Black male teacher, it is your decision who you will be as a teacher. Over 80 percent of teachers and over 75 percent of principals in America's public schools are White; Black and Brown students need us, all teachers of color who care for them, in the classroom. But what students need us for and what school leaders think they need us for may not align. In this chapter, I explore how I managed the tension between my purpose of teaching students critical thinking and the culture of compliance expected at the no-excuses charter school where I worked for two years. My writing shows how my subject-area expertise was disregarded by my school's leadership and the ways that I was expected to fulfill the role of disciplinarian and compliance officer. My story reveals how I violated my pedagogical principles of critical thinking and relationships by following the compliance-focused mandates of my no-excuses charter school. I chart how I became the teacher I wanted to be through acts of resistance focused on meeting students' needs. I write, especially, to the future Black male teachers and other teachers of color who may face similar dilemmas. You will need to ask yourself, who gets to define the teacher you become?

I never chose teaching; rather, teaching chose me. I was unaware of the changing urban school apparatus that included charter schools. What I knew was that numerous people thought I'd make a great teacher. After college, I had access to a school where I could test my chops. It happened to be a college-prep charter school, and while there I earned my certification in social studies, grades 6–12. With a few months under my belt, I realized that I was actually good at teaching. By my second year, I could see the impact I was having on my students. I began to wonder how much I would have emerged from my shell had I had a teacher who looked like me at any point in my K–12 experience. For the very first time, I felt a purpose to my work. I focused on building strong relationships with students and enabling them to think critically about their lives, community, and history. This school afforded me the freedom and autonomy to teach critical thinking and to respond to students' needs. I rarely used textbooks. Rather, I used the works of Joel Augustus Rogers, W. E. B. Du Bois, and Michelle Alexander to teach social studies; resistance was daily. However, there were a lot of politics to be played, and brownnosing was expected. I was a casualty of budget cuts within the organization, but they allowed me to take my talents elsewhere. For my last full school year teaching, I was hired by a no-excuses charter school.

At this no-excuses charter school, there were expectations and mandates for how to instruct students daily. These were communicated during a week of intensive professional development over the summer. The trainings were designed to teach the teachers new to the organization the methods and rationale of how and why to teach in the style mandated by the school, which was geared, supposedly, to ensure student success. What I was told was very different from how I had been teaching up to that point; the trainers emphasized objectives like teaching on task, monitoring, redirecting, and tracking the speaker. It was a method of teaching that focused on compliance rather than critical thinking or relationships. Students' needs seemed to be predetermined by the predominantly White school leadership.

This chapter is based on my experience teaching in two charter schools in Camden, New Jersey. Despite the promises made to parents, no-excuses schools are not vessels for the liberation of Black and Brown students. No-excuses advocates will argue that traditional public schools aren't either, and they're right. We know the track record of traditional public schools; we understand the ways in which Black integration happened, and that municipalities and their school districts disregard the well-being of Black students. No-excuses schools are framed as a better alternative to the traditional public schools that have oftentimes failed low-income children of color. These schools limit their goals to improving the standardized test scores of Black and Brown students. They do not promote liberation and affirm the identities of Black and Brown children within their curriculum and pedagogy. If you decide to teach at a no-excuses school, it is your responsibility to determine the teacher you will be, no matter the guiding principles preached to you by school leaders. I made the decision to resist the no-excuses focus on compliance and standardization in order to act in the best interests of my students and to define who I would be as a teacher. I continue to wrestle with my decision, but not because I made the wrong decision. Rather, the decision to act in the best interests of my Black and Brown students had negative consequences for my students. They lost another Black male teacher.

The Turning Point

One day I saw one of my students not standing against the wall and talking to one of her classmates while waiting to enter her math classroom. One thing preached to us teachers was that students, when switching classrooms, were to be quiet in the hallways and stand against the wall at all times. With that in mind, I approached the student and demanded that she stop talking and stand against the wall. After she attempted a back-and-forth with me, the student stopped talking, but she did not get against the wall. I demanded that she go stand next to the wall in a straight line. Teachers had been instructed to penalize students who did not listen to our instructions or did not follow the procedures told to them at the beginning of the year. When the student didn't listen, I asked for her behavior card. She gave it to me, and I gave her two marks: one for not doing what I said and another for not following procedure. When I gave the card back, she protested what she perceived as an injustice; she was one mark short of a detention. I informed her that if she kept talking, she would get that last mark for a detention. I instructed her again, this time with a raised voice, to go back against the wall and stand facing forward. She simply rolled her eyes and stood still. I gave her that final mark for the detention. As I walked away, she said something under her breath. I turned around and yelled from where I was standing that disrespect and failing to follow the rules would not be tolerated. Immediately after I said that, some kids got quiet, some kids got angry, and others tried their hardest not to burst out laughing. And I asked myself, *what the hell am I doing?*

In my previous years teaching at the college-prep charter school, I never got into an exchange like that with a student. Granted, there were times when I had to discipline students, but it was very rare for me to yell or to give a detention. Prior to this situation, I had never been put in a position to have to legislate how kids walked in the hallway. At that moment I realized that I didn't want to be what I was becoming. I was slowly becoming that disciplinarian that I did not want to be. This no-excuses school had attempted to prepare teachers for an urban teaching environment with intensive professional-development sessions the previous summer. Philosophically, I disagreed with their approach. In that moment when I asked myself what the hell I was doing, I was brought back to those very intensive professional-development sessions during the previous summer when I thought to myself, *I won't be able to carry on doing things this way for the duration of the year.* After the students entered their math class, I walked back to my classroom and I sat down in my chair. I reflected on what had just happened, and I told myself that I would not become that kind of teacher, that I had to go back to being the teacher that I was prior to that school year. I knew I had to resist the culture that I found myself in. I wondered how long I could resist until I was forced out. Leaving my students was something I really didn't want to do, but I could no longer kill spirits in the name of obeying authority. I decided to resist as best I could for the remainder of the school year and reassess how I felt at the end of it.

Later that school year, I was approached by my principal with a request that assumed that my role as disciplinarian was more important than my subject-area expertise and preparation. To assist a coworker with achieving her proper certification, the principal decided to switch my teaching assignment the next year. I would teach third-grade science for half the school year, in addition to seventh-grade world history, despite the fact that my certification is in social studies, grades 6–12. My principal said that she and the administrative team would offer me support throughout the year. I assumed that my principal thought this was a good idea because I was a Black male who had good classroom-management skills, was good with students, and was fairly smart. I did not. What really concerned me was that I would be evaluated on my performance in a class that I legally (and academically) had no business teaching. That summer, I attended a training session to help prepare me for the half year of science instruction. I asked the facilitator how I would get through the content in half a year. She quickly responded that the science curriculum was for a full-year course. My principal misled me; my direct supervisor confirmed that my third-grade teaching assignment was for a full year. I relayed my concerns to my subject-area supervisor; either he didn't get it or he didn't care. I understand that a certification doesn't ensure you can teach well; however, in order to earn your certification, there is a level of competence that you must exhibit or else you can't get certified. This was the situation I found myself in. There was no teacher union I could lean on to advocate on my behalf against this transfer.

The beginning of the school year came, and much to my dismay and despite my protests, I was teaching third-grade science. I did the very best that I could, and there were some bright spots. However, I wasn't the best at managing a third-grade classroom. The struggles that we faced as teacher and students were not our fault. They came from my being asked to teach out of my subject area and grade-level endorsement. My principal seemed to value my identity as a Black male teacher supposedly able to "discipline" over my pedagogical expertise. At the end of September, I left the school for another opportunity, and while that particular teaching assignment was the last straw, the totality of my experiences in that school and organization is what facilitated my exit. I hated leaving my students. As one of the only Black men in the building, I hated leaving at all. I hated leaving my beloved Camden, and I am grateful to that principal and the school community for inviting me back to watch my students graduate from the eighth grade. However, my decision to leave was a decision that I was compelled to make because I was asked to disregard my pedagogical principles.

Being a teacher of color is a double-edged sword. In addition to proving your worth to your White counterparts, you are focused on empowering young people while simultaneously attempting to not get burned out by the students who depend on you as a parent/older sibling/counselor/mentor/advocate. Many days are rewarding ones. The love, respect, and admiration that you receive from students and parents are worth every bit of effort that goes into earning them. Serving your colleagues as a resource is an honor and a privilege. Then, there are other days that make you question why you entered the profession to begin with. According to Dr. Ivory Toldson, of the top ten occupations among Black and White males who have at least a bachelor's degree, primary school teacher was the number one profession of college-educated Black men (number three for White men and number one for Black women also); secondary school teacher was the fifth-ranked profession of college-educated Black men (number fourteen for White men). However, Black men have one of the highest rates of turnover in the teaching profession.[1] The Education Trust released a report in 2016 chronicling the experiences of Black teachers told by Black teachers. The report, titled *Through Our Eyes: Perspectives and Reflections from Black Teachers*, presents the takeaways from focus group sessions with over 150 Black teachers nationwide.[2] The responses of Black teachers in the report are consistent with many of my own contentions. According to the report, Black teachers love serving all students, especially students who look like them.

However, being expected to prioritize disciplining over educating, having to prove their worth, and being devalued as content leaders takes its toll. Black teachers have the cultural competency that makes their presence a strength for any faculty. However, their misuse and being taken for granted push them out of where they are needed most—the classroom.

The Blackwashing of No-Excuses Principles

Much of the language I heard during the summer professional-development week for the no-excuses school wasn't foreign to me. The wording and phrasing of the guiding principles at both charter schools were ideas commonly shared in Black households; I've heard them in my own house. I can't count how many times I've heard my parents tell me that I had no excuse for not performing to the best of my abilities in school. My parents and grandparents told me that I had to work twice as hard as a White person in order to succeed. I've been told by my family and by the community that there was nothing that I couldn't do; that if I put my mind to it, I could do anything that I wanted to do regardless of my skin color. At both charter schools where I worked, Black and Brown students were the whole of the respective student populations. Where the organizations diverged from each other was in their overall philosophy. These organizations build academic programs specific to low-income children of color, Black and Brown children whose families cannot afford to send them to better schools. Many of these charter organizations, particularly no-excuses organizations, are founded and administered by "well-intentioned" Whites interested in "reforming" urban education. No-excuses schools claim their goal is to provide low-income Black and Brown children the same educational opportunities available to White children in the suburbs. However, the type of education these low-income children of color receive is very different from the education White children receive.

The no-excuses charter management organization (CMO) was attempting utilize the adages for success of Black and Brown households through its primarily White teaching force; it made sense that Black teachers and everyone else went along with that language. However, the spirit of the language didn't match up with the implementation of the school culture. No-excuses schools do a good job of taking values, traditions, and ethics found in Black and Brown households and using them to promote the no-excuses philosophy. These schools woo parents of color by using coded language found in households of color, phrases like "no excuses," "by any means necessary," and "work twice as hard." They find such quotes out of the mouths of contemporary and historical heroes like Martin Luther King Jr., Barack Obama, Oprah Winfrey, and Malcolm X, then post them around their buildings. However, the education that these children receive focuses on compliance, law, and order, not critical thinking or liberation. It's a racist frame of mind. Consciously or subconsciously, educating Black and Brown children, regardless of class status, in this way further perpetuates, and even adopts, the belief that Black and Brown children are out of control and dangerous if left without structure, a structure many believe they do not receive at home. Quoting civil rights leaders and putting those quotes around your building to reinforce the mantra of no excuses does not mean that you are for Black and Brown liberation. It could very well mean you espouse a doctrine of respectability politics. Our values and traditions are exploited for our buy-in—for example, school and classroom chants or having a warm but strict tone with students. It's nothing more than exploitation of the African aesthetic to make Black and Brown parents feel that these new "alternatives" are places where their children are welcomed and will be properly educated. However, these schools aren't led by us, and they are still under the purview of state departments of education. It's a new name, but it's the same game.

The Beginnings of Resistance

Without having seen any statistics, I reached a hypothesis: my school's no-excuses approach was not meeting students' needs, wasn't always followed, and wasn't always administered properly—by either teachers or administration. Students could separate the wheat from the tares; they knew who cared about them versus who didn't. I had got caught up in the CMO's way of disciplining students. I blame myself for that because I lost sight of who I wanted to be as a teacher. I believed the hype. I believed that the procedure for disciplining kids would work if done properly, and I started to believe in the power of my own presence. I was told that just my being in the room would be enough to get the desired behavior from students.

Emboldened by the actual lead school disciplinarian, I became a de facto school disciplinarian. Truth be told, it became my role whether I wanted it or not. I was called on to break up fights. I was asked to take the place of a disciplinarian during lunch duty, and there were times when teachers arrived late to lunch duty and I was asked to be in charge while a school disciplinarian had to run and do something else. I was alone with sixty students. Thankfully, I could handle it and I had the respect of the students, but under no circumstance should one teacher be left in the cafeteria with sixty students to monitor. When you are a Black male teacher you're going to be leaned on. I went along with it because I wanted to make sure that I was indispensable, both in the classroom and wherever else I was utilized. However, the CMO's philosophy on disciplining kids for everything started to weigh on me. While I had the other aspects of teaching down, being in constant discipline mode became taxing. The students started to rebel against the discipline procedures of the school and quite frankly so did some teachers, including me.

My resistance wasn't about inciting a mass revolt against the school's administration. Rather, I left behind an "us versus them" mentality with my students and focused on their needs and our relationship. My resistance became less about defying school administration and more about building relationships and trust with the students I taught. To be clear, I enjoyed the collegiality that I experienced at work. What I did not enjoy was feeling like I was being used as an instrument to enforce compliance and control over Black and Brown students. In order to teach Black and Brown students, you cannot come from a place of law and order. Black and Brown people catch enough hell from law and order in the world. Many have been unlawfully killed by law and order. Children of color do not need any of that spirit in the atmosphere of a school building. My motivation to resist was the children. I needed them to understand that the classroom was a place where they were free to be themselves and make mistakes, unlike the world that awaited them at 3 p.m. There was no way of accomplishing that with an overemphasis on complying with procedure. So overemphasizing compliance be damned.

Each morning during homeroom, all teachers were required to send students who were out of uniform to the discipline office. Failing to wear a belt, failing to wear the mandated colored sneakers, failing to have your shirt tucked in; all of these constituted being out of uniform. The no-excuses approach supports sending children home who are out of uniform or improperly dressed, presumably to enforce and promote personal responsibility. Sending a child home doesn't prove a point and doesn't meet students' needs. It only takes away classroom time from a student who needs to be in the classroom. Sending a child downstairs because they're out of uniform and giving them a detention can do more harm than good if that particular child is without the means to get the shoes you want them to have. A kid without a belt is no excuse for making time in the classroom secondary. If a CMO wants to be a uniform school in the city, then it should be prepared to give out free belts, shirts, pants, and even shoes on a daily basis. Again, are we prioritizing compliance or critical thinking?

The uniform policy penalized parents when their children violated the uniform policy; students were sent home and/or parents were required to bring the proper uniform when appropriate. Students also received a detention. If a kid had their shirt untucked, I told them to tuck it in, and they tucked it in. All it took was a simple request. Kids listened because we had a relationship built on mutual respect and care. If a kid didn't have on the mandated colored sneakers (students had to wear black sneakers), I didn't notice. If a child was without a belt, they were without a belt. The discipline office began coming to my classroom to check whether students were out of uniform when they noticed I no longer sent students down to them. Although I was never reprimanded for my resistance, my behavior was frowned upon. Nonetheless, I had built up enough "street cred" with administration for them to "allow" my refusal to follow compliance-related enforcement.

To prevent another incident of me yelling at a student in the hallway, I instructed students to line up in the classroom when class was over, rather than in the hallway, allowing them to talk quietly while they were waiting. Once next period's class arrived at my door, I would stand in the doorway as the current class walked out behind their teacher for next period. These two changes in procedure were about giving to receive—that is, prioritizing relationships and students' needs. My classroom-management style is about being realistic. Students talk; they want to socialize and network. Teaching and learning must happen, but no-excuses doesn't allow for kids to be kids outside of formal learning unless it is a sanctioned activity—that is, lunch or recess. Every minute is to be accounted for so no learning time is lost. However, children are not robots, and to expect them to be in the name of academic success fails to account for the importance of socialization. I decided to practice my pedagogical principles: give students a safe space to be kids without penalizing them for pursuing their own social needs at appropriate times.

The CMO required that teachers follow the mandated curriculum, regardless of students' current academic levels. In my seventh grade, I had several students reading at or below a third-grade level, several with individualized education plans. I was given no opportunity to modify the curriculum and had no special education support. Regardless, I was expected to show "growth" with those students. While the students with individualized education plans received pull-out services for language arts/literacy and math, they did not receive such services for history classes. Considering the current emphasis on making history more language arts/literacy based, I was surprised that those students didn't receive services and that I did not receive additional teaching support. Knowing that I was going to be observed, I did not create an alternate learning activity for the students who could not access the mandated curriculum. I made this choice in order to force the discussion with my vice-principal about meeting these students' needs. Upon having this conversation, the students and I were assigned a paraprofessional who was taken advantage of by the students who needed the help, only to have this individual do the work for them. So, against the wishes of the administration but in order to meet the needs of these students, I slowed down the speed of the course to bring all students along. Unfortunately, this meant that when it was time for students to take benchmarks administered by the CMO, there were some questions they couldn't answer because we didn't "cover" the entire curriculum. My goal was to teach at a reasonable pace that would allow students to learn as much information as possible. It was also my goal to teach my students about the realities of what came with the labels put on their lives and how to challenge those conventions. Unfortunately for me, the performance growth on paper didn't reflect what I knew to be true in my classroom. So I didn't meet pay-for-performance goals, but that really wasn't my concern.

I did receive some reprimands from the administration. I was warned a few times about my actions. I was even told by an administrator that they had noticed a change in me from the beginning of the year. Messages phrased for the whole staff were actually meant for me to hear during staff meetings. For example, we (staff) were told that in order for the policies and procedures to work, we all had to work together. That directive was aimed at me. I could tell by the eye contact made with me by the school leaders delivering it. We (teachers) were also encouraged to point out the teachers who enforced compliance expectations. But what administration couldn't deny was that I wasn't a classroom-management concern; I could be trusted with people and private information, and to always do the right thing for students. Despite criticisms aimed at me, I knew that my actions were for the benefit of students, and the administration knew that I did my job. I stopped reading and participating in school chants and classroom chants; I stopped participating in bogus team-building chants led by the administration; I stopped penalizing students for inconsequential compliance matters that I could handle myself; and I decided that my classroom would be my own classroom. I was unapologetic about how I ran it. By the conclusion of the school year, the relationship I had with my students was where I wanted it to be. As for my relationship with the administration, let's just say we were equally happy that the end of the school year had come. I knew that my departure was imminent.

Being a teacher of color means answering the following questions: Who are you teaching for? Are you teaching for the people or for anyone else? Before you decide to accept a position working in the city, whether at a no-excuses school or not, do your homework on the school and the organization that you could enter into. Learn their philosophy on paper and their philosophy in the atmosphere. Ask whether you can be who you are as a teacher of color or whether you'll have to adjust your behavior to meet the organization's principles. Choose to work in an environment where you will feel most fulfilled. Immediately develop a strategic plan for your career. If you dedicate yourself to children of color, great. But you must have a plan for your development. Find a mentor of color that is not in your building. Never overextend your reach, even if you want to. Do not allow for others to use your Blackness as a tool to compensate for their ineptitude. Find other teachers of color and meet with them regularly for support. If you find yourself in a place where you suddenly have to resist, then by all means, resist. For Black people, resistance is in our blood; it is in our DNA to resist injustice. Resistance is attached to our liberation. May we continue to resist to achieve the liberation of our students.

CHAPTER FOUR

WORKING THE SYSTEM

*Teacher Resistance in a Context
of Compliance*

Alisun Thompson and Lucinda Pease-Alvarez

Introduction

Teachers in the United States confront an enduring tension between professional autonomy and institutional control. While several scholars have described this tension as endemic to the way US teachers have historically experienced their work, there is evidence that the current policy environment has exacerbated this tension.[1] In recent years teachers have had minimal say when it comes to the development of policies that specify what and how they should teach and how they should assess their students.[2] Schools, districts, and governmental entities expect teachers to comply with policy initiatives via strictly enforced accountability measures and external monitoring. Despite claims that these policies will help close the achievement gap that has come to characterize how students of different ethnic, linguistic, economic, and racial backgrounds experience schooling in the United States, there is evidence that these policies are further constraining the opportunities to learn available to English language learners and students of color in US schools.

As teacher educators and university-based researchers, we have witnessed the increased intensity of accountability and standardization policies through our students and our work with teachers and administrators in schools. This chapter describes our experiences observing and working with Educators Advocating for Students (EAS), a teacher collective that is resisting and renegotiating policies of standardization. Many of these policies have undermined professional discretion, requiring teachers to teach and assess in ways that ignore students' instructional needs, interests, and experiences. We joined with teachers to form this collective as a grassroots response to what we perceived to be a draconian policy environment that runs counter to our pedagogical commitments and understandings of good practice. In an effort to better understand how teachers are implicated in the policy-making process through activism and resistance, we focus this chapter on the story of this teacher collective. We pay particular attention to how this group is resisting and renegotiating top-down policies and to the impact this resistance has on its members.

Drawing on critical and post-structuralist conceptions of agency and resistance, we begin with the conceptual framework upon which our inquiry is based. After describing our research approach, we portray the processes, actions, and impacts that have to date characterized our collaboration. We conclude with a discussion of the implications for theory, situated practice, and the professional development of teachers.

Conceptualizing Resistance

In examining teacher resistance, our goal was to better understand the nature of teacher agency within an authoritarian context of compliance. In the social sciences, there has been a long-standing debate over whether structure or agency is more important in shaping behavior. Dissatisfied with this dichotomous framing, we looked to post-structuralist theories to understand how teachers engaged with restrictive policies that ran counter to their pedagogical principles. From this perspective, agency and structure do not function as binaries but are instead dynamically engaged in a mutually constituting process. In other words, individuals do more than merely resist or comply with structural forms.[3] Even in constraining circumstances, actors can creatively respond to the conditions of their environment, often leveraging structural aspects for their own means. The theory of "improvisation," introduced by Dorothy Holland and her colleagues, enables us to explain how and why individuals are capable of impromptu actions that would seem to be outside the social and cultural resources available to them. Rather than focus on agent and structure as opposing forces, the theory of improvisation allows us to show how individuals produce unusual forms of behavior and make use of structure to bring about a contested social end.[4] This dialogic perspective between structure and agency casts individuals as innovative—capable of not only interacting with structure but using it to produce change.

A reconceptualization of agency and structure prompted us to complicate our understanding of how and in what context resistance emerges and how to recognize less overt forms of noncompliance or even appropriation *as* resistance. Given that teaching has historically been (and continues to be) a feminized profession in which teachers' work is externally monitored and controlled, we looked to feminist and postcolonial theory to better understand resistance in a context of compliance.[5] For example, feminist scholars have argued that women's resistance does not always directly contest power but frequently works through diffused webs of influence to confront overt power structures. Resistance does not necessarily manifest as militant action but can also be demonstrated through sustained, daily acts of courage and subtler forms of rebellion.[6] Most notable is James C. Scott's conception of the cumulative effect of everyday acts of resistance among peasants and enslaved populations as having the potential to bring about change: "Everyday forms of resistance make no headlines. Just as millions of anthozoan polyps create, willy-nilly, a coral reef, so do thousands upon thousands of individual acts of insubordination and evasion create a political or economic barrier reef of their own."[7]

Because Scott and others address the cumulative impact of individual and subtler forms of collective resistance, their thinking provides a useful framework for considering the work of EAS, the grassroots organization of teachers that is the subject of this chapter. EAS formed in response to top-down mandates that teachers saw as undermining their pedagogical principles and restricting their ability to meet the needs of their students. In describing EAS's efforts, we offer a story of collective activism and build on the aforementioned literature on agency and resistance.

The Emergence of EAS

EAS emerged as a venue from which to address a compliance environment that required teachers to implement policies focused on the standardization of learning and teaching in the pseudonymous Arden Valley School District. Arden Valley is a bimodal district: the children living in the northern part of the district are predominantly white and middle class, while those living in the southern part of the district are predominantly Latino and from low-income backgrounds. All the teachers participating in EAS over the years have worked in the Arden Valley schools that serve students who are primarily low-income and of Mexican heritage. Over 90 percent of the students are of Latino backgrounds, with over 55 percent classified as English language learners. Most of the remaining students were formerly designated English language learners and are now designated as fluent English proficient. While two EAS members worked as teachers for less than five years, the remaining eight have worked as teachers between fifteen and thirty years. Two teachers in the group are retired but taught for full careers in Arden Valley School District and are deeply committed to the community. Two of the core participants are of Mexican heritage, and the remaining eight are White.

In the fall of 2007, a series of events led to the first gathering of the group that came to be known as EAS. In October of that year, a student teacher told University of California, Santa Cruz, faculty members Cindy Pease-Alvarez and Melissa Stevens that her cooperating teacher was frustrated with various school district policies, including the district mandate requiring elementary school teachers to use the standardized skill-based literacy program published by Houghton Mifflin Company.[8] Melissa, who knew the teacher personally as well as professionally, suggested that she and Cindy meet with the teacher to discuss her concerns. During an informal get-together, the teacher reported her apprehension about these policies and expressed curiosity about how other teachers were responding, saying that she was the only one who had publicly expressed a negative reaction to the mandate at her school. Melissa responded by saying that she had been hearing similar concerns from teachers who were working in other schools in the district. She suggested a meeting for these teachers to discuss their concerns collectively.

After contacting teachers via phone calls and personal emails, the group had its first meeting at Cindy's house in early December. A total of six teachers from three different school sites attended the first meeting. With outreach, over twenty-five teachers attended the next meeting, held in late January of 2008. With the exception of summer, EAS met monthly from 2007 to 2010, with subgroups forming for specific projects. While membership and attendance varied, a core group of eight to ten teachers regularly attended EAS meetings.

In spring of 2010, at the suggestion of the teacher union president, group members agreed to make EAS the professional issues (PI) subcommittee of the union. EAS members advocating for this change thought that a formal affiliation with the union would help maintain the group's focus and coordination. In the fall of 2010, the PI subcommittee convened with five former members of EAS (including the union president), Cindy, and three other members who had at one time or another assumed leadership roles in the union as building representatives and/or former members of the union's executive board. Although former members of EAS who have not participated in meetings of the PI subcommittee have expressed a desire to meet periodically on an informal basis, these individuals have not met as a group since the fall of 2014.

Our Role in EAS

As members of EAS, we have taken on the role of participant researchers. As participants, we take part in all the activities of the group, including attending meetings, volunteering for specific roles, and contributing to discussions. We have also been the documentarians of the group, keeping accounts of minutes, notes, and guiding documents such as the mission statement. As researchers, we have collected and analyzed relevant data and engaged in ongoing reflection about our role in the group. As group members, we are, like all those participating in EAS, committed to changing the status quo as reflected in policies that have compromised the autonomy and integrity of teachers committed to enhancing the educational opportunities of their students.

Nevertheless, we struggle with the level of authority we should assume in the group. Given that we are not currently practicing teachers employed by schools and districts facing policy and economic pressures, there are real and perceived differences in our roles and those of other group members. There have been times when we have pondered our actions within the group, worrying that we have been either too directive or, alternatively, too passive in our efforts to influence group actions. Our roles in the group remained a topic for self-interrogation and reflection throughout the study.

The major data sources for the analysis that follows include field notes and audio recordings of meetings, documents produced by the group, postings on an internet discussion board, and interviews with ten of the core teachers. During these interviews, we asked teachers about their perspectives on district policies, their reasons for participating in EAS, how they benefitted from their involvement with the group, what they found challenging or problematic about the group, and how they thought the group should engage with authority figures and institutions in order to change or mitigate the policies that the teachers thought were problematic. Interviews have also provided us with information about the contexts in which the teachers worked (e.g., the teachers' professional backgrounds, relationships, understandings, and experiences; their students' communities; the school and district cultures in which they worked; and state and federal policies affecting their lives). The following questions have guided our inquiry:

- How is the group negotiating the current top-down policy environment?
- What resistive actions to policy initiatives and/or institutional authority does the group engage in?
- How does involvement in the group affect participants' professional lives and pedagogical commitments?

Impact on Group Members

All the teachers we have interviewed considered the opportunity to engage with and learn from others during meetings the most beneficial aspect of their involvement with the group. They concurred that the time we spent together at meetings were occasions when they did not have to worry about the consequences that their views or actions might have on their professional well-being; the group has always been careful to maintain members' anonymity. Teachers reported that having access to the views of others provided them with important insights that were not otherwise available at their school sites and strengthened their resolve to resist policies that ran counter to their pedagogical principles. As group member Irene stated, attending EAS meetings gave her "arguments to take back to my school and to know that I'm in the right." During one meeting, she shared that parents at her school site did not know about the process they needed to follow in order to request waivers for their children to be enrolled in bilingual classes, and that administrators had not responded to her request to clarify the process. During that same meeting, teachers offered information on how the waiver process was advertised and carried out at their sites. Irene brought this information back to her school, facilitating a change in practice that directly benefitted students and their families.

Grace, a second-year teacher, also appreciated being able to connect with teachers from other school sites and gaining support for engaging in pedagogical practices that were not spoken about at her school. When describing how her participation in EAS supported her, she stated, "It reminds me that I don't have to fit into this box and that I can say no." She also reported to the group's website that because of her involvement in EAS, she was willing to speak publicly about her opposition to district policies and actions. Another member told us that her involvement in EAS helped her realize that she thrives in an environment of collegiality, something that was missing at her school; that realization led her to resign her position and obtain a job teaching in a school known for its collegial faculty.

Through our interviews with teachers, we also found that members of EAS thought that their involvement in the group's various policy actions, such as a public letter criticizing the district's testing and assessment policy, affected their teaching. For example, in the following interview excerpt, group member Maureen describes how her work with EAS contributed to transformations in her teaching: "Most important, EAS has impacted my teaching. I do not feel intimidated by others' ideas that I should teach to the test. I have used my voice in team meetings to say that we no longer need to teach to each individual test. I also began to teach more in Spanish whereas my grade level (due to pressures of state standardized exams) had begun to transition bilingual 2nd-grade students at the mid-year, rather than in 3rd grade as other Early Exit programs do." Being involved with EAS supported teachers in upholding their pedagogical commitments to students and teaching in ways that aligned with their understandings of good practice.

Impact on the Policy Environment

Although a range of actions were discussed during meetings (e.g., proposing a slate for school board elections, making recommendations for textbook adoptions), the group coalesced most strongly around actions related to the district's assessment policies. This began when a member shared a letter she sent to district administrators outlining her concerns regarding the district's assessment and testing policies. After she received no response to this letter, EAS members decided to draw on the letter to write a public statement criticizing the district's testing and assessment policies, explaining how the loss of more than 100 hours of instructional time to testing was impacting the quality of teaching and learning in the classroom. EAS pleaded with the public to "express your concern over instructional time that has been lost to demoralizing, repetitive testing, and ask that teachers once again be included in decisions about how to assess the kids they know best." In addition to spending several hours crafting this statement, EAS members made sure that faculty at various school sites had access to the statement and the opportunity to sign it. Once two hundred teachers signed the statement, EAS members contacted reporters at three different newspapers. Over the course of a three- to four-week period, the statement was published in each newspaper, including a Spanish version of the statement in a Spanish-medium newspaper widely available in Arden Valley.

The group also engaged in other resistive actions focused on district and state testing policies. Several teachers were interviewed about their views on testing and other issues when a local newspaper followed up on their public statement. In addition, a panel of EAS members appeared on a local community television program focused on testing. In late September of 2008, the teachers read the statement in English and Spanish to a group of parents participating in a monthly community gathering in the Arden Valley town plaza. In December, an EAS member drew on the letter to draft a resolution calling for a testing moratorium that would be considered for approval at a statewide meeting of the California Federation of Teachers. After two other group members helped her revise the resolution, she shared it at a district-wide meeting of the union. The union leadership asked the membership to authorize the resolution in a letter/ballot attached to the statement that was disseminated to each teacher in the district. Once authorized by the membership, EAS members submitted the resolution to the PI subcommittee of the California Federation of Teachers, who in turn brought it up for vote at their annual meeting, where delegates unanimously passed the resolution.

According to the president of the local union affiliate, who was also a member of EAS, he and other union leaders drew on the group's perspectives about testing and assessment in contract negotiations. From his vantage point, this was most apparent in the following clause, which appeared in the final version of the 2008–9 contract negotiations and required that the district seek teacher input when developing testing and assessment policies: "The District acknowledges the need to review the total number of assessments being administered throughout the District and to support only those assessments determined to be effective and necessary as a Program Improvement District. The District shall seek the input of the union's assessment committee on this topic." Shortly after the contract was negotiated, the union president asked that three members of EAS join the district's assessment committee. Although these individuals, along with the union president, met periodically with the superintendent of the district, the concerns and suggestions that they shared regarding district testing and assessment practices were not taken up by the superintendent.

Resisting Authority: Negotiating Multiple Discourses

While there was strong consensus that participation in EAS supported teachers and enabled them to uphold pedagogical principles that were under attack by district policy, there were also differences in the ways group members viewed collective action. Our analysis of interviews with EAS members, field notes from group meetings, and conversations while working together on various projects revealed conflicting views about how group members thought they should negotiate authority when attempting to resist policies imposed on teachers. For instance, teachers believed that when working as a group to mitigate or change district policy we should do the following:

- Focus on improving what goes on in our classrooms
- Allow for anonymity, particularly when critiquing the district
- Gain the support of the union
- Make our position known first to authority figures before going elsewhere
- Maintain positive relationships with people at the top to ensure communication
- Try to name a problem as opposed to naming those we find problematic

Analysis revealed that members were not of one mind about how to negotiate authority. Tensions regarding how the group should engage with authority emerged on at least two occasions. First, group members were in disagreement about whether the group should endorse the resolution calling for a moratorium on standardized testing. Some members thought that calling for a moratorium on testing was a futile activity. They thought that it would be much more productive to focus on changes in testing policies (e.g., eliminating the use of standardized testing in primary grades). In other words, they believed a more moderate expectation to reduce testing was more likely to be successful than a full moratorium.

Differing discourses also emerged during conversations focused on a book chapter that the group was asked to write.[9] During these conversations, it became apparent that some teachers felt that it was important for them, as Ann put it, to work "with the system." This would mean attempting to communicate with district authority before engaging in acts of public resistance, like writing letters to the newspaper or appearing on a local television program. Other group members advocated for a more confrontational, preemptive approach that did not entail prior communication with district administrators before engaging in public acts of resistance. Their opinions about these approaches and what they constituted were variable and sometimes accommodated multiple discourses.

The following excerpts from our conversations exemplify how these discourses emerged while group members Barbara, Cindy, Daryl, and Ann worked on the chapter. In the following exchange, Barbara describes her perspective on how the group negotiates authority: "we've always tried—to work *with* the leadership of the district." She juxtaposes an alternative approach, which she finds to be counterproductive when, in line 9, she states, "We're not trying to sabotage or just go scream at them":

BARBARA: Well and also I think that we've always tried—to work *with* the leadership of the district. Um . . .

CINDY: Okay.

BARBARA: As let's change this together. Let's um . . .

DARYL: The . . .

BARBARA: I mean the meetings with Sally.

DARYL: Sally.

ANN: That's true.

BARBARA: We're not trying to sabotage or just go scream at them or . . .

CINDY: Uh hum.

BARBARA: Like some groups do.

DARYL: Information has been presented to the . . . to internal administration before it has been presented to external media for the large part.

BARBARA: But we have always tried to work through them first.

Throughout this conversation, when referencing individuals and entities that have had more adversarial relations with district authority than EAS has, Ann and Barbara use terms such as "whistle-blowers" and "extremists." However, in the following excerpt, an alternative perspective about these individuals also emerges. Ann begins this exchange by taking up and building on Barbara's and Daryl's comments about working with the district before going to outside sources. Ann also references the importance of communication, which is a theme that she previously emphasized in group meetings:

> I think that you're not gonna be heard by just being in somebody's face. And that's the thing about trying to work with the system. And you know look for those moments of opportunity or those windows of opportunity . . . like that assessment clause is a great thing for you to even fall back on now with what you are talking about. *Remember?* The union's gonna have input. Well this is what you know what we hear from teachers. This is what teachers want. This is how we really want this to be presented. You know I mean . . . it's like the communication thing. Go back to communication and what we mean. I just think that to *start there* before you go outside to the newspaper and the other things is gonna be . . . help your voice be heard more.

Later on, Cindy asks Daryl what he thinks of Ann's perspective on working with the system. He responds by positing an approach that accommodates both discourses when he says, "I think for my personality I prefer to be one of the people who tries to cooperatively solve a problem. I think it is often useful to have somebody out on the limb to get friends yelling behind you." In contrast to the terms others use when referencing those who are confrontational in their relations with institutional authority (i.e., "whistle-blowers," "screamers," "in somebody's face"), Daryl uses softer terms like "friends yelling" and "noisy and boisterous people."

Although Ann and Barbara continued to discuss what they found to be problematic with a more confrontational approach,

the chapter the group ultimately submitted includes the following paragraph originally composed by Ann (though vetted by the
entire group), which takes a position integrating both discourses
found in the group:

> When responding to top-down policy mandates that we think
> are harmful to students, we have tended to take the approach
> of working within the system by trying to communicate our
> concerns about district policies to administrators. We have also
> pushed against the system to make sure that our voice is heard
> on those occasions when administrators have not responded
> to our concerns, not provided us a place at the policy making
> table, or persisted in their enforcement of policies that do harm
> to children, families, and teachers.

Conclusions

The teacher collective we describe here emerged as a safe and productive space where members worked together to publicly contest
district and state policies, even when they disagreed on the tactics
for resistance. Our research documents and provides a resource
for understanding how teachers collectively enact agency as they
negotiate the curricular and testing/assessment policy mandates
within the context of a top-down policy environment. Teachers
do not simply comply with policy mandates or the dominant discourses underlying them. Instead, our research reveals teachers
coming together to actively and tactically engage with institutions
and structures about policies in order to uphold their pedagogical commitments. In so doing, they have worked with available
discourses, not necessarily discounting or embracing them but
accommodating them as they address collective goals. At times,
members figured out how to work within the system of institutional constraints in order to ensure the well-being of group

members by, for example, preserving the anonymity of untenured teachers. At other times, members were willing to directly confront and resist district authority, especially on those occasions when administration had not responded to concerns or provided space for teachers' voices.

As teacher educators, we have drawn on our work with EAS and the PI subcommittee of the union to endorse what we term *engaged teacher education*, which provides prospective and practicing teachers with opportunities to assert their agency in the policy-making process. From our vantage point, this approach is embedded within a vision of teacher education focused on the preparation of teachers as civic agents.[10] We further hold that there is a global need to talk back to policies that marginalize students, particularly those from nondominant communities. We draw on a collective perspective of policy making as a process that involves multiple stakeholders, enacting a democratic and transformative vision of schooling.

PART TWO

Professional Principles

CHAPTER FIVE

THE UNITED TEACHERS OF NEW ORLEANS STRIKE OF 1990

Emma Long

IN SEPTEMBER AND OCTOBER 1990, between 68 and 80 percent of New Orleans public school teachers refused to enter city schools over a contract dispute with their employer, the Orleans Parish School Board (OPSB). When negotiators for the school board refused a raise for its paraprofessionals and clerical workers, who were represented by the teacher union, United Teachers of New Orleans (UTNO), all members of the union went on strike—including its teachers. For three weeks, while school board and union negotiators continued at the bargaining table, striking teachers, paraprofessionals, and clerical workers walked the picket line and, in an additional move, collected signatures to remove members of the school board through a recall petition. In what became the longest strike in the New Orleans public school system, striking teachers exhibited principled professionalism through their solidarity with paraprofessionals and clerical workers, and their commitment to professional recognition and living wages for all school employees. Through oral history interviews conducted twenty-five years after the strike, evidence of teachers' solidarity with other school employees is especially clear. While school board documents and teacher contracts readily propose the economic value of their union, interviews with teachers and union leaders tell of the social and political importance the union played for its members. The interviews also reveal how strikers used tactics from grassroots campaigns, including the civil rights movement, to influence public opinion, maintain optimism among its rank and file, and persuade the OPSB and the New Orleans community of their professional worth.

UTNO functioned as a union where teachers had the opportunity to lead; position themselves as socially valuable, as connected to their ability to receive a living wage; and participate in local politics, as exhibited by their attempt to remove members of the OPSB during the strike. Principled resistance exhibited by the teachers, paraprofessionals, and clerical workers during the strike eventually swayed a large percentage of the community to support their pursuit of a raise and to sign petitions for the school board recall. The calculation, planning, and eventual compromise exhibited by union negotiators also reflected a commitment to principled professionalism during the strike—keeping the event from swaying toward chaos by informing teachers each step of the way and negotiating with an end in sight. The strike, a collaborative effort by public school teachers, paraprofessionals, and clerical workers, reaffirmed their role as professionals employed in New Orleans public schools.

UTNO Formation and the 1978 Strike

The UTNO strike of 1990 was not the first time New Orleans teachers refused to enter their schools of employment. In 1966 and 1969, unionized teachers represented by the predominantly black

American Federation of Teachers (AFT) Local 527 unsuccessfully went on strike for collective bargaining rights. In 1978, New Orleans public school teachers struck again, this time successfully after having integrated the ranks of the predominately white Orleans Education Association with the AFT Local 527.[1] As the first integrated education union in the South, UTNO negotiators agreed upon an 8 percent pay raise for the city's teachers, ending the strike after a week.[2] For many veteran teachers who participated in the 1990 strike, the 1978 UTNO strike gave them confidence and experience that applied to decisions in 1990. The success in 1978 persuaded many strikers to join the picket line when they believed their school board could do more to compromise.

The Strike of 1990

Talk of a possible strike began when UTNO and OPSB bargaining teams could not agree upon a new three-year contract in the summer of 1990. During negotiations, the union sought raises for the lowest paid of its membership, the paraprofessionals and clerical workers, rather than its teachers. However, negotiators from the OPSB declined to match the offer, citing a shortage of funds. When negotiators on both sides found little room for compromise, UTNO negotiators, led by African American union president Nat LaCour, suggested a strike.

At a mass meeting before the system's first day of school, the UTNO negotiating team urged union approval of LaCour's recommendation to strike if talks broke down. LaCour advised the teachers to go to work on the first day of school and to continue for two weeks. If negotiators did not reach a contract settlement by September 17, he suggested that UTNO should then strike. His recommendation for union members to strike meant that if the needs of paraprofessionals and clerical workers were not met at the bargaining table, then teachers would come out for the needs of their coworkers—a move that reflects the collaborative nature of schooling and the degree to which teachers, paraprofessionals, and clerical workers rely on each other. Once union members went on strike, the union would pressure for raises for all of its personnel. LaCour's suggestion secured the solidarity needed among UTNO rank and file.

Teachers, paraprofessionals, and clerical workers present at the meeting voiced their opinions on the proposal. However, the energy in the room grew when an African American teacher, Betty Sapp, rose to give an alternative suggestion: present members of the OPSB should be recalled from office. LaCour remarked how the overall mood toward the strike changed:

> One of our teachers went to the mic and she said, "I recommend that we recall the board." And when she said that, the members erupted in support. I mean, they were just screaming. This is an instance where we followed the will of our members. We then started—we launched the campaign through the course of the strike—to recall the board. So, sometimes you have to get behind your members. That came really from the floor of the membership, as opposed from the leadership—a lady by the name of Betty Sapp. She just said, "I think we ought to recall the board." And everybody erupted in support. I had the sense enough to know I had better go along with her.[3]

Sapp's idea would change the fate of the strike. Often unions function with top-down dynamics, in which ideas hatched by negotiating teams or leadership are met with either support or disagreement by rank-and-file members. This dynamic was transformed when negotiators chose to include Sapp's idea from the floor. The exchange, between LaCour (the union president) and Sapp (a teacher represented by the union), also illustrates the gender dynamics of the teacher union at the time of the 1990 strike.

While a majority of the union's rank and file was female, men often assumed positions of leadership. In LaCour's decision to "go along with her," a man in a leadership position acknowledged a woman's important role in the union and strike preparation.

The women who participated in interviews for this project never explicitly saw their participation in the union as feminist. Rather, female interview participants interpreted their role in UTNO as an extension of the civil rights movement. However, when ideas presented by women were given equal weight by UTNO leadership, the union reflected a modest commitment to gender equality. This exchange of ideas also indicates principled professionalism that positions union leaders and teachers as equal professional partners who depended on and listened to each other's input. At the end of the meeting, union members voted to approve LaCour's proposal, with Sapp's addendum. The union would continue to negotiate a contract with the OPSB for two weeks as teachers, paraprofessionals, and clerical workers entered their respective schools the following day.

In early September, each side of the bargaining table remained firm. Teachers across the city began to establish classroom routines and solid relationships with their students. Live Oak Middle school teacher Melanie Boulet, who is white, remarked, "I remember just diving right into teaching. By September [17], I remember kids knew me well enough that they actually wrote me letters when I was on the strike line."[4] Through UTNO building representatives, teachers stayed informed about the ongoing negotiations and confidently worked without much attention to the upcoming strike. But, for most union members, the moment UTNO called the strike, their commitment to their classrooms took a different form as they joined the picket line and pressured for professional recognition and living wages.

On September 17, 1990—the first day of the strike—school records reported that 68 percent of the city's 4,500 teachers did not show up for work, although UTNO claimed more than 80 percent of its membership honored the strike.[5] The first day of the strike also meant the beginning of the recall efforts to remove members of the OPSB. To recall members of the school board, teachers stood outside community centers, churches, and busy streets to collect signatures. At the bargaining table, UTNO negotiators withdrew all compromise proposals that included raises for paraprofessionals and clerical workers and increased health coverage. The union instead pushed for a $45 million contract that added to the original demands, plus a 10 percent raise for teachers for each of the next three years.[6]

For many of the striking teachers who joined the picket line, the protest over wages served as another example of their long commitment to activism in the city. Dr. Raphael Cassimere Jr. picketed alongside his wife, Inez, at her school of employment— Dibert Elementary School in Mid-City. The Cassimeres, both African American, relied on their experiences from the civil rights movement and previous teacher strikes—in the 1960s during the AFT Local 527 strikes and in 1978 during first UTNO strike—as motivation for 1990.[7] UTNO president Nat LaCour also connected his and other union members' efforts in the civil rights movement to their picket line in 1990:

> At the time of the 1990 strike, the district teaching force was overwhelmingly black and most of those blacks, I'm sure, had come through the 1960s, 70s, and 80s . . . So, most of the teachers who were in the system at that time too were actively involved. So, we came along with the civil rights movement. We were part of it. . . . The fact that the union was majority black and black people were concerned about improving their conditions, just belonging to the union and working to make education better, was all part of the civil rights struggle.[8]

At this time, UTNO had a largely female and majority black membership. For many women and minorities, the teaching profession had served as the initial step from the working class into a white-collar work environment. As LaCour and fellow members of the union bargaining team worked to end the strike by negotiating with the OPSB, the teachers' presence—picketing, chanting slogans, and singing on city sidewalks—provided a public display linking the strike to a wider dialogue on injustice in New Orleans.

As director of organizing for UTNO, Connie Goodly spent much of her time during the strike organizing the recall movement. While many in the community, including some teachers, thought the effort was unlikely to succeed, other teachers felt most passionate about this issue of the strike. In addition to collecting signatures on busy streets and in neighborhood centers, UTNO leaders strategically sought out a day when signatures would be easily verified and collected: October 6, 1990, the day of a statewide election in Louisiana. Union members who collected signatures could, on that day, ask voters leaving their polling stations to sign using the same name on their voter-identification card, providing less room for error.[9] This Election Day plan provided teachers with a calculated strategy to recall members of the board, which reinforced their professional standing in the community. As measures to recall OPSB members progressed along with rallies and picketing, some union members expressed excitement over their on-the-ground activism.

While administrators relied on substitutes to ease the commotion in their schools, it was clear that teachers were needed to make the school run as usual. School administrators asked teachers to rethink their commitment to the union. In the first week of the strike, teacher Melanie Boulet received a call from Armand Devezin, her friend and principal of Live Oak Middle School.

Devezin, who also served on the OPSB negotiating team, asked whether she might return to the classroom: "I got a call from the principal the first week of the strike—I can't remember what night it was—begging me. 'Melanie, please come back in. It's terrible in here.' And I said, 'I can't.' And he said, 'I knew it.'"[10] Boulet recalled that she and Devezin had a good relationship—they had begun working at Live Oak at the same time and could rely on each other for professional encouragement—yet her friendship with Devezin did not outweigh her commitment to the strike and to her fellow teachers, paraprofessionals, and clerical workers. Boulet's response to Devezin, despite their friendship, is an example of her principled resistance to the pull of administrative requests, even friendly ones.

New Orleans teachers also engaged in principled resistance when dealing with critiques from parents and the community. Carmen James, an African American, remembered confrontations with parents and relied upon her experience and knowledge as a special education teacher to address their concerns: "You had parents who would come in and say their little things about, 'You ought to be in there with these children instead of out.' Ignore it. I'm a special ed teacher. I teach emotionally disturbed children. The best way to approach those type of people is—ignore them . . . I needed [teachers] to pull together. I needed them not to waiver and think, 'I need to be back in that building.' 'I need you to stay right here.' And we were able to do that."[11] Reflecting her expertise with parents and students, James knew not to heed a parent's harsh words. She suggested the teachers on her picket line do the same. This example of principled resistance is specifically rooted in James's training as a special education teacher. Her professional response to community criticism helped keep the picket line outside of Dibert Elementary School from turning into a war of words.

While awaiting a final contract, UTNO members continued to picket, rally, and stage marches in the city. These opportunities to organize worked to keep members motivated and to remind the public why the teachers remained on strike. On September 31, 1990, as a nod to New Orleans music traditions, UTNO members staged a jazz funeral, instead of a march, for the burial of "Mr. Ed. U. Cation."[12] This symbolic gesture brought attention to the plight of the schools. As the days went by, students continued to receive subpar education, which concerned the city's teachers. But strikers would not return to their classrooms, believing that in the long run, ensuring a living wage for teachers, paraprofessionals, and clerical workers would benefit the New Orleans education system, including its students.

However, some teachers began to worry about their financial stability waiting for a new contract. James, who served as the building representative, listened to the concerns of many teachers on her picket line at Dibert Elementary. Without a steady paycheck, teachers' bills sometimes went unpaid: "This is people's lives we're talking about. Somebody could lose out on their home . . . One chick did lose a car because she didn't get her note in and her husband had to go and plead with the people for that, so there was a lot of circumstances that people don't realize. That when you strike, you know, yeah, you're out there for the group, but you're also putting yourself into a very precarious situation."[13] To deal with tight financial situations, James recommended teachers seek loans through the union, which were provided through funds from the AFT. There were also instances when teachers on the Dibert picket line came together to pay a bill—all chipping in to help their coworker. It was in these moments of strain that James claimed the striking teachers at Dibert felt like a family, which gave her strength as a leader on the picket line.

By October 6, 1990, negotiators had not met at the bargaining table for over a week.[14] This was also the day of the statewide election that marked the major push to gather signatures by UTNO members involved in the board recall movement. While union members stood outside polling stations, UTNO's negotiating team met again to work on a contract agreement with the OPSB negotiators. It was when LaCour and the union negotiators came up with a contract that both sides could agree on that they received a call from UTNO director of organizing Connie Goodly. Mike Stone, teacher and union negotiator, recalls:

> We had taken a break and Connie called the room we had for the union and said, "Uh, how's it going?" Nat says, "I think we're just about through"—we had just about agreed on everything—and she said, "Well don't give up the recall." And Nat said, "Too late, I've already told them that if we get this—we hadn't even capped off and signed off and agreed yet—but I told them if we get this, we'll stop the recall." . . . And she says, "Oh Nat, we got an office here full, stacks of petitions." . . . His plan for recalling [members of the board] had worked like clockwork.[15]

However, the negotiating team made the decision to drop the recall, which became a contested issue among UTNO members once the negotiators presented their final contract to the union at a meeting to vote to end the strike. The recall demand initially presented by Betty Sapp, from the ranks of the teaching members of the union, had been abandoned by union leadership.

On the night of October 7, striking teachers, paraprofessionals, and clerical workers represented by UTNO met to vote to end the strike. The negotiating team presented the final contract to its members. When they asked union members to vote for its approval, many wanted to stay on strike and expand the recall. Goodly remembered a faction of the membership who expressed disappointment in negotiators' decision to drop the recall: "I can remember one guy yelling and screaming—'That was not a bargaining chip. You shouldn't have done that.'"[16] Patti Reynolds, a teacher who struck at McMain High School, tried to persuade this faction of teachers to consider removing board members in the next election, reminding coworkers, "This isn't the end of that story."[17] In a vote that evening, a third of the teachers voted to continue the strike.[18]

This exchange over the recall movement illustrates the potential for principled resistance to point in contradictory directions. A faction of teachers wanted to continue the recall movement, but union leaders did not recognize that the recall had been the most compelling aspect of the strike for some of its members. Meanwhile, the recall petitions had become a very important and necessary bargaining chip in ending the teacher strike. For negotiators at the bargaining table, their interpretation of principled resistance convinced them they could not negotiate in good faith with a school board they were trying to remove. For the strike to end, those who wanted to continue the recall movement had to compromise their beliefs in order to reach a union agreement and get back into the public schools. Professional resistance included some measure of compromise.

Teachers returned to their classrooms on October 8, 1990, after accepting a three-year, $15.7 million contract. The contract included a 3 percent pay raise for all OPSB employees for the 1990–91 school year, a $50 per employee increase toward health benefits in the 1991–92 school year, and a 4 percent pay raise for the 1992–93 school year.[19]

Teachers were overwhelmingly pleased with the outcome of the strike. Boulet remarked on how happy she felt to get anything from OPSB and described the experience of striking with her fellow teachers as unifying: "To tell you the truth," she said, "I think that was a benefit of the strike—that we were unified and we went back in [the school] strong."[20]

Conclusion

This successful three-week strike in 1990 demonstrated the power that UTNO wielded in New Orleans, as well as its members' commitment to professional recognition for all of its ranks. Through the work of UTNO negotiating teams at the bargaining table, union members played an active role in challenging what they saw as economic inequality by negotiating in good faith to achieve a better economic standing.

New Orleans teachers also entered the political realm by collecting signatures from voters in an attempt to recall members of the school board. Then UTNO director of organizing Connie Goodly believed the effort to recall members of the OPSB in 1990 prepared the union for future political work, including the 1991 effort to elect Edwin Edwards over former Ku Klux Klan Grand Wizard David Duke in the Louisiana gubernatorial race.[21] The grassroots work of collecting signatures and endorsing candidates represented an avenue for traditionally disenfranchised communities in New Orleans to demand political change through the platform of a well-known union.

The combined efforts by the union and its members to combat economic and political inequality also highlight the social importance of the union for members of the teaching community in New Orleans. Pay increases and additional medical benefits, granted by the OPSB, reflected an understanding that these teachers conducted work deserving of such benefits. And, as the interviews highlight, the communal experiences of the picket line provided a space where men and women of all races, but the majority of them African American, could come together to share experiences and identify as part of a larger organization—UTNO.

The UTNO strike of 1990 represented a principled effort to convince OPSB negotiators of the importance of teachers, paraprofessionals, and clerical workers to the public school system in the city. Teachers incorporated principles of solidarity by striking for wage increases for their fellow union members in their decision to leave the classroom, reflecting their understanding of the collaborative nature of schooling. In interviews, teachers' reflections about their time on the picket line and at the bargaining table present a planned and organized strike, with a communal sense of solidarity and optimism. Their reflections on a strike that took place decades earlier highlight the principled and professional strategies incorporated to achieve UTNO demands.

Epilogue: The United Teachers of New Orleans Today

The fate of UTNO changed with the landfall of Hurricane Katrina on August 29, 2005. In the months after the storm, the Louisiana State Legislature passed Act 35, which allowed for the state-run Recovery School District (RSD) to take over the majority of the public schools in New Orleans. Weakened by Act 35, the OPSB fired all 7,500 of its teachers, essentially gutting UTNO of its membership. When the rebuilding effort began, RSD leaders opted to hire new, often uncertified teachers to fill its charter schools. Veteran teachers and union members believed they were purposefully left out of the system's rebuilding effort. Through lawsuits against the state and local school board, UTNO members attempted to define legal decisions like Act 35 as a union-busting move, an effort that failed. New Orleans schools remained union-free for eight years.

In 2013, teachers at Morris Jeff Community School unionized and created the Morris Jeff Association of Educators, an affiliate of the Louisiana Association of Educators. While their union became the first teacher union in the city after the storm, it had limited clout and no bargaining rights.[22] In 2014, teachers at Ben Franklin

High School voted to unionize with UTNO. They agreed to a three-year collective bargaining contract with their school board, which was to begin the following year.[23] They became the first charter school union in Louisiana to get a teacher contract. Two years after its formation, the Morris Jeff Association of Educators voted to unionize with UTNO, and a year later, in June 2016, they successfully bargained for a three-year teacher contract. Teachers at Morris Jeff Community School and Ben Franklin High School are the only educators in New Orleans schools to have collectively bargained for a contract with their independent charter school boards.[24]

In May 2016, teachers at Lusher Charter School attempted to unionize after collecting signatures from 60 percent of its employees. The Lusher school board, however, voted against recognition of the union. When teachers went back to vote on the issue, they could not garner enough votes to form a union. Instead, in a separate vote, Lusher paraprofessionals voted favorably for union representation.[25] A similar situation arose that same month when teachers from the International High School of New Orleans voted in favor of forming a union with its paraprofessionals. When its board refused to recognize the teacher union, teacher activists asked the National Labor Relations Board (NLRB) to oversee a vote. At a hearing on the issue, Brooke Duncan III, the school's attorney, argued the charter was not subject to the NLRB's federal authority because the school was formed under state law. UTNO lawyer Louis Robein claimed otherwise and argued that because the charter was a private employer, it must report to the NLRB. While a regional NLRB director ruled in favor of the union, the legal arguments have continued.[26] More recently, in March 2017, teachers at Mary D. Coghill Charter School petitioned to form a union with signatures from over 93 percent of its teachers.[27] In

May 2017, Coghill teachers voted to unionize, and the school's labor attorney, Meg Bigford, said she looked forward to negotiating a contract with the union after the summer break.[28] Unionization for charter school teachers post-Katrina has been a slow but ongoing process.

CHAPTER SIX

PROFESSIONAL PREPARATION

*Principled Responses to an Ethos of
Privatization in Teacher Education*

Margaret Smith Crocco

Introduction

Over the last twenty years, a pervasive sense of national anxiety about global economic competitiveness has catapulted conversations about educational reform to center stage. In the 1980s, *A Nation at Risk* raised the clarion call for standards-based reform.[1] In the 1990s, concerns over globalization produced further questions about the adequacy of American schooling in a globalizing world and set the bar at "excellence and equity for all."[2] Recent reform efforts aimed at promoting the Common Core agenda share a similar orientation: the demand for improvement of teaching and learning in the nation's schools.[3]

Although the public debate about quality has focused chiefly on schools and teachers, teacher education programs in higher education institutions are held responsible for the quality of the nation's teachers. The National Council on Teacher Quality, an organization established in 2000, states that its mission is "to improve the preparation, support, and recognition America provides for our teachers."[4] Another example is the Council for the Accreditation of Educator Preparation, formed from the merger of two other accrediting bodies in 2010 and authorized by the Council for Higher Education Accreditation. Collectively, these efforts to shame, rate, and regulate teacher education have created a measure of demoralization among teacher educators, many of whom believe that they are producing high-quality teachers and also that some aspects of educational reform are ill-advised and even detrimental to K–12 students, schools, and teachers.[5] Teacher educators, like many teachers, believe that problems of poverty and underfunding of schools are more likely causes of the achievement gap between students in wealthier and poorer school districts in this country, and to some extent between high-performing systems in other countries and school districts in the United States.

Of particular interest to this chapter is the impact of what I am calling an *ethos of privatization* on teacher education programs found in colleges and universities, which is a contributing factor to the demoralization among teacher educators. Privatization is an ideological orientation deriving its fundamental principles from market-based approaches to an industry that was previously seen as a public good. Values of efficiency, return on investment, and accountability serve as the chief yardsticks by which an industry is judged. These values have moved aggressively into education over the last several decades, with a discernible impact on institutions of higher education, public and private alike.[6] Among the symptoms of privatization in higher education are substitution of full-time faculty with poorly paid adjuncts, growth in administrative personnel aimed at compliance with accountability mandates, and declining levels of autonomy and control over the content of teacher education. These symptoms reflect the fact that the values of the marketplace are reshaping the relationships, work expectations, and heightened demand for measurable outcomes prevalent in colleges and universities today.

As used here, the phrase ethos of privatization represents my effort to provide a shorthand, if imperfect, term for the myriad forces associated with privatization that impinge on teaching and teacher education worldwide. Within this framework, students become "consumers," and faculty and administrators become "service providers." The relationships between students and faculty take on a transactional quality—that is, an emphasis on the exchange of goods and services, rather than on a humanistic framework in which the "product" of the educational experience cannot necessarily be quantified. Put another way, a commercial mind-set is reshaping education at all levels.[7] I should note that these forces affect teacher education, whether it takes place in a private college or a public university, inside or outside the United States.

Disruption of traditional (i.e., four- or five-year programs located in colleges or universities) approaches to teacher education has been promoted as a necessary innovation for improving outcomes. In K–12 schooling, the introduction of charter schools, even though they are often public-private partnerships, serves as a parallel example of how the ethos of privatization operates in this domain, as do virtual (online) schools run by for-profit companies. In many of these schools, teachers do not need to be certified, and they are rarely unionized like teachers in many public schools. For-profit charter management organizations run networks of schools, offering the oversight elected school boards provide to traditional public schools.

Just as the ethos of privatization is reshaping K–12 schooling, so, too, is it having an impact on teacher education. Calls for new modes of preparing teachers through fast-track programs of five or six weeks, such as Teach for America (TFA), reflect a set of values influenced by the private sector. These alternative programs have been promoted and supported by philanthropic and policy actors with extraordinary influence on federal and state lawmakers in both political parties. These fast-track programs have uncoupled teacher preparation from higher education and contributed to the erosion of demand for traditional teacher education. Alternative programs have relied on the notion that teachers are "born" rather than "made," reducing teaching to a set of techniques that can be easily and quickly acquired through their fast-track summer programs. They have also justified their existence by accusing traditional teacher education programs of having failed to develop teachers who are sufficiently committed to the needs of diverse learners. Such critiques of public schools, teachers, and teacher education are widely disputed by teacher educators and education scholars.[8]

Privatization has been a dominant force in many sectors of the neoliberal economy for decades, fed by the belief that private or quasi-private entities produce better results at lower cost than governmental entities.[9] Alternative certification programs such as TFA, Teachers for a New Era, and Relay Graduate School of Education raise many questions for university-based teacher educators about the degree to which fast-track programs of teacher preparation can adequately prepare individuals for the complex work of teaching, especially at a time in which standards are being raised.

By contrast, many individuals working in traditional teacher education have long been involved in efforts pushing the field in the opposite direction—that is, toward professionalization of teaching, believing it to be an occupation rooted in deep skills, dispositions, and knowledge of various types (i.e., content knowledge, pedagogical knowledge, and pedagogical content knowledge). Moreover, given what the research shows about the requirements for extended

preparation and opportunities for ongoing professional development of teachers in countries with higher-performing educational
systems than the United States, teacher educators worry that the
fast-track programs, uncoupled as they typically are from institutions of higher education, represent a step that is out of alignment
with other educational reform efforts in the United States.[10]

Today many teacher educators, like teachers, see teaching as a
profession under siege, especially from corporate philanthropists,
who put their faith in values derived from business and industry
as the solution to educational challenges.[11] These reform efforts,
as symbolized by those of the Bill & Melinda Gates Foundation,
have yielded disappointing results in effecting school improvement.[12] Increasingly, the politics and rhetoric of the education
reform movement have laid blame on teachers and, by extension,
teacher educators. Whether the critique is about teacher quality,
or that teachers' pensions are too costly, or that teacher unions
serve only to protect teachers who should be fired, or that teacher
education is too complacent, the constant drumbeat of bad press
has left both teachers and teacher educators feeling demoralized
and defensive.

These circumstances—and the emotional toll they exact—have
led teacher educators to join forces across the nation with teachers to promote improvements in practice while defending public
schools and sustaining hope and resilience in the face of a cultural
zeitgeist that seems determined to undermine their sense of self-
worth.[13] Nevertheless, conditions differ somewhat from state to
state in the manifestation or at least the timing of these trends,
which is not surprising given the fact that control over education
in the United States resides at the state and local levels. In many
places, new regulations associated with the accreditation of teacher
education programs are reshaping the ways in which teacher educators work with their teacher candidates, limiting teacher educators'

professional autonomy, standardizing the approach to teacher education, and emphasizing accountability measures that will demonstrate the quality of the overall program. In some states, teacher educators are held responsible for how the students of their teacher education graduates fare on high-stakes tests several years out from their graduation. Given these conditions and the bad press that schools and teachers have been subject to over the last decade, it is not surprising that the number of students entering teacher preparation programs has fallen dramatically.[14] Likewise, some programs of teacher education found in small private colleges are closing down under the twin burden of declining enrollments and heightened accreditation requirements.

Over the last twenty years, I have worked as a teacher educator and scholar in three state contexts. In each setting, I contributed directly or indirectly to the work of teacher preparation, with oversight responsibility for a program or set of programs in the higher education institution. As part of this work, I was responsible for compliance with accreditation demands and state regulations. I had regular contact with state policy leaders, and I was in ongoing communication with practicing teachers and other teacher educators. For this chapter, I have reflected upon and analyzed my experiences within the context of numerous state and federal policy briefs and pronouncements, accreditation reports and institutional self-studies, news accounts, and educational research about teacher preparation. Although my experiences cannot be taken as representative of larger realities, my conclusion is that teacher and teacher educator satisfaction and demoralization vary to some degree from state to state, despite discernible trends produced by policies promulgated by the federal government and the inescapable impact of national media and politics.

Recent research confirms the importance of state contexts in differentiating how educational policy initiatives get implemented.[15] In the section that follows, I briefly describe the policy environments in the states in which I have worked (New York, Iowa, and Michigan) over the last ten years, offer glimpses into the principled resistance of teacher educators working in these contexts, and conclude with a few suggestions about how teacher educators can sustain hope and resilience in dealing with these difficult times.

Educational Reform and Teacher Education in Three States

Over the last several decades, the federal government has gradually assumed greater control over education through the power of the purse strings, in large measure as a result of the 1965 passage of the Elementary and Secondary Education Act (ESEA); its successor, the No Child Left Behind Act of 2001; and the Obama administration's Race to the Top competition.[16] In 2009, introduction of the Common Core curriculum standards further contributed to reshaping the educational landscape, pushing authority away from the states until passage of the Every Student Succeeds Act in 2016, which was an effort to reauthorize ESEA by shifting power back to the states. In the churn of national educational reform, local conditions have induced variability despite privatization efforts endorsed by national political parties and private policy actors. For example, the push for charter schools has manifested itself differently across the three states in which I have worked. However, one condition felt uniformly by teacher preparation programs in these states has been a dramatic decline in enrollment, anywhere from 10 to 50 percent in the number of individuals entering traditional teacher certification programs.[17] More recently, a similar decline in applicants to alternative programs such as TFA has occurred.[18]

Several other differences in state contexts bear noting. By contrast with both Iowa and Michigan, New York has always been more centralized in its approach to curriculum and instruction, standards, and assessment than other states, including its nearest neighbors, New Jersey and Connecticut. A series of exit exams, the Regents, has existed in New York since 1866. Likewise, New York includes the largest school district in the country, New York City (8 million inhabitants, 1.2 million students), whereas Michigan's largest city, Detroit (about 675,000 inhabitants as of 2016), has a student population of just under 50,000, and the state's next largest city, Grand Rapids (around 190,000 inhabitants), has a student population of around 17,000. By contrast, Iowa's total population hovers around 3 million, with only one city of significant size, Des Moines (around 200,000 inhabitants), and a student population of slightly more than 32,000.

All three states have both rural and urban areas that lawmakers and policy advocates must consider in developing school policies, but the mix of urban, suburban, and rural districts tilts toward urban and suburban in New York, rural in Iowa, and suburban and rural in Michigan. In both Iowa and Michigan, online high schools called "virtual schools" have emerged as platforms for earning a diploma in sparsely settled regions with few school options. In all three states, immigrant students are a factor, but in Michigan and Iowa, where population declines and other factors have influenced state politics, new policies to address the shortage of ESL teachers, for example, have not emerged as a legislative priority.

New York

In 2010, New York State won Race to the Top funding from the US Department of Education, which imposed a set of requirements on schools, including adoption of the Common Core curriculum, more rigorous teacher evaluation measures, and elevation of the cap on the creation of charter schools. By 2012, resistance to these policies had begun to build statewide, but especially in New York City. Then mayor Michael Bloomberg and his chancellor of education Joel Klein promoted change on a variety of fronts, doing battle with Michael Mulgrew, head of the United Federation of Teachers (UFT), a teacher union with over 200,000 members. During this period, David Steiner led the state board of education. He later became dean of the college of education at Hunter College and creator of the Relay College of Education, a non-university-based, fast-track program for teacher certification, which has subsequently been replicated outside New York. Steiner's leadership ushered in a new era of teacher preparation, which essentially uncoupled teacher preparation from colleges and universities. New York City already had a sizable presence of TFA recruits, as well as the New York City Teaching Fellows program, an alternative certification program for career changers. During this period, it became a hotbed of privatized experimentation; charter school networks, such as the Knowledge is Power Program (KIPP) and Green Dot, which were imported from other states; and homegrown networks, such as the Success Academy Charter Schools run by Eva Moskowitz.

Teachers, teacher educators, and parents have all expressed concerns—volubly—about the amount of testing found in New York's schools, which became a key setting for the "opt-out" movement against tests in the schools, especially in the affluent suburbs of Long Island. Likewise, teachers raised numerous concerns about the "value-added" measures used for their annual professional performance reviews, which districts can adopt for purposes of deciding about tenure and termination but which have been shown by scholars to be highly unreliable. Teachers joined groups such as the Badass Teachers Association (www.badassteacher.org/) and BustED Pencils (bustedpencils.com/) to voice their concerns.

Many New York City teacher educators joined these efforts and, through letters and blogs, voiced opposition to educational reform that was considered damaging to the needs of children and preservice and in-service teachers. Teacher educators, many of whom are also scholars, contributed their research and evaluation of programs they opposed for various reasons, such as the teacher education evaluation system edTPA.[19] This system was developed and marketed by Pearson, a corporation whose association with high-stakes testing nationally made it an easy target for attack. A recent critique of edTPA suggests that it has little predictive value in terms of good teaching, is expensive for students, and may be undermining the goal of diversifying the teaching force.[20]

Other scholars use blogging as a vehicle for resistance. For example, Alan Singer of Hofstra University on Long Island writes regularly for the *Huffington Post*. He has attacked Pearson multiple times in his blog and, in other venues, railed against what he dubs "the corporate octopus" of educational reform.[21] Some teacher educators such as Celia Oyler at Teachers College, Columbia University, in New York City use their own blogs to give voice to the resistance of teachers to standardized testing, among other topics.[22] In short, many teacher educators in colleges and universities use writing as a weapon of resistance, whether it is on the pages of Facebook, in an online news outlet, or through their scholarship, to explain the situation of public education, teachers, and teacher education today. Their intention is to provide ongoing support for teachers, both future and current, and the daily struggles they face in dealing with ill-advised educational reform measures, especially those related to accountability, high-stakes testing, and scripted lessons.

Iowa

The discourse of educational reform in Iowa shares a few features with the situation in New York, although teacher educators' concerns in Iowa have manifested themselves in a far more muted fashion until quite recently. In 2013, then governor Terry Branstad, a Republican, called for an annual educational summit to gather support for what he called a "blueprint for change" that was rolled out through a series of town-hall meetings across the state over the next several years. The vision for this blueprint came from Linda Fandel, whose work as a journalist for the *Des Moines Register* had called attention to the decline in Iowa's student achievement on the National Assessment of Educational Progress tests, which are seen as the "gold standard" for national achievement tests in the United States.

In 1992, Iowa students' scores in math and reading stood at the top of the fifty states. By 2011, Iowa had slipped to the middle of the pack. Branstad brought Fandel into his administration as special advisor on education and hired a "director" (or chief state school officer) for Iowa's educational system, Jason Glass. Glass didn't remain in Iowa for long, leaving the state in 2013. He was succeeded by Brad Buck, who had, like most of the directors before him except for Glass, come up through the ranks within the state.

Although Iowa was the last state in the nation to adopt state curriculum standards, it shrewdly rebranded them as the "Iowa Core," a tactic that managed to avoid the contentiousness over the Common Core that caused some states, such as Indiana and Georgia, to jettison them when they proved politically unpopular. Furthermore, although debated strongly across the state in a series of town-hall meetings, the educational blueprint crafted by Glass and dubbed "One Unshakable Vision" moved forward through the legislature. At the same time, Iowa served as a governing state for the new performance-based student assessments, known as Smarter Balanced, that were linked to the Common Core. With ACT, Pearson, and the Iowa Test of Basic Skills all operating out of eastern Iowa, the resistance to the educational testing movement in Iowa was, at least at first, virtually nonexistent.

In June 2013, Branstad signed an educational reform law based on his reform blueprint. The law raised the starting salary for teachers, established a "teacher leadership" career ladder, provided tuition remission for teachers in critical STEM areas, increased school funding, extended student teaching to a full year from a semester, expanded online education, provided a "seal" to signify "college and career readiness" for Iowa high school graduates, created pilot programs in competency-based education, and called for teacher evaluations based in part on student test scores. Despite these legislative victories, some members of the state legislature called on the governor to do away with the state department of education, free local school districts from the Iowa Core, retreat from Smarter Balanced, and abandon plans for value-added measures of teacher evaluation. As of 2015, Governor Branstad and Iowa Department of Education Director Brad Buck withdrew the state from the Smarter Balanced consortium of states and promised greater flexibility for school districts. Given rising sentiment against national "overreach," as it came to be known, in policy making about education and other arenas, this development in Iowa tracked close to the trend lines occurring in many other places.

Confident of their ability to work through local elected representatives, state teachers' organizations, and the Iowa Department of Education, teacher educators did not seem to feel as demoralized by reform efforts as did teachers in New York, although they drew on some of the same professional principles and practices—for example, autonomy in decision making, educational research as warrant for policies, and professional solidarity through organizations such as the Iowa Association of Colleges of Teacher Education—to advance their views. In keeping with the ethos of the Iowa caucuses, local school boards, teachers, and parents manifested throughout these controversies a striking willingness to work together to return Iowa to a stronger position in cross-state educational rankings. At the same time, Iowa educators and teacher educators enjoyed distance from the negative portrayals of public education often found in the pages of the *New York Times,* the *Wall Street Journal,* films such as *Waiting for "Superman,"* or the attentions of corporate philanthropists. Charter schools were few; unions remained relatively strong; and educators had plenty of allies, some of whom were former educators, in the state legislature. When the governor asked higher education institutions for an alternative certification program, the three Regents universities (University of Iowa, Iowa State, and the University of Northern Iowa) came together and developed one that they felt did the least harm while being responsive to the need for more teachers of science and math in the state.

The proposals causing greatest concern among colleges of teacher preparation in Iowa were related to Governor Branstad's call in 2011 to raise the grade point average threshold to 3.0, along with changes to cutoffs and requirements related to Praxis test scores. Many smaller teacher education institutions were concerned about the edTPA program that Iowa had adopted, which was developed and piloted at the University of Iowa. As elsewhere, the financial burden and other administrative aspects of this test fell more heavily on smaller institutions and poorer students. In a state with a large testing industry as exemplified by the headquarters of ACT and a significant presence by Pearson, this test did not provoke the outrage that it did in New York.

Nevertheless, teachers and teacher educators became concerned in late 2016 about a piece of legislation that would seriously limit collective bargaining rights for teachers. In February 2017, these groups joined forces for the March for Iowa's Teachers in the state capitol of Des Moines.[23] Although the effort to maintain full collective bargaining rights was ultimately unsuccessful, the threat brought together many teachers and teacher educators in a new group called Iowans for Public Education, which currently has a membership of over 11,000 and is dedicated to defending public education and teachers going forward. In Iowa as elsewhere, the perceived threat to public education, especially once Betsy DeVos became US Secretary of Education, appears to have galvanized resistance in a state where efforts toward privatization via charters, school choice, and vouchers previously had little impact.

Michigan

As a postindustrial state buffeted to a significant degree by economic hardship related to the decline of the automotive industry, Michigan presents an interesting third case of educational reform. High-stakes tests in this state go back to the 1970s, with the introduction of the Michigan Educational Assessment Program. In the 1990s, Republican governor John Engler, who was seen by his supporters as a champion of educational reform, garnered national attention by modifying the teacher tenure law, advocating for interdistrict school choice, championing charter schools, and leading an overhaul of K–12 school finance, which shifted funding for schools from local property taxes to the state sales tax. Although the pace of change slowed considerably during Engler's third term in office, his initiatives continued during the administration of his successor, Democratic governor Jennifer Granholm. In 2011, Granholm's successor, Republican governor Rick Snyder, ended the "last in, first out" approach to teacher hiring and firing in Michigan. Tenure would now take five years to earn and would remain provisional, based upon achieving annual ratings of "effective" in the teacher evaluation process. In 2013, the legislature began considering a new program of teacher evaluation that would include value-added measures (40 percent of the total rating) as well as evaluations done by the principal or a proxy. Although this didn't pass as originally proposed and ended up leaving school districts with some flexibility in how teachers would be evaluated, it did tighten up the process overall.

A unique feature of the Michigan schooling landscape is its "school of choice" program, in which the vast majority of public school districts allow students from other districts to enroll, albeit in limited numbers.[24] This has proved disruptive to school budgets, especially those in urban areas where students typically move into neighboring suburban districts. Likewise, the promotion of charter schools in the state, including a high proportion of for-profit charters in Detroit, has contributed to the siphoning of students from traditional public schools. Charter schools and school choice provisions have not led to higher levels of student achievement in Detroit, according to recent reports,[25] and they have produced accusations of fiscal mismanagement of public funds.[26] Despite the poor performance of the state's charter schools, it's important to concede that several of the chief "authorizers" of charter schools in Michigan have been universities (e.g., Central Michigan, Eastern Michigan, Oakland), who originally saw potential in this form of educational experimentation to improve student outcomes. Today, many of these universities—at least unofficially—concede the failure of these schools. Moreover, a recent study on school financing has shown that the state's choice and charter policies have contributed to the difficult financial straits in which many school districts find themselves.[27]

The drama of Michigan's largest city, Detroit, as it fell into bankruptcy in 2013 has played itself out nationally in a variety of media forums, reflecting concerns about the health of cities more generally. The Flint water crisis and the restructuring of Detroit Public Schools in 2016–17 both provoked heated reactions in the state, which were made even more contentious when legislation related to Detroit Public Schools included a provision allowing for hiring uncertified teachers. Such a provision seemed totally out of alignment with Governor Snyder's call to make Michigan a higher performing state by 2020. Accomplishing this goal would require an enormous leap forward since Michigan now ranks toward the bottom of the 50 states in several measures of student achievement, including early literacy.[28]

For teacher educators in Michigan, the chief foray into privatization came with the Michigan Teacher Corps (MTC), an urban residency program designed to provide teachers for "hard-to-staff" districts. Supported by philanthropic funds and public dollars, individuals recruited into this program worked in a group of Detroit Public Schools for a year, having completed only a brief preparation for schooling during the summer. Much like the TFA model and the New York City Teaching Fellows, the MTC presented itself as a program concerned with equity and social justice and providing "radically simple training" that focuses on "key skills new teachers need to get off to a strong start."[29] The program also emerged as a result of chronic teacher shortages in the city. In early summer 2017, a new superintendent, Dr. Nicholas Vitti, was hired to run the Detroit Public Schools Community District. In speaking to a group of teacher educators from across the state in June of 2017, Vitti pledged to work with traditional teacher education programs in Michigan on improving schools in Detroit. The MTC program has quietly closed down.

As in other states, resistance and resilience efforts took the form of research and writing in opposition to changes perceived as counterproductive to improvement of education, respect for children's needs, and support for teachers' high-quality performance. For example, at Michigan State University, editorship of the *Journal of Teacher Education* has provided a platform for writing editorials about educational reform and the warrant of educational research behind recent initiatives such as edTPA.[30] Scholar-activists such as Jennifer Berkshire advance ideas in favor of principled resistance by writing blogs, using Twitter, authoring op-ed pieces for *Huffington Post*, or creating YouTube videos or podcasts to voice their concerns about teachers exiting the profession.[31] Berkshire's letter appears on Alyssa Hadley Dunn's blog. Dunn, with other colleagues at Michigan State University, recently wrote an article about teacher resignation letters that provide evidence of the demoralization found among many teachers nationwide.[32] Bringing these sad stories to light is an effort to raise public awareness about these issues in the hope that lawmakers, policy makers, and the public are aware of the (perhaps unintended) consequences of recent educational reform efforts.

Sustaining Hope and Resilience

Teacher educators work in privileged and distinctive positions in higher education. Their relative power and freedom to voice their opinions, which is protected by the academic freedom found in most universities, allows them space to use their positions to broadcast the plight of teachers. Many of them are doing this, enlisting a variety of tools to speak out about the state of teaching today. Although they are frustrated and, to a considerable extent, demoralized about the ways in which their work and that of teachers gets portrayed in policy circles and in the media, they are fortunate to have a platform that allows them to work in concert with teachers for change without fear of losing their jobs.

In terms of the challenges teacher educators face with their own work, one illustration of the influence of place relates to accreditation. Changing standards for accreditation have had much less effect in Iowa, where accreditation is done by the state, as opposed to Michigan and New York, where the Council for the Accreditation of Educator Preparation oversees the process. Nevertheless, edTPA, with its considerable cost and negative impact on the recruitment of diverse individuals into teaching, is used in both Iowa and New York. Although the test is currently not required in Michigan, teacher education policies in that state, as elsewhere, are constantly being revisited by departments of education. In short, the future is unclear, despite growing research indicating the manifold limitations of this approach to teacher evaluation.[33]

Across the three states profiled here, certain patterns of principled resistance by teacher educators can be seen. Teacher educators come together with teachers to voice their opposition to damaging policies through established organizations such as the Iowa Association of Colleges of Teacher Education or Michigan's Directors and Representatives of Teacher Education Programs, as well as through newer ones like the Badass Teachers Association or BustED Pencils or Iowans for Public Education. Teacher educators in research institutions use their scholarship to advance the cause of equity, question how policy decisions have been arrived at, and give prominence to preferred reform pathways that will improve outcomes for the least privileged students in public schools. Unsurprisingly, many teacher educators use their teaching to take up ideas around equity and social justice that they hope their students will carry into their own classrooms and that will sustain them as they deal with the difficult circumstances of many classrooms today.

Teacher education has always been engaged in connections to practice to a degree that many other higher education programs and departments have not been. Teacher educators today are closely connected to schools and teachers, through both their own graduates and the mentor or cooperating teachers who host their preservice teachers in their classrooms for the practicum. They share in the feelings of demoralization that are so common in today's schools. Although teacher educators may not be leaving their jobs in colleges and universities to the same extent or with similar public testimonials about the reasons for their departures (at least as far as I know), some teacher educators talk about their desire to "deinstitutionalize" themselves and work for social justice outside academic life. Notable examples of educators taking this course of action are Kevin Kumashiro, previously dean at the University of San Francisco, or Lee Anne Bell, previously director of teacher preparation at Barnard College, Columbia University. This is not, of course, an option available to everyone. In the meantime, many teacher educators continue to write, teach, speak out, protest, and resist the problematic policy legacies of the last several decades.

Pushing back against forces that undermine the quality of teacher education is an ethical as well as a professional obligation, even if the means adopted toward this end differ from person to person and place to place. From the standpoint of history, hope may arise from the reality that policy initiatives in education, like enrollment, seem to have a cyclical quality, a shelf life, if you will, before the pendulum swings in the opposite direction. Although contemporary challenges are different from those of decades ago, the need for hope and resilience in the face of today's assaults on the quality and integrity of teacher education and teaching remains. In many places, resistance and solidarity with teachers are, in fact, the order of the day.

CHAPTER SEVEN

BUILDING FOUNDATIONS FOR PRINCIPLED RESISTANCE

Tom Meyer, Christine McCartney,
and Jacqueline Hesse

TO CREATE MORE EQUITABLE EDUCATION and to resist policies that encroach on their professional wisdom, teachers need opportunities to do the personal and collective work necessary to build the language and confidence to act and advocate as they see fit. As educators, our own principled resistance involves supporting others in gaining the knowledge, skills, and dispositions necessary to reclaim our profession through a yearlong National Writing Project (NWP) invitational institute for educators called Leadership in the Teaching of Writing. Like our colleagues in the NWP network who offer similar institutes, we believe that all teachers are capable of principled leadership, extending their professionalism beyond the classroom door as they engage in dialogue with others. In this chapter, we briefly describe our institute and some ways we invite educators to explore and refine their professional beliefs, name what they are doing in their classrooms, and move toward public, principled actions. In doing so, we draw on James Moffett's ideas about writers' need to write first for themselves before expanding to an audience of "unknown others."[1] Our work extends the conversation about the ways in which writing functions in teachers' professional lives;[2] our institute provides participants with the opportunity to articulate, clarify, and publicly act upon their beliefs. The work of the NWP and this chapter are grounded in the belief that professional development, with professional writing at its core, is an integral part of preparing educators for principled resistance and leadership.[3]

Dilemmas of Practice and Principled Resistance

Teaching is unpredictable and complex; wide gulfs can separate our principles and intentions from the reality of day-to-day classroom practice.[4] Teachers may subordinate their ideals in order to have a chance for tenure; others may ignore their beliefs about teaching and learning to follow scripted modules or to focus curriculum on test preparation. Professional development, designed to help schools realize preset goals, often positions teachers as receivers of information without any wisdom of practice. To disrupt this narrative, we invite teachers to work from inside the system to make meaningful change within their classrooms and schools based on principled practice.

We believe teachers can pursue a principled practice, resist unjust curriculum, and work publicly to advocate for what is right. In line with Henry Giroux, we see curriculum and education as "terrain[s] of struggle . . . shot through with ethical considerations."[5] For this reason, educators must not ignore these struggles, but study them, publicly resisting when necessary. Acting to change the world, however, does not come with a clear set of guidelines; teachers need to be cautious as they resist, in order to honor their professionalism and protect their jobs. Dilemmas of practice are often wedded to particular contexts and specific people, leaving many teachers fearful of overstepping real or perceived professional boundaries and roles. Debra Meyerson informs our thinking, describing "tempered radicals" as "everyday leaders" who foster incremental change from within their organizations.[6] Their actions can be small, such as "refusing to silence aspects of themselves that make them different from the majority," or large, such as working "deliberately to change the way [their] organization does things" or "organizing collective action."[7]

Expanding Professional Voices

Teachers with self-knowledge and practice articulating their pedagogy and principles will be more likely to see themselves as teacher-leaders who can be public in their beliefs and actions, entering into dialogue and collaboration with others. Moffett's conception of "discourse distances" maps writers' natural trajectory of writing first for themselves, then for trusted others, and, finally, for unknown others.[8] Adapting Moffett's ideas to our work, we invite teacher-writers to first make their ideas accessible to themselves, reflecting on their lives and work as they write reflections, narratives, and autobiography. Through analytical conversations and writing, some may elect to share their writing with trusted others. In this process, as they write about aspects of their professional lives and practice, they can sharpen their writing and also their understanding of what they are writing about.[9] As teachers become more confident, some might invite "unknown others" into a conversation about practice in formal publications, by sharing their practice at conferences, and in other public settings.[10] In this conception of teacher development and in our pedagogy (see figure 7.1), as teachers build self-knowledge they become more cognizant about their principles through articulating them; we believe that these new understandings support teachers as they become more

FIGURE 7.1 How teacher development supports principled resistance.

personal and professional
SELF-KNOWLEDGE

practice articulating
(pedagogical & professional)
PRINCIPLES

willingness to move into
PUBLIC REALM

confidence to engage in
**TEACHER-INITIATED
LEADERSHIP**

PRINCIPLED RESISTANCE

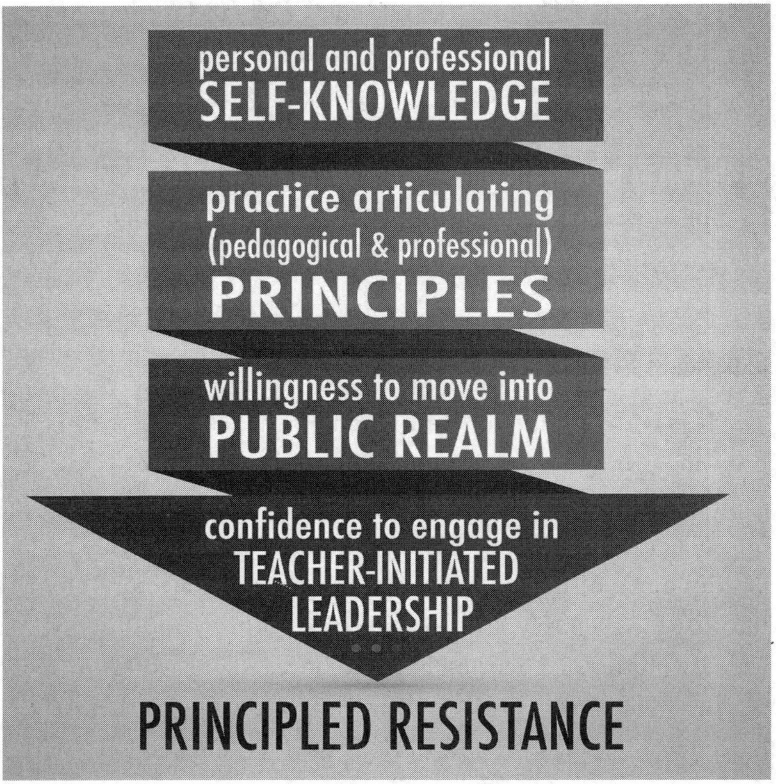

willing to open their doors to others, known and unknown. We then challenge teachers to draw from their professional beliefs to initiate change both within and beyond their classrooms. These principled actions often entail a form of resistance.

The Instructional Setting for Our Work

Since 2013, we have collaboratively designed, facilitated, and revised an NWP-affiliated yearlong institute, Leadership in the Teaching of Writing, comprising three corequisite courses: Teacher as Writer, Teacher as Learner, and Teacher as Leader. Participants who complete the institute earn nine postgraduate credits. In this section, we offer a brief description of the three courses. Throughout the remainder of the chapter, we incorporate several examples of how instruction functions to support participants in articulating, clarifying, and publicly acting upon their beliefs. We draw on three years of experience leading this work, during which time we studied participants' writing, including application essays, coursework, and "letters of reflection" completed at the end of every course. To the degree that we can, we name and briefly explain the instruction linked to particular pieces of writing.[11]

Beginning in May and ending in April, the institute has a blended learning format and includes twenty daylong class meetings and cycles of nonsynchronous learning activities, which we collectively document and curate on WordPress. At the conclusion of all three courses, we ask participants to write a letter of reflection in which they discuss their learning, quoting from their own writing as well as our collective readings. We ask them to point out particular moments that mattered and to identify areas of instruction to "keep, lose, or change."

The institute includes cohorts of fifteen to twenty educators selected on the basis of their written applications and group interviews. In the application, participants describe their schools, their instruction, and hunches about what helps students learn; they also submit samples of student work as a way to illustrate their practice. At collegial interviews, participants read aloud and discuss selected samples of their students' writing in the company of others. The cohorts are composed of educators from a variety of contexts, from the preschool through the college level, who have different areas of subject matter expertise and experience. In a recent cohort of sixteen educators, an interview group included a seasoned community college composition teacher; a midcareer social studies teacher from an alternative, urban high school; and a science, technology, engineering, and mathematics (STEM) teacher who had three years of experience and taught at a rural middle school.

In the first course, Teacher as Writer, we meet in person ten times to build our collective knowledge about composition and the role that writing plays in our lives, classrooms, and communities. The daily instruction begins with "writing into the day" and ends with "writing out of the day." In between, there are shared readings of articles and chapters related to writing and writing instruction. Participants also design and lead eighty-minute writing workshops. Each teacher creates an inquiry workshop, making public their efforts to understand how students develop content knowledge and skills as readers, writers, speakers, and thinkers. In the workshops, teachers invite colleagues to analyze the practice through firsthand literacy experiences and the study of student writing. In the subsequent courses, Teacher as Learner and Teacher as Leader, we meet face-to-face on five fall and five spring Saturdays. The focus of the fall course is action research. Informed by their goals for student learning and writing, teachers try something in their classrooms and write descriptive analyses about "what happened when . . . and why it might matter." During this sustained inquiry process, they "enter the parlor" of ideas through research related to the classroom inquiries they conduct.[12] In the spring, participants design, implement, and reflect on locally meaningful leadership projects, extending their work into the public sphere. The structured, professional writing and learning community provided by these courses allows teachers to strengthen their pedagogy while exploring and acting on their beliefs about teaching and learning.

Building Self-Knowledge

Early in the institute, we read "All Writing Is Autobiography," in which Donald Murray postulates that "we become what we write" and that when we write, we build self-knowledge.[13] Toward these ends, we regularly invite teachers to write, examine, and reexamine stories they tell about themselves as learners and teachers. Along with Murray, Robert Yagelski helps us understand how the process of "professional writing" enables participants to understand their beliefs. He explains, "When we write, we enact a sense of ourselves as beings in the world . . . Writing both shapes and reflects our sense of who we are in relation to each other and the world around us."[14] In some cases, participants write about their actual classrooms or schools. In other cases, the contexts they allude to are more broadly structural or discursive. Here, Emma, a social studies teacher in an alternative high school, reflects on the role that writing can play in mediating the interplay of her beliefs and the "propaganda" she encounters: "Through professional writing, I own my voice and strength as an educator and clarify my beliefs. In many ways it is the most challenging writing, as my beliefs about education are strong—visceral even—and subjected to a constant stream of propaganda that disputes beliefs I hold to be obvious about what is best for children."[15]

Early in our institute, we view Chimamanda Ngozi Adichie's TED talk "The Danger of a Single Story" and engage in a "loop writing" process. Peter Elbow developed loop writing to help writers develop new perspectives by completing several short, prompted pieces of writing in succession.[16] In our variation, we first ask participants to collect language from Adichie's talk; each of the subsequent loops last about eight to ten minutes. First, participants record their initial thoughts about the talk. In the next loop, participants write a story from their teaching lives. The third loop involves rereading what they have generated and underlining a central idea, which they use to start a new loop, allowing the writing to go in a new direction. A next loop involves identifying and writing from the first-person point of view of someone implicated in one of the earlier loops—for instance, a student, a colleague, or an administrator. In the final loop, we ask participants first to read everything they have written and then to write a response to these questions: What themes are emerging in your writing? What are you *really* writing about? One recent participant, a fifth-grade teacher named Renee, wrote, "When we choose to show, or 'see' a person as one thing, and only one thing, that is what they become. How often do we do this as educators? How often is it done to us as teachers? How many times have we done it to ourselves?"[17] Many teachers, like Renee, carry self-constructed stories that are self-defeating, locking them into cycles of disempowerment and doubt. Deficit self-definitions place teachers at risk of internalizing oversimplified stories about themselves as educators, making it difficult to resist when events, people, or ideas conflict with their professional principles and beliefs.

Writing offers educators an opportunity to question fixed notions we hold. Yagelski explains that as we write, we have a unique ability to be in the present, reflect on the past, and imagine the future.[18] Through writing and dialogue, educators can explore their learning while rehearsing intentions and rationales for action. Here, Tammy reflects how, as a younger student, she wrote for grades, which later limited her ability to teach writing. She imagines a new way to teach: "As a student, I was . . . writing only for teacher approval and a good grade. My students' transformation as writers will never happen unless I transform myself. I need to write with them and for them. I need to let them see how I process, how I struggle to pick just the right words. Most of all, I need to let them see how the act of writing something that is meaningful to me transforms me as a human being."[19] Tammy writes to "transform" her teaching practice. Like other past participants in NWP invitational institutes, she positions herself as a "writer among writers," using her own experiences to gain insight into the supports her students need.[20] Her intentions suggest a revision to her pedagogical principles. In embracing the power of modeling, she asserts a broader professional principle: educators must make their own learning visible. Our hope is that through reflective writing, participants can revisit the past and imagine new ways to teach that align with their anchoring beliefs.

Practice Articulating Principles

Our institute invites participants into a professional community that involves reciprocity and vulnerability. With ongoing support from members of the cohort, each participant designs an original teaching workshop and crafts and revises original writing. In these processes of creation, participants speak and write as a way to know themselves, but also as a way to articulate their beliefs with known others. They depend on one another for collegial feedback in various forums, not just in face-to-face whole-group discussions, but also in writing groups and online.

The writing groups, which include up to four participants, initially meet several times during the summer for one- to two-hour sessions. Over the course of the year, participants read excerpts from freshly written pieces, as well as midprocess and finished pieces they have worked on with their writing groups. Like Whitney, who claims that the revision of writing in the midst of others permits the revision (and "transformation") of self, we believe participants have a chance to explore, reframe, and reimagine their teaching together.[21] By routinely inviting teachers to practice naming and writing about their principles and practices in person and on the blog, we support their movement toward more public audiences and actions. This sequence follows Moffett's notions of writing for self, known others, and eventually, unknown others.

Paulo Freire explains that everyone has a right to "name the world"—to truthfully and humanely name the constructs and contexts of the world and identify that which influences and conflicts with his or her principles and beliefs.[22] To gain self-knowledge, we need practice writing and speaking about what we are doing and why. Here, we describe three methods we use to support participants in building self-knowledge with known others in person and online.

About midway through our year, participants craft a piece we call "professional fingerprints." In it, teachers write on our blog about a guiding teaching passion that marks their practice, illustrating how that "fingerprint" manifests in their work. This allows teachers to practice articulating their professional convictions. Emma works with sixteen- to twenty-one-year-old students, who, after encountering significant obstacles in previous schools, generally feel "disengaged from and discouraged about school." Emma describes her efforts to create an environment where students start telling new stories while actively exploring the "power of people to create change" and challenge "dominant narrative[s]":

> I have always been interested in the dual potential of school to reinforce the status quo or to challenge and transform it . . . In my social studies class, students explore social, economic, physical and political aspects of their neighborhood and connect that exploration to learning about the structure of government, its role in our local lives, and the power of people to create change. I use multiple "texts" when looking at a particular topic and use the different texts to interrogate meaning. I want students to examine multiple sources to expose different viewpoints on any given topic, to reveal how easily a dominant narrative can be challenged or made more nuanced. I believe I model an intellectual environment in which students are motivated to see and then re-see things in order to challenge easily made assumptions.[23]

By writing this particular piece for known others in our cohort, Emma built her confidence and ability to articulate her practice and principles; eventually she further expanded her audience, leading a workshop for regional teachers. Her workshop became a platform to both publicly resist the narrative of schools as places that reinforce "the status quo" and share her beliefs and methods for addressing this dilemma with other educators.

We incorporate a paired set of routines to close each of our days called "naming our practice" and "writing out of the day." During the former, we ask the group, "What did we do today? What is the big idea about teaching and learning you want to hold on to?" This conversational process helps the cohort build shared vocabulary while creating a theoretically grounded framework to inform practice. One teacher, Kyle, wrote, "So many times throughout this year, I've thought, I kinda' knew that, but couldn't have named it . . . Naming something, making it conscious, being mindful of the tools at your disposal makes them so much more powerful."[24] Peter Johnston echoes Kyle's sentiments and suggests that when learners name and notice, they are more likely to remember.[25] After naming our practice, we ask participants to "write out of the day" by selecting a central idea to explore further from the day of reading, writing, and thinking together. Early on, they write out of the day in their private journals; then, they write posts on our shared blog; and eventually, they publicly tweet about their learning. This practice of articulating their beliefs and ideas on a public forum moves teachers further from trusted others and into adopting a principled stance that is visible outside of our cohort.

Going Public with Less-Known Others

Drawing on Moffett, we believe that writing for self and known others may offer teachers a path toward principled resistance. In the end of our second and third semesters, after fellows complete action research and public leadership projects, we ask them to compose written descriptive analyses of their work. This involves not just explaining what they did and why, but also what impact these projects might have had on them, their students, and their communities. Participants incorporate and comment on written excerpts and various artifacts to illustrate their work. We believe that these processes enable teachers to position themselves as knowledgeable, professional, and public intellectuals.[26] Here we offer three examples of teachers' principled actions; two teachers resist notions of a standard English language arts curriculum, notions that are carried through policy initiatives and held in place by socially constructed expectations. A third teacher uses writing to pave a path away from a hostile workplace.

In the first case, Sophie describes her desire to have students demonstrate their comprehension of Holocaust literature through poetry writing: "Students come to me with their own ideas about English Language Arts class. I like to challenge those ideas and propose that we can exceed the standards while not being, well, standard."[27] She experimented with having students literally black out text in order to leave behind the essence of literature that they read. This nonstandard method challenged her students' notions of assessment and reading comprehension. Sophie created a gallery of student work and eventually presented versions of this work at regional and state conferences, where she publicly articulated how and why she resisted traditional notions of summative assessment. She entered dialogue with "unknown" others, justifying the choices she made in the best interest of her students. Here, Sophie reflects on the importance of sharing this work: "It's easy to stay in the bubbles of our classroom and our schools, sharing trials and tribulations with our closest school confidants. It is much harder to look closely at what worked and why in more public settings, listening to and thinking with others about the moves we made as leaders and learners . . . The public has a perception that we unwittingly support by remaining silent outside of the walls of our schools. Teachers need to reclaim the narrative of our profession before it is too late."[28] Sophie suggests that teachers must be willing to go public to confront narratives that devalue teachers' knowledge and lifelong work.

Like Sophie, Johanna, an urban high school teacher, went from building self-knowledge to publicly articulating her practice. She resisted state-mandated curricula and traditional notions of test preparation. In September of the school year, Johanna began a months-long inquiry that stemmed from a summer intention to resist scripted curricula: "Last July, during our Institute, I decided I would *not* follow the state curriculum modules after realizing how uninteresting the texts were to my students. I wondered: what would happen if I let my tenth grade students pick the topic about which we would read, write, and research? How would they perform on the state exams after spending a chunk of time immersed in this work? Was I ready for any consequences of not following the modules that other teachers were using?"[29]

Given Johanna's commitments to student-driven learning, she resisted her school's adoption of state-mandated curricula. Johanna initiated a plan privately, but she eventually shared the results with known and trusted others and, finally, with many unknown others:

> After talking through my intentions to my principal and colleagues, I opted to follow my principles. For several months I guided my students in analyzing and studying a range of contemporary resources about modern day slavery, convinced that the student-selected topic was important, and that the process of studying and presenting the material would be a richer experience than following the New York State modules for tenth graders . . . Our months long project culminated in a "Modern Day Slavery Awareness Fair," during which nearly 200 guests joined us to learn in a variety of formats my students developed.

Laila's resistance looked different from Sophie's and Johanna's. Laila, a social studies teacher, envisioned a school where educators, parents, and administrators collaborated to help students define their own futures and in turn to influence the community and world. In her eyes, this was a matter of equity and justice.[30] But her hands were pedagogically tied and her innovations dismissed. She laments, "I see bleak similarities between the feelings of hopelessness and predestined futures between my students and the primary source documents that represent the feelings, thoughts, and emotions of children who labored in factories during 18th and 19th centuries."[31] Laila describes administrators who criticized her for starting class with writing time rather than reciting relevant Common Core Standards and for having her students examine "fixed" versus "dynamic" learning theory.[32] The administrators were concerned that the depth with which she approached content would sabotage her students' success on state exams, and on a formal observation, an administrator labeled Laila as "a deep ocean swimmer, whose students are only in the deep end." By December, Laila confided that she was considering leaving the profession, writing, "Have I misunderstood my role as an educator? Am I off at the bottom of the deep ocean? Is it wrong to have a dream for my students . . . and the future of education in America today?" By the time she capitulated to the school's expectations, it was too late.[33] Laila was positioned as a resister, unwilling to discard her deep commitments. Feeling ill-equipped to navigate these workplace dilemmas and what she describes as consistently low expectations for students and teachers alike, Laila left her job and secured a position more aligned with her beliefs. Writing for others helped her cement her commitments, which later led to principled action: leaving her job.

Implications

We have argued for the centrality of writing in teachers' professional development and leadership. Given time to safely explore their principles, educators benefit from publicly revealing their thinking to known and, eventually, less-known others. Our model of professional development permits teachers from different schools and communities to identify their self-knowledge and to explore and articulate their professional commitments, while also planning principled actions in a community of practice. Similar work takes place at the more than 180 sites of the National Writing Project. It is replicable and represents a starting point for change.

In our institute, teachers posed questions and studied their classrooms with known others. Christine Dawson suggests that "as teacher-writers invent text, they are also, in a way inventing and being invented, by themselves and others, within the social context of writing groups."[34] Each made several strategic moves on the way to principled resistance, exploring and articulating beliefs over the year through practices like "naming our practice" and "writing out of the day." Participants wrote "professional fingerprints" and descriptive analyses of action research studies and reflective narratives about their leadership projects. Emma offers a rationale for the role teachers can take in education: "Educators are in a unique position . . . to plant meaningful seeds—not just seeds of knowledge as in content, but seeds of feelings, and habits of mind or heart—and ultimately we have some role, whether big or small, in shaping students' sense of self. This is big, very human, work."[35] Both Sophie and Johanna engaged in principled resistance by publicly rejecting an externally imposed curriculum. Based on their professional principles, they built curricula that honored their professional wisdom and students' interests.

The teacher-as-writer movement started decades ago with a simple premise: teachers of writing need to write, as opposed to simply *assigning* writing. In ensuing years, teachers of writing studied and wrote about their teaching. More recently, teachers have used writing to propel their work as public intellectuals and advocates.[36] Writing isn't always easy. Sometimes the writer has to confront painful, emotional hurdles, as Laila describes: "[Writing became the] vehicle I needed to help me reconnect with the roots of my past struggles, pain, and feelings of inadequacy."[37] Writing, though, can offer teachers a platform to reassess and adjust their notions of who they are as learners and professionals. Teachers writing and rewriting in the presence of others may allow the writers to gain authority in this age of policy encroachment, where teachers' professional voices are silenced. Teachers face conflicting messages from legislators, administrators, union leaders, and colleagues, each of whom call for more teacher leaders yet prioritize standardization. Many teachers struggle to negotiate workplace dilemmas and find that their hands are pedagogically tied and their innovative ideas dismissed. Rather than offering alternatives to problematic ideas, they are asked to fall in line and implement externally imposed curriculum.[38]

Our teachers are pragmatic public leaders who want to keep their jobs *and* honor their principles. Here, Sophie plans to publicly offer her ideas for those who may take them: "I don't want to tell people *they should teach differently*. I want to share options and ideas and let people figure out a way forward for themselves. Because of our institute, I have learned to share my ideas with people who are interested. They can take or adapt what they will, but if they chose not to, we are still better for the conversation. We can share our ideas, and maybe we can be inspired to work toward a new path, together."[39] Going public involves putting ourselves and our ideas into the world while participating in conversations with others who are doing the same. The teachers we want to work with take an inquiry stance about teaching, writing, and working toward a personal and just philosophy and practice.[40] Teachers can reclaim their professionalism by finding and taking a seat at the table as professionals, recognizing and addressing educational dilemmas. Teacher-initiated leadership, with professional writing as a motor, offers an authentic path to principled resistance.

CHAPTER EIGHT

TEACHER RESISTANCE

Personal or Professional?

Jocelyn Weeda

I WAS RUSHING AROUND trying to prepare for my school day when an announcement came over the PA for all staff and faculty, including teachers, secretaries, custodians, cafeteria workers, maintenance crews, and bus drivers, to report immediately for a meeting. A sense of dread washed over me. Meetings called at the last minute were typically about something tragic that had happened over-night to a staff member or student. Little did I know this staff meeting was about *me*.

To begin the meeting, our principal shared that he had a pre-pared statement to read from the central office. Then he said, "I must preface the statement with, we all know and love Jocelyn. She has been a longtime friend and member of our faculty. She recently wrote a letter that many have read, and although I personally agree with what it said, I have a job, professionally, that I have to do in which I can't say everything that I personally feel."

After twenty years of teaching, that was the first day that my professional ethics were called into question. Throughout my career, I had often been held in esteem for my professionalism. I had received my National Board Certification, taught graduate classes for local universities, been encouraged to teach staff-development sessions, and been asked to be a member of many district-level committees. I had even earned my PhD in education. I was the poster child for professional commitment. So what could I have done that would cause such a bold statement from my principal, who supposedly loved me? What were hundreds of staff members in my district being warned against doing that was so egregious? I wrote a letter to my state's board of education that sprang from the moral center of who I am and what I professionally believe about education, about being constrained from doing good work. I wrote a letter that was, at its core, principled resistance to current reforms. Below are the first and the final paragraphs from this letter that caused such controversy:

> Dear Ohio's Board of Education members, Department of Education officials, Legislators, and most importantly, Ohio's parents:
>
> I am a 20-year teaching professional in Ohio, and after reading the recent release from the Ohio Department of Education's "Information on Student Participation on Testing," I was flabbergasted by the intent of the release. Why? Because the release was written in attempt to bully parents, teachers, and school districts into compliance with standardized testing that has the highest of stakes attached to it. I have taught my middle-schoolers that bullies must be confronted. Therefore, this letter is intended to outline why I, even with my job clearly being threatened in this release, still am encouraging parents to refuse state-mandated standardized tests for their children.

My final paragraph informed caregivers of their right to refuse the state tests on behalf of their children and let them know why, as a professional, I believed this was an educationally sound choice:

So, the bottom line is this: *I ask that you stand with me and in support of me (and your child's teacher), by exercising your right to refuse*. It will allow me to go back to directing your child's education based on their actual needs, not on the needs of the test or a testing company. I say this to you knowing that it will most likely hurt my evaluation. But know this, the testing is ALREADY hurting me and your child so much more. I am willing to take the harshest of punishments doled out by the state, so your child no longer has to be punished daily. Why am I willing to do this? Because I have been forced to be a bystander to this bullying in the past. I have watched over the years as children have cried because they don't understand a word that is on the test and I am not allowed to help. I have watched children get physically sick because they are worried about how their parents will view them after they see their scores. I have watched as 8 year olds ask if they can bring stress balls into the testing environment (I'm pretty sure that we as adults did not have these concerns when we were 8). I have watched as students beg not to have to take a test that makes them feel so stupid. I have watched as student incidences of seeing counselors due to school anxiety issues rise during testing periods. These are but a few of the things I have witnessed as results of high-stakes testing. I can no longer be a bystander. I cannot in all good conscience continue to watch our kids being bullied without standing up. Take shots at me, I'm an adult, and I can handle it, but stop allowing the State to take shots at our children by refusing to give them the data they need to continue to bully us all.[1]

My principal pegged me as someone who followed my personal beliefs instead of my professional ethics, but he was wrong. Prior to this year of teaching, I had come to feel an internal dissonance about the educational reforms taking place in my state and nationally. I had chosen to go back to school to get my doctorate to see if I could find the elusive easy answer to "fix" what was wrong in education. What my research uncovered instead was a strong professional commitment to good work in teaching and an equally strong philosophical belief about the purpose of education. That ideal of "good work" was not in sync with the corporate education reforms being instituted in schools. James A. McLellan and John Dewey's words became a calling to me as an education professional: "It is . . . advisable that the teacher should understand, and even be able to criticize, the general principles upon which the whole educational system is formed and administered. He is not like a private soldier in an army, expected merely to obey, or like a cog in a wheel, expected merely to respond to and transmit external energy; he must be an intelligent medium of action."[2]

Becoming "an intelligent medium of action" is a challenge to teachers to bring about change on behalf of children by questioning the systems in place presumably in the best interests of children. Personally, it would have been easier to go along with things as they were, not examining or questioning too much. Professionally, it is difficult to stand up for the types of experiences that children deserve and are not getting, which requires going against those systems that are in place. The ideal of being "an intelligent medium of action" informed my research at the university and fueled my professional ethics as I wrote the letter to the state board. But I was not a lone soldier in this battle. My doctoral research provided me the opportunity to connect with others who could no longer be a "cog in the wheel" and instead resisted the system as a part of their professionalism.

The Personal/Professional Binary

I find it necessary to trouble the distinctions between the "professional" and the "personal" for this chapter. My own sensibilities have difficulty making these an either/or scenario when, as with much of teaching, it is so much more complex. Teaching is both personal *and* professional. With respect to teacher identity, the personal attributes of teachers very much influence the professional knowledge, skills, and discourses that they use daily. Likewise, the professional identities of teachers and the meaning they place in that role as teacher affect their daily personal life. Many teachers believe that the professional and the personal are one and the same. I am not advocating for these to be separated, and I see them as layered and nuanced. But for this chapter, the distinction lies in the perception of the personal as being individualistic and opportunistic, suiting the needs and whims of the individual. On the other hand, the perception of the professional as being of the collective responsibility to uphold the integrity of teaching as a profession and for the students that the profession affects daily. Oftentimes teachers whose actions are resistant to the status quo are seen as psychologically deficient or self-interested. Thus, it is my contention that it is imperative to change the discourse in education in which the idea of teacher as resister moves from an act of deviance and defiance to one of authorship and professionalism. Teachers who question and differ are no doubt the ones that can bring forth the idea of a democratic voice to the educational system.

Research on Teachers That Engage in Principled Resistance

Teachers who are engaged in resistance can be found at the intersections of identity, professionalism, and democracy as they integrate these three for the public good. In my doctoral research, I interviewed teachers who were leading their states in helping parents opt their children out of state testing, teachers who had connected with others via social media to protest legislation and reforms, and others who were willing to speak up by writing articles for newspapers. These teachers had followed a path similar to my own. They found their professional voices as they engaged in principled resistance. Here, I focus on four teachers, highlighting experiences they have in common that justify their work as professionally, not personally, driven. These teachers described various aspects of principled resistance:

- A dissonance in what they knew was good teaching and what was being asked of them within the classroom
- The need to become professionally informed about corporatized educational reform and legislation
- A need to defend their students and their profession by dis–rupting discourses that labeled them and their students as failing[3]
- Being dismissed as personally, not professionally, driven when they brought up these issues within a school setting
- The need to connect with like-minded professionals to share their professional voice about what was happening to their schools

Dewey states, "Except in dealing with commonplaces and catch phrases one has to assimilate, imaginatively, something of another's experience in order to tell him intelligently of one's own experience."[4] These interviews have helped me to frame my own acts of resistance as part of a larger chorus of principled resistance.

The following vignettes highlight these teachers at different points in their journeys. I focus on aspects of their narratives that resonate with professionalism. These teachers who engaged in resistance requested that their first names not be changed. To be named and identified along with their stance against corporate educational reforms is integral to their identities and integrity as educational activists.

Growing Discomfort

Rosemarie is smart and passionate and has a magnetic personality. It is easy to see her commitment to good work. Rosemarie was a K–1 teacher, certified as a reading specialist, and taught for ten years. Although she still identifies as a teacher, her role now is as a parent-activist and United Opt Out administrator. Rosemarie talks about becoming a resister as a political act. Her story, like mine, started in a faculty meeting. She vividly recalled being told that, if she wanted to be treated like a professional, she better be able to cite research to back whatever she chose to do in her classroom. It was important to her professional commitment to continue to build on that research to add new methods and ideas; she viewed her classroom as a process that continued to be refined daily, always focusing on her students' needs. She learned one of her first lessons about a teacher's responsibility for professionalism from a teacher education professor: "If we wanted to get respect, then we had better constantly be reading, learning, challenging our own assumptions so that we are giving kids the best education possible. We need to be collegial and keep our doors open because your good ideas can impact other children, not just the ones in front of you, and you can learn from those who have experience to share." This professional ethic was taken with her into the faculty meeting where she first learned about the Florida Comprehensive Assessment Test (FCAT) and how it would be used to rate schools by scores.[5] She felt the need to speak out professionally on behalf of students across the state and said, "This is not good. This is bad for schools. We are now going to be competing. We all know what schools are going to be A schools. We know what schools are going to be F schools, and those schools are going to be punished. This isn't good for our profession." She watched as other teachers immediately began dismissing her concerns. To her, the teachers began to look at her as if she "had three heads." Many teachers made patronizing comments about her concerns, saying, "Oh honey, it's just a test! No big deal! Don't worry about it!" Rosemarie worked in a district in which her students would be the least affected by the FCAT, but she felt the ethical responsibility to speak up for all kids. She knew professionally that this was just the beginning. It didn't take long for her to begin to feel a lack of control over critical curriculum decisions in her classroom.

The dissonance that Rosemarie described was typical for the others that engaged in principled resistance. Most had an incident, often in a faculty meeting, in which they recalled being asked to interact with students in a way that went against their professional knowledge and moral ethics. New reforms disrupted their classrooms, their pedagogical practices, and their students. These uncomfortable feelings led them to gather information to better understand the macro discourses in educational reform and the institutional barriers preventing them from doing good work. In short, their professionalism was challenged, which pushed them to become more vocal and engage in resistance.

The Red Pill Moment

Becca, a twenty-four-year veteran teacher in a public school in the Northwest, needed to understand reform mandates that focused on quantitative measures of what students achieve, how teachers are rated, and how schools are ranked because they were negatively affecting her profession. Most of the teachers in my research that engaged in principled resistance had taken to heart the democratic ideal of being part of an informed citizenry. Becca's strong background, education, and experiences reveal her professional commitment. She has taught music and technology; she is active in her teacher union; and she has been involved with Save Our Schools, United Opt Out, the Badass Teachers Association, and the Washington Badass Teachers Association. Becca named Save

Our Schools as the one group that "brought me in (and) opened my eyes" to the responsibility of resistance. As part of her ongoing professional inquiry and development, Becca participated in a webinar in which historian of education and education activist Diane Ravitch was the guest speaker. Becca called this her "red pill" moment—a metaphor from the movie *The Matrix* in which the lead character has the choice to take the blue pill and live in ignorance or take the red pill and learn the truth. Becca recalled, "I even wrote [Diane Ravitch] a letter that said this was my red pill moment. I knew that I needed to be vocal now. Somebody has to be talking out for the kids because this . . . this tsunami is coming, and we aren't going to be able to stop it, but we need to stand up to it."

Becca began researching, reading, and connecting through social media to learn more about new educational reforms and confirm her suspicions about how what was happening to schools could affect her students. Becca began the research before testing came to her district, because, she believed, "If it can happen there, it can happen here." This research led her to follow podcasts of the speeches from the United Opt Out National, Inc.'s first direct action, Occupy the Department of Education in DC. Becca saw the need for principled resistance as an active endeavor. As a part of her professionalism, Becca has kept informed of what is occurring in other states and her own, gathered more information, set up rallies, and shared that information with colleagues, parents, and community members.

Teacher Bashing as a Sport

Nearly thirty years ago, Parker Palmer claimed, "Teacher bashing has become a popular sport."[6] When those that engaged in principled resistance spoke out, many were immediately put down or dismissed by others. The stakes are higher today and can come from within the profession. Disrespect of teacher professionalism isn't just on a small scale at faculty meetings; it has become a pervasive part of our culture. This disrespect has been offered by media, policy makers, and the general public, who think that they understand the job of an educator because they were once students themselves.[7]

Dawn came to my attention after an article she wrote on standardized testing was published in the *Washington Post*. She wrote from the heart about the harms that her students faced from the number of state-mandated tests and the hours spent preparing for them. She wrote as a concerned twenty-six-year teaching professional who taught fifth-grade language arts in an urban school district in the Midwest.

Because her discourse was public, complete strangers began to question her professionalism. One person commented on the article, "I grew up in New York and I took tests that were an hour long test, and I would finish it in thirty minutes. I don't understand what all this griping is about. This is nothing for them to be wetting the bed over." Dawn was infantilized, condemned, and dismissed in the quick retort by someone who didn't know her personally or professionally.

Dawn called her state department of education when her district released the calendar that showed twenty-two state-mandated tests to be given before students finished third grade. The state official argued that the state had required only seven tests for the students. Dawn pointed out that they had to take fifteen other end-of-the-year tests for teacher evaluations. The official said, "Well that's not our department." And Dawn exclaimed, "But it's the *same* child!" The state official questioned Dawn's creditability in assessing the situation, because the two departments were different and, therefore, were not connected. Dawn's moral and ethical professionalism did not allow her to look away or ignore the bigger picture. She, like all those teachers that I researched who engaged in resistance, felt the need to connect with others who could also see the damage that is being done by outsiders to our profession.

Do-It-Together Activism

Within my research, teachers that engaged in principled resistance felt that they were a party to or witnessing morally wrong acts against children. Many, who have voiced their concerns for years, are just beginning to see the fruits of their labor in the formation of online communities. Social media has been an important professional tool for keeping informed, feeling solidarity, and sharing knowledge with others. Using social media in a type of do-it-together activism allowed these teachers to politically transform themselves as a larger part of a collective social movement.[8] Within the groups like Save Our Schools, United Opt Out, and the Badass Teachers Association, each of these teachers found the support they were looking for and confirmation that this was not a lone personal journey. They began to see themselves as professional whistle-blowers or change agents. Many have used this solidarity to attend rallies, write to and testify before legislators, publish articles and blogs, and have one-on-one discussions with community members affected by these reforms.

I met Brittany through one of these social media groups. She is a teacher from the Midwest, licensed in elementary and special education. She began teaching twenty years ago and is a sixth-grade language arts teacher. Brittany began engaging in principled resistance through a political action campaign against a state bill that put limits on the ability of public employees to collectively bargain.

Brittany spoke passionately about her professionalism, "her kids," and how needing to act on their behalf pulled her into a social media group, the Badass Teachers Association: "We were actually *doing* something about it. I live for the actions. I feel like

. . . telling Bill Gates something isn't necessarily going to change my situation, but it is cathartic. I feel this release of tension. It has really fed me in a way I can't explain." Brittany described the role of the Badass Teachers Association as a community-building group of professionals: "I really feel like I am not Chicken Little; I'm not the crazy alien with three heads. It validates my professionalism and what I see occurring." Brittany and the other teachers talked about finding groups that made them feel supported and empowered. Bringing others into this community was another important aspect of the movement. It helped them feel a sense of belonging and solidarity.

Emotions as Sites of Power

Although emotions and feelings are often devalued and derided in our culture, they are addressed in feminist literature as important sources of knowledge, power, and resistance. In *Feeling Power: Emotions and Education*, Megan Boler writes, "Emotions are sites of control . . . which reflect our complex identities situated within social hierarchies, 'embody' and 'act out' relations of power."[9] Society teaches women and teachers to control our emotions. Yet, emotions are honored in feminist research because "they reflect linguistically-embedded cultural values and rules and are thus a site of power and resistance."[10] These teachers (myself included) feel their resistance is rooted in moral and ethical feelings of dissonance and passion.

The teachers who engaged in principled resistance talked about the idea of rocking the boat as something that was difficult. It went against their personal nature, as they would have preferred to follow the rules as they did when they were successful students. But ultimately, as professionals, many felt the need to "fix it." Most felt that the idea of resisting had become central to their principles about professionalism.

Brittany pointed out that she could not and should not be neutral. She discussed that stopping to do test preparation was something that was commonplace in her school, but something she felt morally conflicted about: "I feel like they are saying, 'It is my responsibility to give them their best shot (on the test) and shame on me if I never show you how they word questions.' I really feel that way. Do I *like* feeling that way? No, but they make me complicit in it. And that is a real f— you moment! How dare you come in and make me do something that I know isn't good and I know isn't right to do?" Brittany felt that not acting when she felt something was wrong supported the status quo. For teacher resisters, supporting the status quo with silence is just as political as acting against it.

Brittany, Dawn, and Rosemarie all felt so passionate about the profession of teaching that they got choked up when talking about leaving it. Dawn and Brittany understood that they may someday need to join the ranks of teachers who have become conscientious objectors and resign from the profession they loved.[11] Rosemarie did decide to take that time away from teaching, but she reflected emotionally, "I really want a profession to go back to. I really thought at this point I would be back teaching kindergarten because I, [becomes teary eyed] it's what I do, and I can't . . . it just hits me here [motions to heart]."

All of the teachers talked about teaching as a part of who they were, not just a job, not just a paycheck, but also something worth fighting for. Rosemarie had second thoughts about recertifying when her credentials were expiring, but ultimately she decided to renew her certification: "I am a teacher. It is my professional identity, it's what drives my activism, and it is what I still read about and study to this day. I thought by not recertifying I was letting the reformers beat me and push me out of the profession I love and would love to return to at some point. I didn't want anyone to somehow take away what I had done or diminish my knowledge by noting my certification wasn't current. I had to do it for my own self-respect. It's too much a part of who I am."

Each of these educators objected passionately to the public discourse about schools and current reform movements but also vowed to stay in the profession, speaking from within on behalf of students.

Psychology researcher Jessica Kindred suggests that acts of resistance are a form of authorship and ownership, of survival and self-preservation, and of empowerment: "Although resistance is most often considered a sign of disengagement, it can in fact be a form, as well as a signal, of intense involvement and learning. In the simultaneity of negation and expression, it is an active dialogue between the contested past and the unwritten future, between practice and possibility."[12]

Conclusion

Resistance is an important part of participation in a democracy. Kindred reminds us that "the engagement of resistance—not its repression or its avoidance—is critical for . . . the kinds of participatory shifts that support practical and actual organizational change . . . [the expression of resistance] may be the entry act itself, a point of orientation from which further learning can proceed."[13] This resistance allowed Rosemarie, Becca, Dawn, and Brittany to keep fighting professionally on behalf of their students. This same resistance gave me the courage to turn and say, as I stood up to leave the meeting, "This was not personal. If it was personal, I would have chosen to stay silent. Personally, it would have been easier to say nothing instead of putting my job on the line. Personally, it would have been easier for myself and my family to just keep going with the status quo. Professionally, I had no choice."

I walked out of the room feeling completely alone. No one said a word to me that day except an occasional "sorry" in the hallways. I returned to my classroom with an email inbox full of letters of support from others outside my district that had read the letter I wrote to the state board. I turned to social media to feel connected and less alone. I was buoyed by the good work of those that were resisting alongside me. The road after the letter has been an interesting one. The experience kicked me in the stomach, but it also gave me the resolve to continue being the professional I know I am by doing good work and continually standing up for kids.

Connecting with other teachers engaged in principled resistance has since become even more important to me. Social media has been the center of that connection. Knowing there are other professionals that are engaging in principled resistance who are taking this same type of public bruising on the behalf of their students, their colleagues, and their profession gives me hope. Through social media, I have reconnected with former students who reached out to say "thank you" and "keep going," and that students without a voice needed more teachers that engaged in resistance. But I've also had to root myself back in my own good work with students in which I am fully present with them as much as I'm fighting outward. To know that I am one of many who engage in professional activism and to connect with them via social media has made the difference. This democratic process of embracing dissonance, seeking information, connecting, and acting with others has allowed me to restore myself professionally and personally.

PART THREE

Democratic Principles

CHAPTER NINE

DEDICATED, BELOVED, AND DISMISSED

Teachers as Public Intellectuals in New York City Public Schools of the 1950s

Lizabeth Cain

Introduction

On January 3, 1952, Mildred Flacks received a letter from her principal at Public School 35, located in the Bedford-Stuyvesant neighborhood of Brooklyn, New York, where she had been an elementary teacher for nineteen years. In the letter, her principal commended her work, noting in particular the leadership she had provided to the elementary faculty: "From my informal visits to your classroom during the past several years, I have been long convinced that your sincere and effective work, coupled with your skill in the newer methods of elementary education, have been in large measure responsible for the excellence of our elementary department."[1]

Twenty-eight days later, Flacks was dismissed from her teaching position by William Jansen, superintendent of the New York

City public schools, who charged Flacks with insubordination and "conduct unbecoming" a teacher. She had been summoned to the superintendent's office nine months before to answer questions about her membership in the Communist Party. She had refused to answer directly, instead reading from a prepared statement, which included excerpts from teaching evaluations she'd received from supervisors who described her work with glowing praise. In her prepared statement, she described what these evaluations did not capture: "These reports, and many others in the files, do not reflect the sincere love I have for my profession and for the children in PS 35. I have had many opportunities, during the past 19 years, to transfer to other 'better' schools. I have refused such opportunities, believing that the most satisfying moments of my career were spent with my underprivileged, 'forgotten' children."[2]

Flacks was one of nearly 250 New York City teachers who were fired between 1950 and 1955 under the provisions of the Feinberg Law, a New York State law that required districts to actively seek out and dismiss members of a list of organizations that were defined as subversive. No teacher who was fired under the Feinberg Law was accused of any kind of professional misconduct; merely being a member of an organization classified as subversive was sufficient grounds for dismissal.[3] All the fired teachers were members of the Teachers Union (TU), a New York City professional organization founded in 1916 and disbanded in 1964.

While the dismissed teachers were members of the TU, the union had little power to protect their jobs, and the teachers understood that they would be dismissed as a consequence of their principled resistance. Teachers' rights to collective bargaining had not yet been won, so while unions offered their members significant solidarity and moral support, they had little legal standing or official recognition. Districts were under no obligation to offer their employees due process; teachers could be summarily fired for little or no reason, and with no legal recourse. It was in this climate that these teachers refused to answer questions about their political affiliations. By refusing, these teachers maintained their integrity. By writing and speaking eloquently about the injustice, they maintained their identities as public intellectuals, obliged by their democratic principles to think and speak beyond their school-day duties as teachers. However, they lost their jobs.

This chapter illuminates the importance of their chosen actions and focuses attention on the words they used to describe their role as teachers in a democratic system. By many accounts, this was an exemplary group of public school teachers who defended their principles by refusing to answer questions they deemed irrelevant to their work as teachers. In so doing, they endeavored to protect and defend democratic principles, carving out space for teachers to maintain personal democratic principles and teach according to the pedagogical principles that flowed from the democratic. These teachers were committed to protecting intellectual freedom and dissent, for themselves, for their students, and for every other citizen. They brought this commitment into their classrooms, through consciously and thoughtfully inviting multiple perspectives and constructive dissent into teaching practices. Animated by these deeply held beliefs about the important responsibilities teachers have in strengthening and maintaining democratic systems, these teachers chose to resist in a way that they knew would result in their dismissal. They did not engage in naive resistance; they protested with full awareness of the probable costs of their actions, which they understood would be loss of livelihood.

Because these teachers were convinced that the school district had no legitimate ethical grounds for inquiring about their political affiliations, they appealed to the public, the superintendent, the parents of their students, and their colleagues in open protest letters, which they disseminated to the public through newspapers, petitions, and public meetings. Through their protest letters, these teachers described specific contributions they had made to their schools that they particularly valued, contributions that the schools and the students would lose when teachers were fired from their jobs. Unsurprisingly given the circumstances of their firing, these teachers did not highlight the politically infused aspects of their practice in public protest letters. Although there is no evidence that these teachers were attempting to subvert the US government or indoctrinate students, the potential for which was the rationale for their dismissals, there is ample evidence that they did instill in their students an understanding of the democratic structure of the US government through public schooling, including specific actions their students could take to express their views, bring attention to the needs of their community, and leverage public opinion on the political system. These teachers believed that their students, many of whom were of color and lived in substandard housing, could be liberated from the circumstances and limitations of their birth through public education. In the period immediately after the Second World War, some saw any kind of political dissent as dangerous. Although many citizens of the time, having been influenced by the broader political climate, viewed communist, socialist, and other collectivist beliefs as threats to democracy, these teachers took a different position: that democracy is strengthened in proportion to the degree to which its citizens are able and willing to express pluralistic and critical beliefs.

These teachers, all of whom were Jewish and part of a tradition of social justice–oriented intellectualism shared by many urban Jews of the time, may well have been members of the Communist Party, although conclusive evidence of that is thin. It is more likely that administrators of the New York City public schools had long ago grown tired of the gadfly efforts of the TU. The Feinberg Law provided them with a means to eliminate the most politically active teachers from the schools.[4] Postwar fear of Communism offered a justification for going after certain vocal and active teachers. The principles of the teaching profession had long included an emphasis on critical thinking and democratic participation, at least in some circles and some classrooms. That emphasis was tolerated and appreciated by the public, until teachers who acted on behalf of their students in accordance with their democratic principles were cast in a new, damning light by widespread concerns about political subversion.

The TU teachers, therefore, were fired in a moment of intense political pressure, in which the principles that had served as the cornerstone of their teaching were in conflict with the principles of the political machine that dismissed them. For many teachers, this presented an ethical dilemma: teachers who were called in for questioning were permitted to keep their teaching positions, provided they were willing to resign from the Communist Party and provide information about their colleagues.[5] Those teachers who refused to answer the superintendent's questions, knowing they would be dismissed, took a principled stance against being asked questions unrelated to their teaching, and they steadfastly refused to provide investigators with names of like-minded colleagues. Their principled stance was taken on behalf of their fellow teachers, in order to protect professional principles about the limits of administrative reach into their personal lives, and important democratic principles about the importance of dissent. These principles have been shared by many in the teaching profession. In effect, these teachers acted as conscientious objectors to politically motivated actions that limited their intellectual freedom and that of their students.

In writing the protest letters, the teachers appealed to the public with descriptions of classroom events and teaching practices, presumably believing that the public would be more sympathetic to the pedagogical principles that the teachers espoused, rather than the democratic principle of ideological pluralism. For example, teachers described their commitments to developing sympathetic relationships with students, tailoring classroom instruction to the needs of students, and creating curricula connected to the lived experiences of their students. Without naming these practices as progressive, these teachers were describing fundamental tenets of progressivism. While many of the principles articulated in the protest letters identify specific classroom practices that were also evidenced in their classroom-observation reports, the teachers did not mention every aspect of progressive or democratic teaching practice that they implemented in their classrooms. Rather, they likely emphasized the classroom practices that they thought would be most effective in appealing to their readers, whether those readers were colleagues, parents, students, or the public. The teachers argued that their work in classrooms, with students, was more relevant than their political affiliations to their continued employment in the public schools.

Democratic Principles

To varying degrees, these teachers actively and consciously prepared students for participatory democracy. They encouraged thoughtful dissent, critical thinking, and collaborative projects in their classrooms, and they taught students how, when, and to whom to make their voices heard in the larger political system. Through these classroom practices, they taught students how to recognize and resist injustice where they found it.

Sam Wallach, who taught high school social studies, appealed to his colleagues for their support in a lengthy letter outlining moral, legal, and pedagogical arguments against the politically motivated dismissals of teachers. His letter clearly articulated his commitment to the pedagogical ideals of teaching, which included connection to students and the differentiation of instruction that flowed from those connections, as well as a teacher's responsibility to foster democratic ideals in students:

> When I first started as a young teacher, I took seriously the high ideals of our profession about the need to understand children, the individualization of instruction, the inculcation of a devotion to the democratic way of life. Very quickly I found a tremendous gap between the theory I had learned in college, the examination questions of the Board of Education, and the realities in the schools. I saw some teachers who accepted these things and adapted themselves to them. But I determined to fight for the ideals I believed in.[6]

Wallach acknowledged in his letter that his professional principles were not every teacher's principles, and he illustrated that some of his colleagues had chosen to conform to a public school system in ways that he believed were inconsistent with pedagogical principles that had informed his preparation as a teacher. It is notable, however, that this was a letter he wrote to his colleagues, so one presumes that at least some of his fellow teachers were sympathetic to these tenets of democratic classroom practice. Wallach considered his refusal to answer the questions put to him by the superintendent's office to be consistent with his pedagogical principles. Both his teaching and his refusal to respond to these questions demonstrated his commitment to democratic principles of the teaching profession. His principles and commitment to the democratic possibilities of classroom practice informed his decision to resist the inquiry of the superintendent's office. Wallach drew a connection between his classroom practices and the professional principles that informed them: "This whole procedure . . . is contrary to everything I believe in and to the very principles in the Bill of Rights, which I have endeavored through the years to have my pupils understand and live by. No person, no government agency has the right to pry into the personal beliefs or associations—religious, political, economic, or social—of a teacher."[7]

He went on to take issue with the superintendent's argument that progressive and democratic classroom practices could be subversive, instead asserting his dissenting position that these practices were the best means for strengthening democracy. He decried the stated position of the superintendent's office that "the teachers and their union are subversive when they engage in a fight to expand intercultural and interfaith education, to stop the banning of books, to develop democratic methods of teaching and to teach children to think critically."[8]

The TU teachers were working in a politically fraught time. While today's teachers often imagine that the friction between the political system and the public education system is new, or at least newly intense, the history of public education in the United States illustrates that public education has been a perennial battleground, in which teachers, parents, students, and the public constantly debate and discuss the proper purposes and practices of education. Unsurprisingly, no teacher used a protest letter to draw attention to his or her commitment to developing in students the critical capacities that would allow students to resist injustice, although this value was clearly evident in a pamphlet Wallach prepared for teachers, *Teaching Democracy Through Subjects and Methods.*[9] The letters usually focused on the teachers' dedication and personal commitments to students, rather than political ideologies. The TU teachers believed that democratic, egalitarian classroom practices had the potential to liberate their students from life chances limited by poverty and race. Many of them, like Mildred Flacks, whose experience is described in the opening vignette, had chosen to work in impoverished schools and settings specifically because they believed their work could contribute to better lives for their students.

Pedagogical Principles

Much of what the TU teachers carried out with students in their classrooms will be recognized by the reader as progressive teaching practice. These teachers demonstrated in their protest letters that they valued individualized instruction, student engagement with curricula, and a degree of intellectual autonomy for their students. Stella Eliashow, who taught high school Latin and English classes in schools throughout the city, often embodied this principle. This excerpt from a classroom-observation report illustrates that her students were invited to make decisions, with parameters supplied by the teacher: "Home reading—read a book for fun. There may be complete freedom of choice, but choice must be justified."[10] Eliashow had been offering students choices in her classroom for many years by this time, and at least one of her supervisors early in her career had proffered an understanding of why a teacher might do that: "The pupils had a share in the decision about the form of the final manuscript. Such participation by them gives a sense of possession and an interest in the cooperative enterprise."[11] In the observation reports, there are many instances of teachers offering students meaningful choices in a reading assignment, or written homework, or in solving or resolving some classroom challenge. Over and over, these teachers describe their practices with a deep commitment to their students and their life chances.

Harlem elementary school teacher Alice Citron wrote a great many letters to editors of various New York City publications long after she had been dismissed from her public school teaching job. In these letters, Citron often described her classroom practices, attempting to bring attention to the most important pedagogical principles she held as a progressive teacher of materially disadvantaged children. For Citron, the role of the teacher went beyond delivering the curriculum to students; she believed she had a responsibility to her students that went beyond what they might learn or experience in her classroom. She worked to teach according to her pedagogical principles, even when doing so meant putting in more hours and going to greater lengths than were required for continued employment or expected by building administrators. In a letter to the editor of the *Christian Science Monitor*, long after she had been fired, Citron referred to the TU effort to create unbiased curriculum, an effort in which she was a leader: "With the cooperation of the Association for the Study of Negro Life and History, some of us did our own research, reeducated fellow teachers and altered the curriculum. Some of us wrote dramatic scripts, organized research groups among the children and through varied activities changed their attitudes toward themselves!"[12]

While Citron's intention was to draw the reader's attention to the development of antiracist curricula, she also noted two key democratic classroom practices, including setting up opportunities for students to work collaboratively in small groups, and constructing curricula connected to the lived experiences of students. Importantly, she also offered a rationale for democratically infused classrooms: the effect they could have on the attitudes and life chances of students.

In her response to a published review of a book about the role of parents in teaching young children to read, she offered a dissenting view based on her teaching experience: "There are children who come from economically and culturally deprived homes. My personal experience as a teacher of such children is that the role of the teacher is decisive. The world of the child has to be enlarged. The curriculum has to be stimulating and exciting. The school has to bring all the arts into their lives."[13]

Dorothy Rand made a similar connection between her democratic principles, her refusal to answer questions about her political convictions, and her work with students. In her protest letter, Rand described her students and her conscious, deliberate work to fully enfranchise them through education: "I have taught in Harlem since 1936. The sorry condition of Harlem schools is notorious. I have made every effort to improve the welfare of the children of that community . . . I have taught my pupils, all of whom are Negro or Puerto Rican, to take their places as American citizens of the future. I have tried to instill in them a pride in their heritage, an understanding of their contributions to our country, and a desire to assume their rightful places in the life of our country."[14]

Stella Eliashow described her personal dedication to the teaching profession and talked about her commitment to the intellectual and emotional development of the girls in her classroom. She asserted the need to consider the specific circumstances and abilities of students in developing a differentiated approach to classroom practices when she described a class of girls who had consistently scored below average on standardized IQ tests of the day: "These girls are steeped in a sense of failure. Their reading and speaking difficulties are frequently tied to deep emotional problems. They know that in my class no one will ever make them feel foolish or stupid because they do not understand. They know that they can sit with me after school to go over their difficulties, that I will coach them patiently and at the same time respect them as individuals."[15]

Eliashow's empathy for her students is clearly evident in the words she used to describe their difficulties, even as she unflinchingly acknowledged their documented failure to achieve scholastically. She went on to describe her relationship with her students, noting that it was this kind and understanding relationship, established from the start of the school year, that her students lost when she was dismissed from the classroom: "For what is a mark on a paper or on a report card, unless it is followed up by an analysis of mistakes and a pointing out of new directions? How can I get to those girls who have failed *this* *time* the idea that failure is not a static condition, that together the teacher and the student can work away from failure towards success? No substitute taking over on April 13 can really do this job for me."[16]

These teachers' emphasis on creating active and conscious citizens through classroom practices might easily have been misconstrued as evidence for subversion by both the superintendent's office and the public to which they appealed for support. They used their protest letters to position themselves as conscientious dissenting actors, declaring that their refusal to answer questions about political affiliations was part and parcel of their commitment to principles of freedom and dissent, principles which they never denied they had brought to their classrooms. Their fury is often palpable in these declarations, as they attempted to shame the superintendent's office into recognizing their value to the New York City schools:

> Actually my only "crime" has been to refuse to submit to official questioning about my personal beliefs and affiliations. This I have done because I myself sincerely believe in the provisions of the American Constitution, which deal with freedom of speech and freedom of conscience. These are principles which I have tried hard to have my students understand and respect. To have relinquished them now would have been to belie my own teaching and to show disrespect for the great Americans who struggled to establish and defend these freedoms.[17]

Although Eliashow mentioned her goals for the citizenship education of her students in this excerpt, this brief mention does little to evoke a classroom in which students were encouraged to thoughtfully dissent. By far the stronger image is of Eliashow herself, a full-fledged citizen, describing her democratic principles, following her conscience in refusing to answer questions about her political affiliations, and asserting her conviction that inquiries into her political beliefs were un-American. Eliashow's concluding remarks to the board of education further amplified her commitment to her democratic and pedagogical principles: "I challenge you who are about to judge me to take Dr. Jansen's criteria and apply them to me. I submit that, judged by these criteria, I am eminently fit to teach. At no time in my career have I acted in any way contrary to the interests of my students, of my fellow teachers or of my country. I stand proudly on my record."[18]

These protest letters can be seen as the considered and conscientious efforts of a group of teachers who faced an ethical quandary. Mildred Flacks, making a similar statement after summarizing her teaching career, dissented from the fundamental premises of the inquiry into her fitness to teach: "Thus I believe that, since my character and fitness to teach are above reproach, and that you have no legal right to question me about my political beliefs or associations, I must respectfully decline to answer any such questions about my political beliefs and associations, and insist that my 'character and fitness to teach' be judged solely on the basis of my record and performance in the classroom."[19]

Developing critical capacity in students was perhaps the only aspect of the work of these teachers that might have been called subversive, although the teachers would have argued that critical thinking was an essential trait for citizens of a participatory democracy. In this respect, the questioners in the superintendent's office and the TU teachers were engaged in a debate not about whether radical beliefs rendered a teacher unfit for the classroom but about the very nature of democracy. Presumably, the teachers understood that developing critical political consciousness in students would be seen by some as a subversive classroom practice, and they therefore chose not to highlight this aspect of their teaching in their protest letters intended for the public. These teachers lost their jobs in part because their professional principles included an appreciation for dissent and critical thinking, which they applied to their own lives.

These teachers went out fighting, using the writing and speaking skills essential to the practice of the teaching profession. Their actions then allowed their story to extend into the present, offering a powerful example of principled teacher resistance. While these teachers could not have predicted that their words would appear in print decades after they wrote them, they did know that the intellectual skills developed in the classroom, of thinking and writing, of honing an argument and finding the means of disseminating it, are powerful political tools crucial to democracy. They worked to share those skills with their students, and they extended that knowledge to the public sphere when they believed that they had to take a stand for the principles of their profession. Ultimately, in describing and defending their democratic and pedagogical principles, these teachers protected their professional ethics and maintained their professional integrity. Clearly this was not without risk, as many of these teachers never worked in public schools again. However, public opinion and even the political sphere eventually found in favor of these teachers, and they were reinstated many years later. While this came too late to allow them to return to the classroom, some of them were able to reclaim their pensions. More importantly, they were pioneers of intellectual freedom for public school teachers.

CHAPTER TEN

STAKING A CLAIM
IN MAD RIVER

Advancing Civil Rights for Queer America

Karen Graves and Margaret A. Nash

THE COVER OF A 2015 ISSUE of *Equality*, the Human Rights Campaign magazine, announced "A Historic Victory . . ." in reference to *Obergefell v. Hodges*, which guaranteed same-sex couples the fundamental right to marry. An accompanying timeline noted that the Supreme Court's 5–4 decision upholding the constitutionality of same-sex marriage was rooted "in a long history—every setback and every victory bears heavily on our moment today."[1] The timeline includes critical events in lesbian, gay, bisexual, and transgender (LGBT) history in the United States, stretching back to the 1950s founding of the Mattachine Society and the Daughters of Bilitis, marking the Compton's Cafeteria and Stonewall Inn revolts, and documenting key Supreme Court cases such as *Romer v. Evans*, *Lawrence v. Texas*, and *United States v. Windsor*. This snapshot captures a wide swath of political and social terrain, but the field of education, an important sector of LGBT history, is missing. Generally, significant and fierce battles in schools are absent from popular press coverage of the struggle for gay civil rights.

Since the Cold War, queer perceived/identified teachers in the United States have worked under strict public scrutiny. As the political terrain has shifted from gay purges to civil rights battles, LGBT teachers have adopted a number of strategies to maintain their jobs. In courtrooms across the country, principled teachers and other school workers have taken visible stands to challenge dismissals based on flawed claims of immorality, at great personal cost. At times these acts of political resistance have resulted in legal steps toward equal employment protection for LGBT educators, even as the individuals named in the cases were not able to reclaim their own jobs.[2] In this chapter, we chart a history of LGBT educators' struggle for employment, with particular attention to *Rowland v. Mad River Local School District*. Although the Supreme Court allowed a lower court ruling against a teacher fired for her sexuality to stand, Justice William J. Brennan's dissent, the first acknowledgement by a Supreme Court justice that First and Fourteenth Amendments rights extend to homosexuals, established a foundation for the critical victories celebrated by the LGBT community three decades later.

Charting Political Currents Against LGBT Educators

If becoming a teacher meant anything, it meant literally becoming a certain kind of person . . . [One's] very identity remained under constant public scrutiny.

—Kate Rousmaniere[3]

Intolerance for LGBT teachers is a relatively recent phenomenon, emerging in the mid-twentieth century. As Jackie Blount shows in her watershed publication, *Fit to Teach*, scholarly literature as well as elements in early-twentieth-century popular culture contributed to the slowly developing backlash against LGBT teachers. As late as 1929, it was possible for prominent researcher Katherine Bement Davis to publish *Factors in the Sex Life of Twenty-Two Hundred Women*. Teachers and superintendents constituted just over half of the 1,200 single, college-educated women in the study. Among these educators, 22 percent reported experiencing intense emotional relations with women and another 25 percent reported experiencing intense sexual relations with women. Davis's study marked the end of a period when candid discussion of one's sexual expression was possible, however. By 1932, Willard Waller's popular text, *The Sociology of Teaching*, warned against employing homosexual teachers, claiming that homosexuality was contagious.[4]

At the end of World War II, Cold War politics framed the most repressive period in US history for gay and lesbian citizens, and educators became a particularly vulnerable target. This period was marked by a widespread purge of gay and lesbian teachers, professors, and students. The most relentless attack occurred in Florida during the Johns Committee investigations.[5] Between 1957 and 1963, the state investigative committee actively pursued lesbian and gay schoolteachers, subjected them to interrogation, fired them from teaching positions, and revoked their professional credentials. By 1963, the committee reported that it had revoked seventy-one teachers' certificates, with sixty-three cases pending, and had files on another hundred "suspects."[6] A combination of factors led to the committee's demise in 1965 but, as Stacy Braukman shows in *Communists and Perverts Under the Palms*, the ideology that powered the Johns Committee's crusade simply went underground.[7] A 1977 reprisal of homophobic ideology in Miami pushed Florida to the center of the national spotlight on the gay rights movement.

Some communities in the United States began to inch toward civil rights protections for gay and lesbian citizens in the 1970s, overturning sodomy laws and prohibiting job discrimination. These political actions triggered antigay organizing by conservative political groups. Among all public employees protected by newly minted antidiscrimination laws, lesbian and gay schoolteachers drew the most contentious reaction. In 1977 and 1978, national attention was riveted on the battles taking place in Miami and California.[8] In Florida, anti-LGBT forces challenged a law that protected gay men and lesbians from discrimination in employment, housing, and public accommodations, strategically narrowing the scope of the referendum to focus on gay and lesbian teachers. In California, an anti-LGBT referendum was based entirely on the question of who could teach in public schools.

The Florida referendum was a resounding defeat for the gay rights movement, a "stunning setback" that would reverberate across the nation.[9] It was followed by similar retrenchment in Minnesota, Kansas, and Oregon, making the 1978 statewide vote in California increasingly important. There, gay rights groups organized effectively while antigay forces overextended their political reach, targeting all teachers who supported gay rights. This time voters rejected the referendum, handing the gay rights movement a critical victory.

At the same time, however, state senator Mary Helm introduced a bill in Oklahoma that was a virtual twin of the California law. It passed in the House by a vote of 88–2 without debate and was approved in the Senate unanimously. The new law allowed school districts in Oklahoma to fire gay men, lesbians, and any other educator who engaged in "public homosexual conduct," defined broadly as "advocating, soliciting, imposing, encouraging or promoting public or private homosexual activity in a manner that creates a substantial risk that such conduct will come to the attention of schoolchildren or school employees."[10] In other words, the law prohibited teachers from supporting gay rights. The National Gay Task Force challenged the law on multiple grounds: that it violated freedom of speech, freedom of association, freedom of religion, the right to privacy, and the equal protection clause of the Fourteenth Amendment, and that the law was too vague and too broad. A federal district judge upheld the law, and the case went to the Tenth Circuit on appeal. In a 2–1 decision, the appellate court struck down the part of the law that restricted free speech. Dissenting judge James Barrett was furious, writing that a teacher who advocated on behalf of gay rights was less deserving of constitutional protection than one who advocated "violence, sabotage and terrorism."[11]

When the case reached the Supreme Court, six justices voted to hear it. The court had a history of turning away cases brought by gay citizens who wanted to claim civil rights. In this case, the appellate court's decision in favor of gay rights advocates would stand unless the Supreme Court ruled otherwise. *National Gay Task Force v. Board of Education* thus became the first Supreme Court case to address gay and lesbian teachers. Because of Justice Lewis Powell's absence, the decision was tied 4–4, meaning that the National Gay Task Force victory at the appellate court was affirmed. The part of the law that infringed teachers' freedom of speech was ruled unconstitutional.

Prior to the political organizing in Florida, California, and Oklahoma, individual teachers had begun going to court to challenge dismissals based on their sexual orientation. Backed first by the American Civil Liberties Union (ACLU) and then the National Education Association (NEA), plaintiffs fighting for their jobs tested legal arguments designed to keep LGBT educators out of schools. These early decisions turned on morality and privacy assumptions that had long circumscribed all teachers' autonomy and employment rights. In some cases, teachers gained ground in the effort to secure nondiscriminatory employment protections, but, as Jackie Blount has observed, in all cases the individual teachers whose jobs were on the line were displaced.[12]

Three of these cases reached the Supreme Court. In 1972, Joseph Acanfora was completing his student teaching assignment at Penn State when, as part of a news story on the university's gay student group, he noted that he was gay. College officials subjected him to intense scrutiny regarding his character before forwarding his application for a teaching certificate to the state department of education. Acanfora accepted a job teaching eighth-grade science in Montgomery County, Maryland. About a month into the school year, the Pennsylvania Department of Education held a news conference, announcing it was approving Acanfora's request for a teaching certificate; with news of his homosexuality now public, Acanfora's principal promptly removed him from his teaching duties. Although there was strong community support for Acanfora, the district court handed down a mixed opinion. It protected homosexuals' right to teach but noted that Acanfora had violated the "duty of privacy" he was to maintain as a public school teacher. The United States Court of Appeals for the Fourth Circuit rejected that reasoning and upheld Acanfora's right to freedom of speech. But it held that his dismissal could stand, given that he had failed to list his membership in the gay student group on his job application. The Supreme Court declined to hear his appeal in October 1974, allowing the lower court ruling to stand, and Acanfora left teaching.[13]

In October 1977, the Supreme Court also declined to hear appeals of lower court decisions in two more cases: *Gish v. Board of Education of the Borough of Paramus* and *Gaylord v. Tacoma School District No. 10.* James Gaylord, a Phi Beta Kappa graduate of the University of Washington, was a high school history teacher who had established a strong record of teaching over a twelve-year period. He had not disclosed information about his sexual orientation and was not charged with any sort of immoral conduct, but when his vice-principal asked whether he was gay, he said yes. Gaylord was fired in December 1972 on charges of "immorality." The Washington Supreme Court upheld the dismissal on the basis of Gaylord's status as a gay man, a ruling the US Supreme Court did not review.[14]

That same day, the court declined to hear an appeal in *Gish*. In 1972, veteran high school English teacher John Gish organized the Gay Teachers Caucus of the NEA. Later that year, the Paramus, New Jersey, school board ordered Gish to take a psychiatric examination. Gish refused. Supported by the ACLU, he began a five-year legal journey that ended when the Supreme Court refused to hear the case, leaving the New Jersey Superior Court's decision intact. Relying on the 1952 *Adler v. Board of Education of the City of New York* ruling that had since been superseded, the New Jersey court found that school boards maintained wide latitude in determining the fitness of teachers. They considered Gish's "actions in support of 'gay' rights" a deviation from "normal mental health which might affect his ability to teach, discipline, and associate with students."[15]

Each of these cases had been set in motion in 1972, just as the gay rights movement was gaining traction. Over the course of the decade, two lines of argument emerged, anchored in the First Amendment freedom of speech and the Fourteenth Amendment equal protection clauses. By the time the Supreme Court had its next opportunity to weigh in on the matter of employment rights for gay and lesbian teachers, Justice Brennan was fed up with the court's persistent refusal to consider the important constitutional questions at stake. In 1985, he issued a dissent in *Rowland v. Mad River Local School District* that would provide an important foundation for legal breakthroughs in the future.[16]

Turmoil in Mad River: Rowland's Resistance and Brennan's Dissent

I just knew something was up, because there was a hush around the secretary's office, which was outside of my office.

—Marjorie Rowland[17]

Marjorie Rowland began work as a counselor at Stebbins High School in Riverside, Ohio, in August 1974. In November, she told her secretary that two particular students did not need to have special permission to see her, and that if Rowland was available, the secretary should allow either of those students to come in. The reason, Rowland disclosed in confidence, was that each of these students had come out to their parents as gay; the parents had not responded well, and the students needed support. The secretary peppered Rowland with questions, leading to Rowland saying that she was bisexual and was currently in love with a woman.[18]

The secretary told a supervisor and the school principal that Rowland was bisexual. When Rowland refused to resign, she was called to a meeting with the superintendent. Supported by an ACLU attorney and a teacher union representative, Rowland again refused to resign and was immediately suspended. When a federal judge blocked the suspension, district officials reassigned her to a job where she would have no contact with students. At the end of the year, Mad River School District did not renew Rowland's contract.[19]

It is important to consider Rowland's decision to contest her dismissal in civil court from her perspective in 1974. She wasn't a self-proclaimed "activist educator," seeking an opportunity to confront employment discrimination against bisexual, gay, and lesbian school workers. Rather, the actions that launched her ordeal stemmed from her professional concern for the well-being of two students struggling with familial reactions to their own sexuality. As a trained counselor, Rowland had a more advanced understanding of human sexuality than was commonly expressed in US schools in the 1970s, particularly in regard to same-sex attraction and desire. Her knowledge led her to speak directly with her professional colleagues, in confidence, about the students' counseling needs.

Soon enough it became clear that Rowland's trust was misplaced, and her openness might be read as naive. However, the local context was more complex than that. Rowland lived in Yellow Springs, Ohio, home to Antioch College, "a very liberal community."[20] She was out in Yellow Springs and actively involved with speaker groups from the college, who gave community presentations on sexual orientation. The educator was an activist, after all, but she is best described as an "accidental activist" where her work in the schools was concerned.

Rowland's personal character provides another clue as to why she decided to pursue the civil case to reclaim her job. Pragmatically, she realized there was no point in arguing with the school administrators who suspended and then transferred her before the school board fired her in the spring of 1975. Looking back, Rowland explained, "I was angry, but I wasn't mean. I was determined."[21]

Like other gay and lesbian teachers fighting for their jobs, Rowland experienced the loss of career and income, received threatening and obscene phone calls, and went bankrupt as her case made its way through the lower courts. While waiting for the judge's ruling, Rowland learned of a secret indictment against her for food stamp fraud; her lawyers advised her not to go home as she likely would face arrest. During the years before the trial, unable to work in public schools and with three young children to provide for, Rowland had gone to law school; a felony conviction for food stamp fraud would make her ineligible to practice as a lawyer.

According to Rowland, the same prosecutor of the fraud case also tried to influence the judge in her lawsuit.[22]

In 1981, a jury trial found that Rowland's equal protection and free speech rights had been violated. US magistrate judge Robert Steinberg explained that Rowland had "a constitutional right to be different, to express her inner-most personal thoughts, her doubts, her fears, her insecurities, her likes, and her loves to fellow workers and to friends so long as she does not impede the performance of the public school function. The fact that these expressions may be repugnant to some and shocking to others is of no consequence in and of itself."[23] In 1984, a divided United States Court of Appeals for the Sixth Circuit overturned the ruling. Chief Judge Pierce Lively dismissed First Amendment protections because he determined that Rowland's speech did not address "matters of public concern." The equal protection claim fell victim to the court's opinion that there was no evidence that Rowland had been treated differently than heterosexuals.[24] That, in effect, teed the case up for Justice Brennan.

It takes four justices to move a case forward at the Supreme Court. With the support of only Brennan and Justice Thurgood Marshall on *Rowland v. Mad River Local School District*, observers noted that the court was giving its "usual silent treatment to [a] . . . case that might have changed the status quo."[25] But this time, Brennan took the opportunity to issue a blistering dissent, joined by Marshall. Brennan framed the case as a question of the constitutional rights of public employees to maintain and express their private sexual preferences. Since the lower courts were in disarray on this point, he argued, it was time for the Supreme Court to address the issue. Brennan noted that the facts uncovered at the jury trial were clear. Rowland had been dismissed solely because she told a secretary and some fellow teachers about her bisexual status. This speech did not interfere with her proper performance of duties or the regular operation of the school. The dismissal was a violation of Rowland's free speech rights in accordance with the *Pickering* standard, which held that speech of public employees not related to the performance of their duties was protected by the First Amendment, and her Fourteenth Amendment right to equal protection under the laws.

Brennan was clearly irritated with the Sixth Circuit ruling that Rowland's speech was not protected because it was not a matter of public concern, and he noted that the lower court dismissed Rowland's equal protection claim in error, without citing precedent. His analysis of the case issued a parting shot regarding the circuit court's "crabbed reading of our precedents and unexplained disregard of the jury and judge's factual findings. Because they are so patently erroneous, these maneuvers suggest only a desire to evade the central question: may a State dismiss a public employee based on her bisexual status alone?"[26]

Brennan wrote that Rowland's case raised a substantial First Amendment claim. It was settled law that a state cannot condition public employment on a basis that infringes on free speech. The circuit court had cited *Connick v. Myers* to uphold Rowland's dismissal, claiming that her speech did not address a "matter of political, social, or other concern to the community."[27] Brennan raised two objections: Rowland's speech *did* address a matter of public concern, and even if that were not the case, the Pickering-Connick rationale would apply. That standard seeks to balance "the interest of public employees in speaking freely and that of public employers in operating their workplaces without disruption."[28] Since Rowland had not disrupted the school environment, her speech was protected. Brennan concluded that it was "an entirely harmless mention of a fact" that "apparently triggered certain prejudices held by her supervisors."[29]

While the school disruption test is standard practice in free speech cases involving teachers and students, Brennan's affirmation that Rowland's speech addressed a matter of public concern advanced public rhetoric in support of gay rights. Brennan suggested a parallel with racial discrimination, writing, "I think it impossible not to note that a similar public debate is currently ongoing regarding the rights of homosexuals. The fact of petitioner's bisexuality, once spoken, necessarily and ineluctably involved her in that debate. Speech that 'touches upon' this explosive issue is no less deserving of constitutional attention than speech relating to more widely condemned forms of discrimination."[30]

Brennan then turned to Fourteenth Amendment equal protection considerations, arguing that discrimination against homosexuals and bisexuals might well meet the standards for establishing a "suspect class" or be found to impinge upon fundamental rights. He recognized that homosexuals constituted a "significant and insular minority" of the population, and suggested that they met the criteria for strict scrutiny: "Because of the immediate and severe opprobrium often manifested against homosexuals once so identified publicly, members of this group are particularly powerless to pursue their rights openly in the political arena. Moreover, homosexuals have historically been the object of pernicious and sustained hostility, and it is fair to say that discrimination against homosexuals is 'likely . . . to reflect deep-seated prejudice rather than . . . rationality.'"[31]

Brennan argued that discrimination based on one's sexuality had already been found by some courts to infringe on fundamental constitutional rights, such as privacy and freedom of expression. Although he believed that many precedents support the argument that public employees have a fundamental right to "private choices involving family life and personal autonomy," the Supreme Court had not yet weighed in on such questions.[32] Brennan's 1985 dissent stands today as one of the most critical gay rights statements issued by any justice, along with Justice Anthony Kennedy's majority opinions in *Lawrence v. Texas* and *United States v. Windsor.*

Conclusion

I treasure this dissent. I was seen and I was heard, and it wasn't just me, it was the message that I was trying to carry out there.

—Marjorie Rowland[33]

Marjorie Rowland stood in a long line of LGBT educators expelled from the teaching profession on the basis of professional standards warped by homophobia. While individual teachers found limited avenues for resisting the teacher purges of the early Cold War period (e.g., guarding the details of their personal lives, avoiding social gatherings, remaining silent or stonewalling when questioned), Rowland belonged to the generation who leveraged the law to challenge their dismissals publicly.[34] The option was not feasible before 1964, the year the ACLU began supporting LGBT citizens in discrimination cases. The NEA assisted LGBT teachers fighting for their jobs beginning in 1974, the year Mad River School District suspended Rowland. It was not until the 2003 *Lawrence v. Texas* decision that educators in all states could work relatively free of the fear of losing their credentials as statutory felons, simply because of LGBT status. At this writing, Congress has yet to pass a federal law prohibiting employment discrimination on the basis of sexual orientation and gender identity, and only eighteen states and the District of Columbia have adopted such legislation.[35]

Although generally unacknowledged in LGBT histories, the principled resistance of Rowland and the other educators who demanded their day in court advanced both the LGBT movement and the democratic principles that define American schooling at its best. Rowland didn't set out to alter the course of judicial history when she followed her conscience, simply doing her job as a counselor in Mad River School District. Four decades later, she described her commitment as anchored in the local community, but it is now clear that her action laid the foundation for important work to follow.[36] Brennan's dissent in *Rowland v. Mad River Local School District* was the first articulation of First and Fourteenth Amendment claims that later courts used to realize civil rights for LGBT Americans. It has been cited in over seventy opinions, including the landmark 2013 case in which the court found unconstitutional a federal law seeking to restrict marriage to opposite-sex couples, *United States v. Windsor.*[37] Known as the "conscience of the Court," Brennan was a stalwart protector of individual rights. "Brennan believed that majorities could take care of themselves through the legislative process. He was less convinced that solitary human beings, particularly those marginalized by society, could do so."[38] Justice Marshall, with his own unparalleled legacy of principled resistance, was the only other justice to join the dissent.

At the time of Brennan's and Marshall's dissent, few others could appreciate these LGBT educators' commitment to the enduring ideals of democratic education. Indeed, LGBT teachers may have seemed to be the dominant ideology's version of a triple threat—perceived as dangerous to children and youth because of an assumed pathological, sinful, and criminal nature. Relatively few could see beyond these destructive assumptions, which were only just beginning to crumble. As workers in the public sphere who are called upon to protect and nurture the nation's most cherished principles, all teachers fall under strict public scrutiny. As the gay rights movement was getting underway, LGBT teachers found themselves with a particularly significant role to play, both in the movement and in their profession. In Rowland's case, and we suspect, many others, the motivation was pretty simple: "How could I resign for being me?"[39]

At the core of citizenship education in the United States is the teacher's responsibility not only to ensure that students' rights are protected but also to protect their own constitutional rights, setting an example for interpreting the meaning of civil liberties. Here the democratic meets the pedagogical principle. Earlier in the twentieth century, Justice Felix Frankfurter famously called teachers the "high priests of democracy," whose job it is "to foster those habits of open-mindedness and critical inquiry which alone make for responsible citizens, who, in turn, make possible an enlightened and effective public opinion."[40] The principled resistance of Marjorie Rowland and countless others provides an important lesson for the generations that followed.

CHAPTER ELEVEN

TEACHING AND LEADING AS A PRINCIPLED ACT

How Ethel T. Overby Built Foot Soldiers
of the Civil Rights Movement, 1910–1957

Adah Ward Randolph and Dwan V. Robinson

IN 1909, ETHEL THOMPSON GRADUATED from the Year Beyond program at Armstrong High School in Richmond, Virginia, which was established to train African Americans as teachers in the Richmond public school system. From that time forward, Thompson, later known as Ethel T. Overby, began to resist that very system of de jure segregated urban schools by educating her charges about their rights as citizens in a democracy.[1] While many historians have written about how the civil rights movement comprised many constituencies of the African American community, including students, the principled resistance of the teachers and school principals who developed these foot soldiers has received relatively little attention.[2] This chapter highlights Overby's resistance and how her educational philosophy and social activism fostered democratic change inside and outside of schools in Richmond, Virginia. Her democratic principles were manifested in her work with varied community organizations, including schools, the Young Women's Christian Association (YWCA), the Urban League, and the Richmond Crusade for Voters.

Old Dominion: A Site of Principled Resistance

According to June Purcell Guild, author of *Black Laws in Virginia*, "the Negro in Old Dominion, whether indentured servant, slave, free person of color or citizen; has always been an enormously disadvantaged human being."[3] Virginia was a slave-holding state, and segregation was imposed "in Richmond when slavery was abolished, however, it was not rigidly enforced until the early 1900's."[4] In 1892, Overby was born in Richmond, Virginia, the state capital. Her grandparents had been slaves. More importantly, she was born into a family who had acquired some degree of social, economic, and cultural capital because they could read and had skilled labor positions. This was significant in the late nineteenth century because it allowed those African Americans who had literacy to empower themselves.[5] Unlike her grandparents, Overby was born into freedom. However, it was a contentious freedom.

Overby was born into the urban de jure segregated community of Richmond. Its tripartite structural system limited her opportunities in life as a raced, gendered, and classed human being by law if not by circumstance. As the state capital, Richmond's "urban public services for blacks, including schooling evolved from exclusion to segregation."[6] During Overby's teaching career, "segregation enhanced separateness and thus provided a cloak of protection even as it inflicted an inferior status; within the bounds of segregation, blacks could be self-sufficient in a number of ways; in churches, social clubs, schools and businesses . . . the schools, however inferior to white facilities, offered employment and later served as a training ground for black activists."[7] From their segregated neighborhoods, the Black community continued to seek first-class citizenship, their civil rights, and the privileges available to others in the de jure segregated urban context of Richmond. Members of the African American community, including Albert V. Norrell, who had been one of the first African American principals in 1883, campaigned continually for their rights as citizens of Old Dominion.[8] Richmond's African Americans "enacted their understanding of democratic political discourse through mass meetings."[9] They lived within legally mandated segregation, but because they also lived in a democracy, segregation only circumscribed their existence; it did not determine it. Democratic principles provided a framework for their resistance to racial oppression. Overby learned to resist against unequitable and unjust treatment for herself and her community as she witnessed that treatment. Further, she, like so many other educators, sought to be "an agent of change" and fought for social justice in the community through education.[10] The racial discrimination of the segregated South would continue to be her nemesis until her death in 1977.

Overby consistently resisted the expectations of second-class citizenship as an African American woman, as an educator, and most importantly as a human being who was committed to the actualization of a lived democracy for herself and her community. Consequently, examining Overby's life's work can tell us a great deal about what African American educators have done "behind the scenes" or "offstage" to improve educational access and opportunity, thereby serving the public good within and beyond their communities. As an African American educator in the twentieth century, Overby was inextricably connected to her community:

they truly fell and rose together.[11] Overby represents a model of a social activist educator whose life's work was infused with the democratic principle of resisting oppression.

Demanding More Than a School Library

Toward the end of her career Overby wrote, "to be a good teacher, you had to be a good citizen" because "all citizens in a democracy are entitled to understand their worth, to understand that all men and women have a right to participate in society, to rule themselves, to be free, to seek peace, and as members of a democracy be respected and valued as racial, cultural, and political minorities."[12] Thus, the principle of an actualized, lived democracy rather than a theoretical democracy undergirded all of her teaching, both in school and beyond. Overby often discussed with her students their rights and access to the benefits of a democracy. She asked the students real-world questions based on their lived experience. For example, she taught students to question why there were so many things that they cannot do. One of the students answered, "because to be a Negro is to be the last thing on earth?"[13] Through public actions, Overby demonstrated to her African American students that they were worthy of equal rights, and she taught them that they must fight for those rights. Beyond her classroom, Overby worked with the community through the YWCA and the Urban League to achieve one of her goals: access to the segregated public library. It was a demonstration to her students, her foot soldiers, that you could change the world.

Overby viewed literacy as the linchpin to freedom, not just for African Americans, but for all Americans.[14] She loved to read and understood that reading and different forms of literacy opened up the world, not just for White males, but for all. For Overby as an educator, different forms of literacy supported different aims.

Functional, critical, cultural, and voting literacy were important tools to resist oppression. Whereas she was barred from access to the public library as a child, and while the Richmond Public Schools funded and supported libraries in White schools, there were no libraries in all-Black schools. Consequently, Overby acquired literary materials for her classroom, effectively starting her own school library.[15] Her development of a classroom library was a sign of self-determination and resistance. Overby developed her own school library to educate her students on their full rights as citizens in a democracy. She employed multiple forms of literacy including functional, critical, and cultural literacy through the curricular materials acquired for her in-school library. For example, Overby acquired materials through the Association for the Study of Negro Life and History on the contributions and achievements of African Americans, providing students critical and cultural literacy and instilling in them the belief and knowledge that African Americans had achieved and contributed much to the development of the United States. Consequently, she told her students they would, too. However, tax dollars from the Black community went to support the main, Whites-only library. Paradoxically, although they helped pay for its massive collections, Overby and members of the Black community could not avail themselves of them.

In 1926, after continual protests, the Black community finally acquired a segregated branch of the public library named after the first African American teacher in Richmond: Rosa D. Bowser. The Rosa D. Bowser Colored Branch had restricted hours and a limited collection; it therefore offered the Black community insufficient access to literacy. However, as Overby noted about her own classroom library, "It was better than nothing."[16] While the Black community benefitted somewhat from the Bowser branch, they never accepted that it represented *all* they should have in a democracy.[17]

The Bowser branch was never enough. While Overby was teaching at Booker T. Washington School, right down the street from the main library, her struggle for her community against oppression was fueled by the lack of access to tax-supported resources. The struggle began in 1936, when the Black community sued for access to the main library; the suit was thrown out.[18]

In 1942, Overby advocated for improved library access by enlisting the Urban League and other community groups to expand the hours of operation of the Bowser branch. Minutes from an Urban League meeting note that "a committee was appointed to confer with Mr. Thomas P. Ayer, City Librarian, and Miss Belle Boyd of the Bowser Branch Library. Definite request was made for the extension of the hours during which the Bowser Branch would be open; a change in method of securing books from the main library was proposed and a special service to the schools was suggested."[19] The committee secured longer hours of operation for Bowser. As a community organization committed to access and opportunity, the Urban League, with Overby as its secretary, took "pride in reporting the part we played in helping to bring about this enlarged service."[20] Overby and her students moved closer to their goal of desegregation.

In 1946, "a committee at the request of the Y [YWCA] group submitted the issue to the Richmond Civic Council," but their efforts again failed.[21] The different groups all argued for access based on their rights as tax-paying citizens and the limitations of the Bowser branch in the African American community. The Bowser library was insufficient to meet the needs of the Black community. It had 2,284 subscribers, while Richmond had more than 60,000 African American residents.

Overby again enlisted the Urban League to acquire full access to the main library. In 1947, the *Baltimore Afro-American* headline read, "After 11-Year Fight Library Opens Door to All: To Admit

All over 16."[22] Overby's efforts with her community, including the Urban League, the YWCA, and the Young Men's Christian Association (YMCA), all came together to bring an end to the racial discriminatory policy of the public library in Richmond. Overby's commitment to political mobilizing to further democratic principles guided her actions as a member of the YWCA and Urban League.

A Principled Principal at Elba

Another key aspect of Overby's principled resistance was citizenship education and voter literacy. On August 5, 1933, the *Norfolk Journal and Guide* reported that "Richmond's school board named two colored principals . . . the only female principal elected was Miss Ethel Thompson, instructor at Booker Washington School. . . . Miss Thompson will be in charge at Elba School."[23] It had been approximately fifty years since the African American community had first protested to secure Black leadership in the segregated schools of Richmond. Overby become the first African American woman hired by the board of education for a leadership position in the schools, and she would go on to lead two schools in the system. Her leadership in the schools requires us to reexamine the historical contributions of resistance fostered by Black women educators. Their professional and personal lives were shaped by the intersection of race, class, and gender, which limited the opportunities available to them in the larger White communities. More importantly, their principles led them to resist inequitable treatment embedded in the structure of their society and advocate through covert and overt actions for community uplift and liberation from oppression.[24]

In December of 1933, the *Norfolk Journal and Guide* alerted Richmond residents to the poll tax and the fact that the bills were

"Sent Only to White Richmonders," thereby reducing the number of possible "Negro Voters."[25] The article further indicated that through this practice "some people are led to believe that they are qualified with the payment of one year's taxes, only to find otherwise when they go to the polls. It is too late then to correct the situation, and the purpose for which the practice was instituted has been accomplished." Segregation and disenfranchisement undergirded the inequitable social structure of Richmond. As an educator of citizenship education, Overby rejected the structure of inequitable access to democratic participation. As the principal at Elba, she had already begun to institute citizenship and voting education as early as the third grade.[26] Students learned not only how to cast votes but also what was needed to register to vote, and they learned about the necessity of paying poll taxes. A former teacher under Overby, Virgie Binford, indicated "Overby had children bring a penny a day or $12.00 a year" to pay poll taxes.[27] Another teacher, Naomi Morse, recalled that Overby had her foot soldiers canvass the community, awarding parents who had paid their poll taxes with gold stars to display on the front doors of their homes.[28] Even after retiring from the principalship, Overby enlisted community organizations to support her quest to have "100 percent"[29] of Blacks in Richmond as registered and participating voters. One of those organizations was the YWCA.

The Phyllis Wheatley YWCA and Citizenship Education

The YWCA, as part of the social gospel movement of reform ideology, appealed to many African American women. It served women like Overby, who embraced her stance on racial equality and sisterhood as a vehicle she could use to foster change in her own community and the larger society. African American women believed the YWCA could be a means "to meet immediate needs and to advance the race."[30] For black women in particular, the YWCA became a center for advancing civic participation: "By 1920, the YWCA was the third-largest autonomous American women's organization and provided an arena where women struggled over definitions of 'the race problem' and its solution. In these contexts, White and Black women articulated differing assumptions about gender, race, and Christianity."[31] The purpose of the YWCA was "to advance the physical, social, intellectual, moral, and spiritual interests of young women."[32] An important YWCA principle that underpinned their public affairs program was the "assumption of responsibility to secure for all people, regardless of race, creed, color, sex or national origin, the benefits of democracy guaranteed by the Constitution, the Bill of Rights and Supreme Court decisions."[33] These principles aligned with the guiding principles of Overby's life. As the segregated branch, the Phyllis Wheatley YWCA was established by African American women in Richmond and offered community-based options in its curriculum, including business education similar to that offered by the White YWCA. It differed in that it also addressed concerns specific to the Black community, including citizenship education, interracial cooperation, and self-help strategies for young Black women. Overby utilized the Phyllis Wheatley YWCA as a vehicle of cultural, political, economic, and educational change.[34]

While the Phyllis Wheatley YWCA was segregated, it was the principles of the organization that attracted African American women to it. Overby probably viewed the YWCA as an organization where African American Christian women could be what Addie Hunton espoused as "constantly at work for the uplift of her race."[35] By the time Overby graduated from Virginia Union University with her BA in 1926, the Wheatley branch had a membership of 1,051 people and had served 24,000 African American citizens in Richmond that year.[36] Besides working to offer citizenship education through the YWCA, by 1936 Overby was also chairwoman of the organization's Business and Professional Club, where she sought to provide African American women with the skills and knowledge they needed to secure education and employment opportunities. The Phyllis Wheatley YWCA had become a positive organization in the lives of the Richmond's African American community.

Overby's determination to imbue African Americans with stronger understandings of the power of citizenship extended to her perspectives on voting as a vehicle for self-determination. Overby's voting education addressed three essential issues in support of the African American community. First, voting was a privilege, a right, and a responsibility of all citizens. Second, there were bread-and-butter reasons for voting, including its potential to open up more opportunities, protect jobs, ensure a future for African American children, and address how tax dollars from the African American community were spent. Third, there was a civic rationale for voting: to create a better government; use your voice; implement a government of, by, and for the people; provide individuals with stature and prestige; and finally "keep crackpots in their place."[37] Overby organized field trips to the Virginia General Assembly and the city council in Richmond to learn about government functioning and to petition for changes to inequitable conditions. She took her foot soldiers from the Elba School and the Phyllis Wheatley YWCA, along with many community members and parents, to the city council to campaign for "$350,000 for a new school to replace the old Elba School,"[38] which was in intolerable disrepair. The campaign was a success. Consequently, Overby infused the curriculum at Wheatley with programs related to citizenship, voting, and Black history. Because of the expansive organizational reach of the YWCA, Overby was able to extend its programs to benefit the entire community.

While many people think of the YWCA as a place of leisure where women could find classes on "social dancing, knitting, home science, practical sewing, dressmaking, art and stenography,"[39] the Wheatley branch also offered intellectual, cultural, and political education for people of all ages in the Black community. At Wheatley, constituents of the community could find out where the neighborhood boundaries for the Black schools were located through the educational program "What Do You Know About Richmond?"[40] While a school principal and chair of the Business and Professional Club of the YWCA, Overby developed programming to increase the knowledge of young women and girls about employment, education, voting, and citizenship. In 1937, as chairwoman of the Industrial Committee, Overby organized a program about religion, health, recreation, and the history and philosophy of the labor movement.[41] Overall, the programs she organized through this committee and the Educational Committee informed the public about their rights in a democracy and how to resist oppression through social action. Overby was also the chairwoman of the Inter-club Council and Industrial Committee, through which she was honored for her activism at Wheatley.

Another concern close to her heart was interracial cooperation. Overby worked tirelessly to connect the races socially to further racial understanding and cooperation. In 1948, the Industrial Girls of the Wheatley branch and the all-White central branch of the YWCA held a joint conference with a "Spotlight on Citizenship."[42] The subthemes of the conference were the Marshall Plan, human rights, social security, housing, food control, fair employment practices, and equal pay for women. In her 1975 autobiography, Overby asserted that the only way to secure change was through the vote. Hence, the interracial conference was a way to work toward equality among all women and races regarding who should be educated about their rights and opportunities in a democracy. Time and time again, Overby used the outreach of Wheatley to inform the African American community about citizenship and voter education. Her efforts at Wheatley supported her efforts in the schools, including the school she would retire from: Albert V. Norrell School.

Albert V. Norrell and Beyond

As noted earlier in this chapter, Overby started educating children about their rights in a democracy before becoming a principal at Elba School. She presented knowledge about "city, state and national government, according to the maturity level of the pupils."[43] Overby believed in the importance of teaching as a means for helping students understand the inequitable societal structure and to help them to prepare for life circumstances. Further, she impressed upon them the importance of the vote as a means for empowerment and resistance.[44] In 1950, Overby became principal of the Albert V. Norrell School and continued to work together with her teachers "in the best interest of the children and the people of the community."[45] She worked to provide citizenship and voter education through the curriculum in the school.

Inside and outside of the schoolhouse doors, Overby used a slip of paper to resist oppression. The slip of paper, no bigger than a 3 x 5 inch card, contained what citizens needed to know to register to vote. It read, "For Your Family TO VOTE IN RICHMOND'S 1961 ELECTION." Southside residents learned where to pay their poll taxes. The directions began, "GET YOUR FAMILY REGISTERED." The instructions were clear:

1. Go to Room 106, City Hall and ask for Poll Taxes due for 1958, 1959, 1960.
2. Go to the Treasurer's Office, Room 109, City Hall and pay Poll Taxes. Poll Tax payment without penalty, December 5, 1960. Absolute deadline, May 5, 1961.
3. Go to Room 8, City Hall basement and Register.[46]

Voting was not just an individual concern but a concern for the family and the community. On the other side of the small paper were further directions. These directions indicated that "family members will be required to answer these questions on a blank piece of paper," including their name, address, age, date of birth, place of birth, and occupation. Additionally, citizens had to answer the following questions: "Have you previously voted? If so, the State County and Precinct in which you voted? Have you lived in Va. for one year or more? Note: If you become 21 yrs. of age this year you can register without payment of Poll Tax." [47] In her autobiography, Overby writes that she taught people to remember these questions and the answers so they could register, because if they could not answer them all, they could not vote.[48] Beyond her classroom, Overby again joined forces with the Richmond Crusade for Voters, the Phyllis Wheatley YWCA, and the Urban League in her campaign to ensure that poll taxes were paid and that members of the community were registered voters.

As a teacher, principal, and community activist, Overby also leveraged the local newspaper to highlight her activism. She brought attention to one success story: "Ambition fulfilled for Miss Peyton Green, whose first ambition upon becoming 21 years of age was to become a registered voter . . . After registering at City Hall, Miss Green was surprised with a birthday cake bearing 21 candles. The cake was presented by Dr. William Thornton, president of the Crusade for Voters, on behalf of that organization."[49] Overby was one of the original organizers of the Richmond Crusade for Voters, and she worked out of her home as the financial chairwoman of the organization. Clearly, she purchased the cake to present to Miss Peyton.[50] This article indicates how committed she was to ensuring her community, including young people, registered to vote and voted.

Overby continued her efforts to resist oppression through democratic means and by working with multiple organizations, including the National Association for the Advancement of Colored People (NAACP), the Delver Woman's Club, and the Richmond Crusade for Voters, where she had a role in creating the organization and served as its secretary.[51] She was a lifelong worker and not just a member in these organizations. The principles of democratic participation were infused throughout her work to resist oppression in any form and for all people. In 1976, she was recognized by the Virginia General Assembly for her efforts to make Old Dominion a true democracy. An article in the Richmond *Afro-American* that paid tribute to Overby stated that as a principal, she "perhaps has done most toward projecting her school into the governmental life of the community." The article went on to address other aspects of Overby's leadership, including "her efforts to equalize teachers' salaries" and her emphasis on citizenship and "instilling race pride in her pupils and on the importance of their taking an active part in the government of the city, State and nation."[52]

Conclusion

Before becoming a principal in 1933, and for more than forty years after that achievement, Ethel Thompson Overby was a champion for social betterment. Until her death in 1977, she worked toward a society better than the one she was born into. Because Old Dominion did not provide African Americans "equal footing in a democracy,"[53] Overby worked to ensure equal access for all people to the benefits of living in a democratic society. She is significant because she believed that true democratic processes could and would alter the structure of racism, sexism, and classism in the de jure segregated South. She is significant because she is a local figure rather than a national figure. One could argue that her work was done "in the trenches" rather than in the academy. Overby moved beyond the school to enlighten her community as well.

More importantly, she was successful in many domains: the fact that she was educated at the graduate level at a time when it was rare for anyone of any gender or race to earn a bachelor's degree speaks to her tenacity and her belief in the power of knowledge to open doors of opportunity.

Overby's principled resistance as an educator is significant because she demonstrates to us that educators are not victims of their school systems and policies. They can be fierce advocates if they choose to be. Overby had fortitude and determination when, as an African American and as a woman, she was expected to have neither. She fought for and lived by social justice, and "like so many in the African American community" she "worked with Black communities and across cultural boundaries."[54] She did not complain. She made "bricks without straw" and lived by the motto that "it is better to light a candle than to curse the darkness."[55] She was an activist, educator, and leader. At Elba, at Norrell, and through organizations such as the Phyllis Wheatley YWCA, the Urban League, and the Richmond Crusade for Voters, Overby created foot soldiers who would go on to fight in the civil rights movement. Her contributions of principled resistance are many, and any teacher or school leader, regardless of race or gender, can take courage from her efforts to change the inequitable policies and practices that limited the life chances of the African American community. Her urban and southern context insisted that Black children learn, through schools and other social avenues, that their role was to be second-class citizens. Overby challenged this limited ideology on many fronts to demonstrate to students, and the community as a whole, that they had a role to play through functional, critical, economic, cultural, and political literacy, to confront oppression, and to manifest self-determination within the structure of a democracy.

CHAPTER TWELVE

TWEETING TO TRANSGRESS

Teachers on Twitter as Principled Resisters

Jessica Hochman, Doris A. Santoro,
and Stephen Houser

Introduction: Finding a Voice on Twitter

The moral concerns of teachers are making headlines. Acts of resistance such as opt-out campaigns in New York and Seattle and teacher strikes in Chicago have gained national attention. News stories, such as the *New York Times* piece "Teachers Are Warned About Criticizing New York State Tests,"[1] describe teachers articulating their moral concerns for the well-being of their students despite the possibility of reprimand by their state's board of education. In an attempt to raise concerns about preparation for standardized testing's impact on instructional time and student learning, one group of New York teachers learned that they could not voice these concerns as public school teachers and state employees, but only as private citizens.

While major media outlets are reporting on educational issues through articles like this one, the teachers themselves have found a platform on Twitter. This chapter explores the moral dimensions of teachers' tweeting practices. We argue that making teacher voice public through social media is a form of resistance.

Based on qualitative analysis of teachers' Twitter activity, we explore the content of teachers' tweets and the community teachers build through their tweeting practices. Our study found that Twitter is a site of principled resistance,[2] where teachers take action to bring attention to changes in education policy that affect teachers, students, and their communities and to retain the integrity of the profession. By participating on Twitter, teachers raise their voices, participate in conversation, and engage in dialogue with each other and the public.

In what follows, we give some background on why teachers tweet, explain how we collected the tweets of teachers, and discuss the methods we used to analyze the tweets. Finally, we explore our findings: that teachers are building communities of resistance on Twitter and raising awareness of the effects of policy on teachers, students, and their communities in this public forum.

Teacher Voice, Dialogue, and Participation as Resistance

Many teachers' tweeting practices include questioning, resisting, or challenging current education reforms through activism, and in some cases tweets contribute to distinct discourses of resistance. We define discourses of resistance as the conversations, commitments, and cultures developed when teachers question and problematize current narratives of education reform. By researching discourses of resistance expressed by teachers on Twitter, we are able to distinguish the concerns that motivate teachers' criticisms of education policy. We are also able to identify core values that support their teaching practice. The following questions framed our research:

- How do teachers use the unique features of Twitter to resist what they view as challenges to their work?
- How do teachers use their tweeting practices to challenge dominant narratives of teaching, learning, and educational policy?
- How do teachers use Twitter to make their reasoning for resistance known?
- When and how do teachers use Twitter to bring the discourse of resistance to online spaces and, in some cases, to on-the-ground activities?

When teachers' voices are excluded from public discourse around their work, simply claiming a voice and making it public is a form of resistance. This simple claim underlies our study of teacher participation on Twitter. The literature on teacher resistance notes that some teachers engage in "principled resistance," and that some resistance may reflect "good sense."[3] Teachers practice principled resistance when they take a political stance, stake a moral claim, push back against the demoralizing effects of education policies, and shape their pedagogy around their beliefs about good teaching. We identified two crucial elements to teacher resistance via Twitter: dialogue and participation. Both of these elements contribute to the formation of communities of resistance

We approach dialogue in a Freirean sense, as a critical tool. Paulo Freire, the twentieth-century Brazilian educator and critical theorist, describes dialogue as "the encounter between men, mediated by the world, in order to name the world." This naming must be based in a community's lived experiences and realities.[4] Authentic dialogue on a subject such as teaching, therefore, must be initiated and driven by teachers. In an era when teachers are being asked *not* to speak publicly about their work, teacher voice becomes a crucial tool of resistance and empowerment, as this tweet demonstrates: "Difficult teaching our students to have a voice, when we as teachers tend not to use ourselves #teachersmatter."

We look to the tweets of teachers as authentic statements that describe their lived realities in their classrooms, schools, and communities. The language teachers use in their tweets, particularly their moral claims about their work, contributes to dialogue on social media. This tweet, for example, demonstrates that teachers take to Twitter with their thoughts and concerns about their work. They engage with others through social media to name their world or to define its terms based on their own experiences: "@mychaelobowen @lacetothetop @BadassTeachersA Cut scores are a political tool when assessments are used in a high-stakes manner."[5] When the conversation on Twitter runs counter to dominant ideology about education, or the currently accepted narrative, teachers' dialogue constitutes resistance and contributes to the formation of communities of resistance.

For dialogue to occur, subjects must participate. Within research on social media participation, there is a debate over what kinds of online actions constitute participation. Both popular literature and some academic studies characterize practices such as retweeting (i.e., reposting the content of another Twitter user to your own followers) or clicking "like" on Facebook as "slacktivism," or merely identity curation as opposed to participation.[6] However, more recent empirical studies found that those who participate in online political groups are more likely to participate in political actions offline.[7] Further, and closely related to our own methodological questions, Vitak and colleagues found that "liking" political content on Facebook or engaging politically on Twitter are often connected to offline political engagement.[8] In this spirit, we frame both tweeting and retweeting political content, or tweeting about the political action of others, as signs of political participation. At times they can also be acts of resistance. By creating an account and tweeting about one's teaching practice, or using an account to amplify the voices of others, teachers on Twitter are claiming a voice and participating in public dialogue about their profession.

Twitter as a Site of Resistance

We chose Twitter for this study because much work has been done on Twitter as a site of resistance and organizing for collective action as well as on preK–12 teachers' use of social media in their classrooms.[9] Through our exploration of the tweets of teachers, we found that teachers' tweeting practices are aligned with those of other activist groups.[10]

As a networked space, Twitter connects users to one another. These connections mean that users can easily share and replicate content in a persistent, searchable space with a large audience of people both known and unknown to them.[11] Through tweeting, users can alert followers to an upcoming event ("@Lawrence THIS Thursday, 9/17 Support #ParentStrike #WearRed4Ed http://t.co /J6QhD3Ocw1"), share an interesting article or link related to work topics ("Growth mindset! Serena Williams says US Open match was a win, not a loss (from @AP) http://t.co/zXtXX9mqw3"), make a statement about their work day ("RT @STEAMmakerCamp: Got to hang out w some COOL 3rd graders yesterday and tinker around with some stuff"), or make a joke immediately understandable to insiders ("@amberlough How do we like our stakes? High & well done! Get it?? Ahahahahaha. Oh, how I crack us up :))"). We observed teachers using Twitter to meet all these ends.

Twitter expands the geographic and organizational limits that teachers encounter in their schools and districts, allowing them to compare notes and build alliances across geographic boundaries. For some teachers, social media may be the only space in which they can find political allies or connect with others who work in similar positions in other schools. Teachers can also identify policy trends that may appear localized but that are actually more pervasive and, potentially, organized or instituted on a broader scale. In this way, Twitter provides an opportunity to educate others and to be educated about the profession. Thus, Twitter empowers users to form communities in new ways.

Returning to our Freirean lens, we view community as the connections and relationships built through dialogue that works toward mutual understanding. While communities are based on shared interests and beliefs, it is within communities that people work to solve problems and build consensus. In order to make community-building connections, teachers use hashtags to mark relevant content and connect to an ongoing conversation. Teachers may also participate in Twitter chats, which are synchronous structured conversations moderated by community members that focus on a particular topic and take place at specific times. By marking one's tweets with the chat's designated hashtag, one can join the conversation in real time, from anywhere. By joining these conversations, teachers share ideas, find others with similar interests or challenges, build rapport, and create a space for dialogue. They can also review these conversations at a later time by searching the hashtag.

Retweeting also helps teachers amplify their voices and those of their colleagues. Because Twitter users do not always personally know all of their followers, and their followers can retweet beyond known networks, tweets may be spread well beyond the horizons visible to their originators. Thus, on social media, community extends quickly beyond one's inner circle. Twitter offers a platform where teachers may find that they have a stronger voice with more direct access to educational leaders and policy makers; some refer to this as Twitter's "megaphone" effect. And since content on Twitter is enduring, and highly searchable, users can find content that interests them, retweet it to their own followers, and keep the conversation going. This retweet of Chicago Teachers Union activist Karen Lewis may therefore reach and resonate with users nationwide, not just her local constituents: "RT @KarenLewis-CTU: We were taught that teaching to the test is unethical. Now our jobs require unethical behaviors. Any wonder why we resis . . ."

One critique of Twitter is the tendency of communities formed there to be particularly homogeneous. That is, individuals tend toward connections with people like them, or "birds of a feather flock together." Much social media research has shown that people tend to form groups online much as they do IRL (in real life): with people like themselves.[12] However, it is precisely because Twitter is a space where communities of practice can gather and exchange ideas that it is an interesting space to conduct research about teachers and teaching.

Our research demonstrates that there are multiple communities of practice among teachers on Twitter that form around different interests. Many of these communities overlap and engage with one another. This indicates that through dialogue and participation on Twitter, teachers are encountering those with views different from their own and forming communities where these new ideas are discussed.

What Teachers Are Talking About on Twitter

As casual users of Twitter, the principal investigators were already engaged in the practice of reading teachers' tweets. We started to notice a discourse of resistance in their tweets and wanted to take a closer look. The first phase of our research involved collecting the feeds of one hundred self-identified teachers. We then selected a subset of twenty-six user feeds that included high volume, mid-range, and lower-volume tweeters. We read and described these tweets, working toward developing a code book.

Our coding scheme includes three layers of codes. We specifically use types of tweets, as opposed to types of tweeters, because our goal is not to categorize people but rather to focus on the practices teachers engage in through tweeting.[13]

Coding Scheme

Purpose: What is the tweeter generally communicating with this tweet?

- *Content curation.* Tweet that does not contain any original content. User is retweeting or sharing content from another source.
- *Commentary.* Any comment on a policy, a current event, another person's blog, etc.
- *Record of action.* Tweet reporting on action that already occurred IRL (as opposed to online).
- *Humor.* Funny posts about teaching, education policy, or teachers, generally geared toward a teacher audience. (These tweets always include an additional code since they need to be contextualized as educational humor.)
- *Platitude.* Easy answer to a moral problem; an inspirational quote or image that is empowering in a surface way.

Content: What is the tweet about?

- *Educational Policy.* Tweet exploring policy-related matters. These tweets may be perspectives on policy or how policy affects teachers in their work.
- *Politics.* Tweets about elections, elected officials, government.
- *Structure.* Tweets about how power works in schools or education policy as it affects the lives of educational stakeholders.
- *Professional development.* Helpful teaching tips, inspiring or uplifting thoughts for teachers about their teaching and

practice. (Many of these tweets occur in formal chats and/or are denoted with hashtags.)

- *Teaching practice.* Tweets relating to day-to-day life with students in the classroom.

Engagement: Who or what does this tweet engage? What is its subject?

- *Action or effort to organize.* Tweets proposing that people take action either in person or online, or that they organize around an issue or cause. These tweets tend to be future oriented.
- *Community.* Tweets developing a sense of "we" or "us." Tweets are used to build community, connect with others, bring people into a conversation, get people to follow one another. (Those that include hashtags tend to be community tweets because they are reporting out from a shared space for educators.)
- *Moral claim.* Claims about what is right or good, or just about schooling and/or teaching.
- *Self-promotion.* Tweets about one's own work, speaking appearances, conference talks, or other accomplishments, or retweets of what others say about their accomplishments.
- *Voice.* Teachers' own stories; first-person accounts of living through education in these times. Voice tweets are always in the first person.
- *Students.* Teachers' tweets about their students or about their work or experiences with schooling.

Additionally, we developed thirteen fine-grained codes that provide additional detail about the tweet—for instance, school funding, school closures, performance reviews, or high-stakes tests.

Of the over 2,000 tweets we analyzed, only 5 percent of tweets were discarded as irrelevant. This left a huge number of tweets on a related topic, and it raised important questions about how teacher identity, in addition to teachers' principled resistance, is shaped and articulated through public practices such as tweeting. The tweets also proved to be rich and varied texts, as most tweets were coded with more than one code. This demonstrates that tweets can contain many messages; they can be highly communicative, informative, and political.

Teachers' Communities of Discourse

The conclusion of the first phase of our research resulted in our producing a code book that enabled us to analyze the ways that some teachers were utilizing Twitter. We quickly learned that the analysis would be painfully slow and limited if we relied solely on human analysis. We wanted to know more about the communities of discourse that teachers formed when engaging in principled resistance by using their voices on Twitter. In the next phases of our study, we focused on cases when teachers "stake a moral claim" in their tweeting practices. We examined the tweets of 507 self-identified teachers gathered between the summer of 2014 and the summer of 2015. Phase II analyzed 508,000 tweets, and phase III examined over 1 million tweets.

Our goal was to learn whether teachers were making moral claims with their tweets, as a form of principled resistance, and whether they were forming communities based on the kinds of moral concerns they raised. In order to focus our analysis of this enormous data set, we developed a list of moral terms to look for in the tweets that was derived from our analysis in phase I. Words and strings (portions of words) that communicated values about what is good, right, and just in education, such as "care," "love," "democra*," and "deserve," were labeled as moral. We also included frequently used words and hashtags that would help to contextualize the moral concerns communicated in the tweets. See figure 12.1 for the machine-learning dictionary. Bolded words in figure 12.1 indicate the terms we designated as potentially signaling moral content.

In our analysis of more than 1 million tweets, it again became apparent that teachers use Twitter to talk about teaching. Within the tweets we studied, the two most frequently occurring words were *teacher* and *student*. It is also significant to note that of the top twenty-five terms, four of them were words we designated as moral (bold terms in figure 12.2). This suggested that teachers were making moral claims as a form of principled resistance as they tweeted.

We prepared the 1.2 million tweets for machine-learning analysis by tabulating how often each user employed the terms in our dictionary (see figure 12.2). The machine-learning algorithm then

FIGURE 12.1 The machine-learning dictionary.

academic	community	gentrif	policy	**stake**
academy	**compl**	**good**	politi	**strike**
activis	**crisis**	#hiphoped	**poor**	students
advocat	**cry**	**honest**	**poverty**	succ
alec	#ctq	implement	**privat**	suspen
asian	**deform**	include	**privilege**	teach
assess	**demand**	inclusion	proficiency	test
#bat	**democra**	job	**propaganda**	#testing
#bats	**deserve**	**just**	**protest**	tfa
better	dewey	**know**	public	time
bilingual	#edchat	koch	race	**tired**
black	educat	latin	**racism**	**tragedy**
#blacklivesmatter	#educolor	listen	reform	**trust**
#bookaday	ell	**love**	**refuse**	**underfunded**
boycott	engag	**moral**	retain	**underrepresentation**
budget	**ethic**	multilingual	**rich**	**underserved**
care	evaluat	nctq	**right**	**unfunded**
cc	expel	**need**	rttt	union
ccss	expulsion	**neoliber**	school	vam
#ccss	**fair**	#nerdybookclub	score	**voice**
change	**fidelity**	**oppress**	**shame**	**we**
charter	**fight**	#optout	share	white
class	fund	**overrepresentation**	**shortage**	work
classroom	gates	parcc	**should**	**wrong**
#commoncore		participate	skills	

FIGURE 12.2 The top twenty-five words teachers use, from phase II.

teachers	schools	**need**	thanks	#tbats
students	great	**love**	teacher	want
new	kids	time	day	see
like	us	**know**	learning	public
one	education	people	**good**	think

sorted the users' unique "signatures" to determine how similarly and how differently the teachers were using these terms, if at all.[14] We then created network visualizations to show who was using these terms and how they connected and separated the 507 users. Then we analyzed the distinctive words in those clusters—that is, those used more frequently or less frequently than in other clusters (see figure 12.3). We learned that in both dialogue and participation, teachers were forming distinct teacher communities with particular interests in their principled resistance.

The clusters assembled through the machine-learning analysis revealed a thematic driving concern for the users in each category. We saw that they were using Twitter to create distinct discourses of resistance. Over 500 teacher accounts are not necessarily "birds of a feather," but they might be different species who nonetheless tweet to each other. We interpreted the word usage in each cluster to determine the prevailing concern addressed by the users in this category. We also spot-checked users included in these categories as a measure of validity. We assigned the following names to the

FIGURE 12.3 Clusters of word use from phase III. Themes were assigned to clusters based on word usage. 0: Care/Classroom as Locus of Control; 1: Intersectional and Institutional Justice; 2: Civic and Democratic Justice; 3: Communicative Action; 4: Disengaged Tweeters.

Legend: ■ Less than Average Word Count; More than Average Word Count. Moral words are displayed with an asterisk (*) before the word.

0	1	2	3	4
class	ccss	*fight	overrepresentati	overrepresentati
change	*deserve	*democra	underrepresentat	underrepresentat
classroom	*activis	optout	multilingual	nctq
*love	gates	charter	nctq	*underserved
*need	*should	public	*underserved	*unfunded
*good	latin	*refuse	*unfunded	ctq
cc	academic	*propaganda	ctq	multilingual
work	*demand	commoncore	bookaday	bookaday
*know	tfa	gates	expulsion	expulsion
*right	*cry	*shame	expel	expel
succ	*advocat	politi	rttt	*fidelity
*compl	*poor	*deform	*fidelity	hiphoped
share	suspen	*privat	hiphoped	rttt
listen	*racism	koch	nerdybookclub	nerdybookblib
time	reform	*strike	teach	testing
*better	*moral	*activis	testing	*deform
ell	*shame	fund	*we	*underfunded
engag	evaluat	race	school	bats
school	include	*poverty	proficiency	bilingual
students	policy	*protest	*deform	*neoliber
job	*privilege	tfa	*underfunded	gentrif
teach	*crisis	reform	bats	asian

five clusters: Cluster 0, Care/Classroom as Locus of Control (197 accounts in phase III; 48 in phase II); Cluster 1, Intersectional and Institutional Justice (127 accounts in phase III; 68 in phase II); Cluster 2, Civic and Democratic Justice (97 accounts in phase III; 224 in phase II); Cluster 3, Communicative Action (68 accounts in phase III); and Cluster 4, Disengaged Tweeters (44 accounts in phase III). The first three clusters—Care/Classroom as Locus of Control, Intersectional and Institutional Justice, and Civic and Democratic Justice—were the most populous categories in phases II and III of the research and were consistent in their themes.

Users in Cluster 0: Care/Classroom as Locus of Control focused on their classroom as their locus of control and area for concern. The word usage indicates that their principled resistance takes the form of communicating ideas about their knowledge about students and the relationships they develop in their classrooms. The word usage of the teachers in this category is less outward-looking than that in Clusters 1, 2, and 3; these accounts reflect a concern for principled resistance based in their practice as teachers.

Clusters 1 and 2 were remarkably similar in their attention to concerns about justice and how policies affect the institution of school and students beyond their own classrooms. The users in Cluster 1, however, focused their concerns on what we are calling matters of "intersectional" justice—the ways that multiple aspects of identity affect individuals and communities. They used language that suggested they were concerned about how policies affect students and schools in terms of racial categories, class, and privilege. We hypothesize that the accounts may be the product of teachers who work in high-poverty schools, who view themselves as activists, or who may view teaching as activism. However, like the accounts in Cluster 2, they also highlighted major players in educational reform such as "gates" and "tfa."

The tweets in Cluster 2: Civic and Democratic Justice, how-ever, seemed to approach concerns about these reform influences from a perspective that focused on the purpose of public school-ing as a civic and democratic institution, rather than the ways communities and individuals with racialized and socioeconomic identities experienced them. The accounts in this cluster focused on privatization, especially its impact on teachers. We hypoth-esize that these accounts may be held by teacher activists who are located in more suburban areas and who use the "all students" discourse more often than they speak in intersectional language.

Cluster 3: Communicative Action included teachers who seemed to use Twitter to achieve a particular purpose. They might have used Twitter to form community around a book club "book-aday" or to move beyond institutional isolation, especially in re-gard to subject-specific interests (e.g., "multilingual"). This smaller group of accounts often tweeted at an institutional entity in order to achieve an action in response. It was more frequent to find tweets unrelated to teaching in this group—for instance, tweeting at the local gas company to ask about an outage. We hypothesize that the accounts in this group may not be using many of the words designated in our machine-learning dictionary.

Finally, Cluster 4: Disengaged Tweeters. Many of these ac-counts had not been active for some time. We hypothesize that the users may have opened accounts but then let them lapse. The declining use of Twitter in our sample of accounts is indicated in figure 12.5: the full network of phase III.

To learn more about how teachers dialogue and participate on Twitter, we created network visualizations using only the tweets containing moral terms by each account. Each node (or dot) rep-resents an account.[15] Figure 12.4 shows a visualization of phase II, halfway through the study. There are two "tight crowds" pictured

FIGURE 12.4 Network based on use of moral terms (phase II).

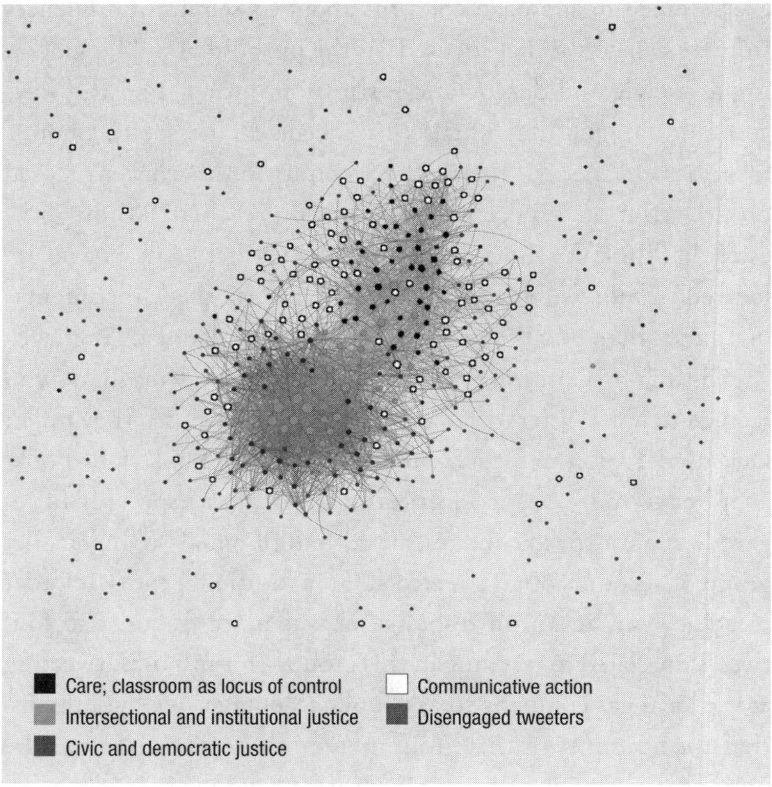

Care; classroom as locus of control — Communicative action
Intersectional and institutional justice — Disengaged tweeters
Civic and democratic justice

here: the Intersectional and Institutional Justice cluster (light gray) and the Care/Classroom as Locus of Control cluster (black). Tight crowds indicate groups of like-minded individuals. Based on the number of connections and lines, it is clear that each cluster contains heavy users of Twitter engaging in lots of dialogue. The phase II full network, however, is a polarized crowd: two groups having a conversation about the same issue in very different ways. There are some bridge accounts, or users who are in dialogue with others outside their cluster. Intersectional and Institutional Justice, the largest cluster, contains many bridges making connections into the Care/Classroom as Locus of Control cluster. Interestingly, we found that many Intersectional and Institutional Justice tweeters had multiple connections with individuals in the Care/Classroom as Locus of Control cluster. In some cases, they had more bridge connections than connections with members of their own cluster. This finding pushes back the concern that teachers' social networks are echo chambers where birds of a feather are speaking exclusively to each other. It was clear to us that Intersectional and Institutional Justice and Care/Classroom as Locus of Control were deeply engaged in dialogue during phase II.

Figure 12.5 shows the full network, again created using only moral tweets from phase three, which included 1.2 million tweets. This visualization shows that the network has evolved over time. Participation by teachers who tweet persistently, or continue tweeting over time, is consolidated. As the circular band of dots around the network shows, some teachers give up tweeting over time or are not consistent in the practice. By cross-referencing the two full network visualizations, we were able to ascertain that some accounts from the Care/Classroom as Locus of Control cluster became Intersectional and Institutional Justice tweeters during our research period. Many of the accounts that shifted categories were connected to the bridge accounts we noted between these two clusters during phase II. We read this change to mean that through participation on Twitter, some teachers experience a change in their moral concerns around teaching. Twitter dialogue among teachers, therefore, has an impact on the views of participants, and these conversations can cause communities to shift and change.

What It All Means

Our findings shed light on practices of teacher resistance through Twitter in several ways that emphasize that dialogue and participation

FIGURE 12.5 Network based on use of moral terms (phase III).

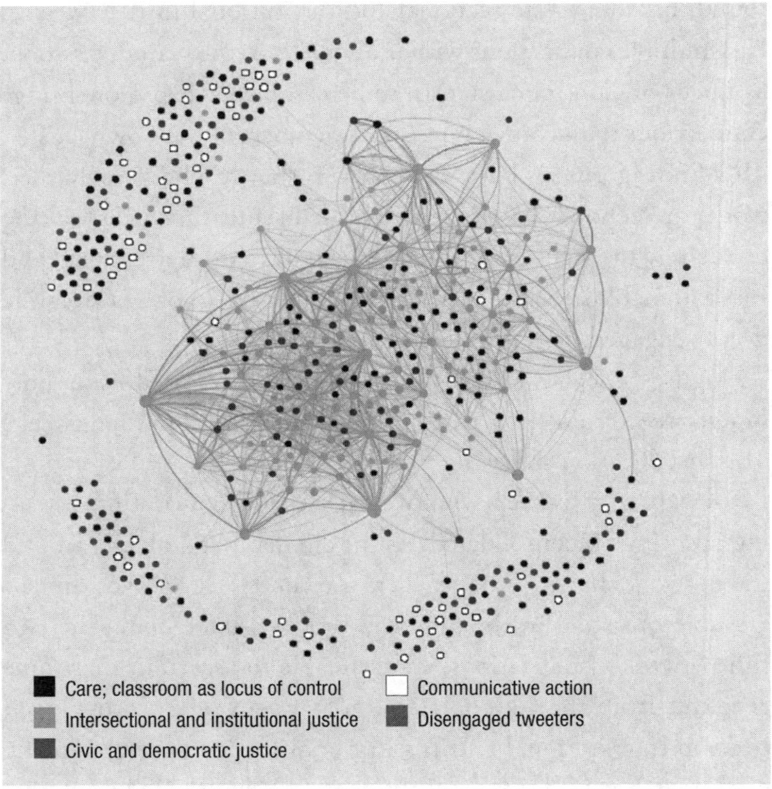

■ Care; classroom as locus of control   □ Communicative action
■ Intersectional and institutional justice   ■ Disengaged tweeters
■ Civic and democratic justice

form communities. First, and perhaps most importantly, our study found that teachers are tweeting about teaching. Their tweets are about their work, which is noteworthy because many Twitter users tweet about a wide range of topics, not only their views about their occupation. By looking at the moral content of these tweets, we were able to learn more about *how* teachers use language to change the conversation about moral aspects of teaching, and we came to recognize teachers' tweets as acts of resistance. By inhabiting their teacher identity online, teachers take a powerful step toward claiming their professional expertise in a public space. This means that their tweets contribute to an important public dialogue about teaching and make claims about what motivates their work.

Second, teachers are using moral terms to describe their work. As our table of most frequently used words shows, words with a moral valence are some of the terms most commonly used by teachers on Twitter. These two facts make a strong case for our view that teachers use tweets as acts of resistance to the dominant narrative about teaching, which is often shaped by non-teacher voices. Reading this finding through a Freirean lens, these dialogues of resistance are a mode for sharing their lived realities, of exercising influence within the teacher community online, and of calling for change based on this expertise.

We also found that the tweets that contain moral terms create dialogical networks of Twitter users. Our network visualizations show that through Twitter, teachers build communities. Twitter is also a space where, through dialogue, they can bridge communities. As we discussed above, it was significant to note that members of the Intersectional and Institutional Justice cluster were frequently in conversation with members of the Care/Classroom as Locus of Control cluster and eventually brought many of those teachers into their conversation. We interpret this dialogue as community building. The fact that it is happening within a social media space provides the possibility that teachers can expand their networks beyond geographic limits and engage more users in the conversation. These networks demonstrate powerful potential for participation in dialogue, as well as possibilities for engagement offline.

While our clusters demonstrate that birds of a feather do indeed flock together, the interplay between clusters demonstrates that dialogue across groups also happens on Twitter among teachers. We therefore read teachers' participation on Twitter as responses to the social conditions that many teachers in the United States face today: isolation, moral blame, and de-skilling. Their work on Twitter intervenes in these conditions and attempts to alter them. By talking about their professional lives in an online public space, teachers articulate their expertise and professional identity and create a participatory space for moral expression, which is itself a form of principled resistance.

CHAPTER THIRTEEN

NAVIGATING DILEMMAS
IN A DEMOCRACY

Lizabeth Cain and Doris A. Santoro

WE HOPE THAT AFTER READING our introduction and the dozen chapters we compiled to illustrate the range and complexity of teachers' principled resistance, readers are convinced that teachers' resistance *may* be motivated by principles, which include but are not limited to democratic, pedagogical, and professional principles. We also hope that readers have recognized the commitment to professional ethics expressed by the teachers represented in these chapters.

Readers learned what these teachers already knew: resistance can entail costs for those who resist. "Dedicated, Beloved, and Dismissed," on teachers' principled refusal to answer political questions, and "Staking a Claim in Mad River," which discusses Marjorie Rowland's principled refusal to resign after being outed as a bisexual, show that teachers who engage in principled resistance may risk their livelihood and their continued participation in the profession.

As more states, such as Florida, North Carolina, Kansas, Wisconsin, and Louisiana, eliminate tenure protections for experienced teachers regardless of their past work performance, it is possible that more teachers will have to choose between their desire to take a principled stand and the pragmatic and immediate needs facing their careers and their families. At-will staffing, at charter schools or in entire states, may muzzle teachers who want to resist policies that they believe are harmful to students and their communities. We can imagine that without tenure protections, Jocelyn Weeda might have lost her job, in addition to being belittled, humiliated, and ostracized, when she informed parents of their rights to opt out of her state's test. Marjorie Rowland's LGBT students lost an important ally when she lost her counseling job.

In other places, students lose when principled and committed teachers can no longer stomach conflicts between what they believe and what they are asked to do. While Randy Miller's contract with his charter school was renewed, he walked away from that school because he could not abide by its no-excuses disciplinary practices. Of course, it is reasonable for an employer to expect some degree of allegiance from an employee in any field, but we argue that it is necessary to carefully consider the ramifications of silencing those who have unique insight into the effects of educational policies and practices on some of the most vulnerable members of a community. Simply put, teachers know things about teaching and students that cannot be gleaned in any way other than by listening to teachers.

It is likely no coincidence that the historical chapters in this book enable us to clearly see the democratic principles at stake in cases of principled resistance. Many would regard the teachers in "Dedicated, Beloved, and Dismissed" and "Staking a Claim in Mad River" as ending up on the right side of history—standing up for political pluralism, civil rights, and the right to privacy. Yet at the time of their resistance the teachers in both of these chapters were considered threats to democracy, the teaching profession, and the young people in their care. With hindsight, we see that the dismissals of these teachers were misguided and damaging.

How can we decide which of the current efforts to dismiss teachers' concerns are misguided and damaging? If you agree with Randy Miller, you think he was right to leave and right to bring public attention to discipline policies at his school. If, however, you think that the best avenue for bridging the gap in education outcomes between middle-class White students and less wealthy children of color is through strict discipline, uniforms, and an extended school day, you might think his students were better off without him. Because education in the United States has not yet been able to bridge this persistent gap, we don't yet know whether Miller is right, although we have our own suspicions grounded in our years of practice and education.

We're left with a conundrum: How can we determine the worthiness of teachers' resistance without the benefit of historical distance? How are we to assess the validity of the professional principles teachers invoke when there is little agreement that teaching, at least in the United States, even *is* a profession? Who stands as the arbiter for determining whether teachers' pedagogical concerns are warranted? As certain as we are that teachers know things about teaching and education that the public needs to hear, we are equally certain that teachers are one stakeholder among many in the practice of public schooling. We need some means of interpreting and assessing their concerns in light of the needs of parents, students, and the greater good.

Arguably, the current policy landscape affecting teachers in US public schools is the result of a lengthy democratic process of give and take, in which some stakeholders have had more influence than others. If democratically elected officials and their appointees create laws and set education policy as part of a representative democracy, isn't it teachers' duty to follow the laws and policies created in this process? This is a reasonable question, but one that may not be applicable to the cases presented here. Many of the teachers represented in this volume have broken no laws; rather, they have violated norms and expectations, some unwritten and unspoken. Principled resistance does not necessarily entail a refusal to abide by the law. Some of the early-career teachers interviewed for Clive Beck and colleagues' "Principled Resistance to System Mandates" made curricular modifications to address their students' needs and interests; Michelle Strater Gunderson and the Chicago Teachers Union went through formal union procedure to bring their concerns about the Common Core to the American Federation of Teachers (AFT) annual convention; Adah Ward Randolph and Dwan V. Robinson showed how Ethel T. Overby worked legal and community channels around de jure segregation in Virginia to resist efforts to disenfranchise and disempower the Black community.

Let's imagine, however, that a teacher engaged in principled resistance in response to laws that required teaching a topic still considered controversial in some localities, whether it be evolution, climate change, or sexual health. Could a teacher engage in principled resistance in the face of laws, rules, or policies that had been implemented through the democratic process? Yes, a teacher could resist on principle, and that teacher could face consequences.

In this book, we have obviously included cases about which we are at a minimum neutral, if not sympathetic. Yet there could be cases of principled resistance with which we would vehemently disagree. Our claim that teachers engage in principled resistance does not mean that those who invoke the phrase get a free pass or an automatic endorsement. Instead, we have intended to show that there are principles—central to the work of teaching—that may motivate teachers' resistance. This point is missed when teacher resistance is viewed solely as an expression of self-serving obstruction born out of stubbornness or an inability to innovate.

Democracy does not guarantee ethical laws and policies. US democracy tolerated chattel slavery and lawful segregation. It prevented women from voting until 1920. In more recent memory, laws have been enacted that leave families hungrier and less healthy. In a democracy, principled resistance is one way to challenge bad laws, rules, and norms, and the ideas from which they are grown. Historically, teachers have often been at the forefront of social movements, but that doesn't mean that they have always been on the right side of history.[1] For instance, teachers have been at the forefront of abolition, but they have also supported corporal punishment. Some of Ethel T. Overby's fellow teachers of Black children probably believed they were doing their best for their students when they promoted vocational school for them, rather than the liberal arts education that would qualify them for college.[2] In Ocean Hill–Brownsville, Black and Latino parents who wanted community control of their schools and more teachers of color for their children were opposed by White Jewish teachers, who went on strike in an effort to protect the status quo.[3]

Pluralism and the freedom to engage in collective action are two of the hallmarks of US democracy. In "Building Foundations for Principled Resistance" and "Working the System," we see teacher educators supporting practitioners in developing their distinctive perspectives and learning how to engage in civic action. These chapters, along with "Tweeting to Transgress," reveal that many teachers approach teaching challenges and ethical dilemmas with integrity and that they want to work productively through the concerns that arise from their professional ethics. These are not teachers who would do what they are told without question, but neither are they teachers who would simply refuse to administer exams, enact policies, or teach with standards because they don't want to. These teachers have all demonstrated a commitment to integrating their ethical concerns within the parameters of public education.

As those who have been paying attention to the ways in which education policy in the United States is shaped will already realize, the premise that educational laws and policies are born out of the democratic body politic may be a rather romantic notion. As educational publishing companies like Pearson engage in extensive lobbying to further their interests with lawmakers, and as philanthrocapitalists like Bill Gates are invited to directly intervene in public education, our democracy might be better described as a corporatocracy.[4] While this observation has long been made of many US industries, the direct influence of moneyed interests on makers of public education policy is relatively new. In the face of these powerful forces, it is reasonable to ask what impact principled resistance might have in this political environment, one in which the voices of ordinary individuals are actively diminished, even when their resistance is organized.

Principled resistance, as we have seen, offers no guarantee that teachers' values will be heard or prevail. The purposeful, strategic, and persistent principled resistance of Camden, New Jersey, teacher Keith Benson offers an important case to consider. Benson is, in many ways, an exemplary principled resister: his critiques and concerns are grounded in his teaching practice and in his commitment to his students and their families, and they are further developed through his research. From 2015 to 2017, Benson published a minimum of ten opinion pieces that articulated his principled resistance to state and district policies and mandates on democratic grounds. He argues consistently that the Black and Brown residents of Camden were excluded from democratic decision making about school reform in that city. His dissertation research, which he conducted at Rutgers University while he taught at Camden High

School, analyzed community responses to the charter-based reform efforts. Benson was elected president of the Camden Education Association, a local chapter of the National Education Association, in 2017 on a platform that demanded democratic community engagement in school reform decision making. As union president, he has won some battles and lost others. This year, Benson's school, despite spirited and sustained community opposition, was slated to be closed, torn down, and eventually replaced.[5] However, Benson also spearheaded a successful community information campaign that has made it possible for more Camden parents to register their children at the schools they choose.

Principled resistance does not guarantee success. Professional ethics may be no match for corporate-style reform. For some teachers like Benson, and there are many, silencing their professional concerns is not an option, no matter the opposition. In those cases, educational researchers and teacher educators might consider how they might amplify and broadcast teachers' voices. Clive Beck and colleagues made this argument succinctly: because teacher educators and researchers enjoy protections implied by intellectual freedom that classroom teachers lack, we have a responsibility to devote at least some of our time, research, and voice to the concerns that teachers would raise more often and more loudly if they could do so without risk. Alisun Thompson and Lucinda Pease-Alvarez described another way for teacher educators and researchers to support classroom teachers: by providing an in-person forum for connection and discussion. Teacher educators might envision ways to help preservice and practicing teachers better understand and navigate the private economic interests that dominate public schooling today. Perhaps how and when to offer principled resistance, and why, should become a foundational concept in teacher preparation programs, much as developmentally appropriate practice and individualized instruction are now.

In the face of these powerful forces that undermine the expertise and ethical commitments of those who do the work of educating, teachers might think strategically about what counts as a "win." In Gunderson's "Chicago Teachers Union's Rejection of the Common Core," we see the Chicago Teachers Union determining that the win would be bringing their resolution to the floor of the AFT annual convention—not that all delegates would adopt their call to drop the Common Core. Their decision to be the ones to decide whether they'd won is an important self-preservation skill many teachers could cultivate. Many of these chapters describe resistance that never prevailed, or that prevailed only after a lengthy, years-long battle. If we want more teachers to stay in the profession and fight for the ethics that animate so many of us, we need to develop the ability to play a long game, and to sustain ourselves and each other through setbacks and triumphs.

Principled resistance can challenge teachers' commitments and resolve. The Chicago Teachers Union guards against disillusionment through its collective action, in addition to setting the terms of victory. "Professional Preparation" shows the ways in which teacher educators can act in solidarity with teachers in order to combat demoralization in an ethos of privatization. In "United Teachers of New Orleans Strike of 1990," the alliance between teachers and their schools' paraprofessionals and clerical workers influenced the union's leadership platform and activated their civic empowerment. Addressing problems of professional ethics as a collective may improve outcomes as well as support individual teachers' ongoing engagement.

We cannot help but notice that while a few of these teachers acted alone, for many others a community of practice was vital to their principled resistance. We see that when teachers find community, in their districts, across districts, or through social media, the principles that undergird their resistance are more clearly formulated and articulated. Perhaps most important, teachers find solidarity with other like-minded teachers when they talk about the ethical challenges they face in the practice of teaching. And yet we also know that time to talk, time to plan, time to consult with one another is very limited for most teachers and virtually nonexistent for some. Because we believe that the principled resistance of teachers is an essential part of the role teachers play in keeping our public education system on its ethical rails, we also believe that the profession can and should do more to help teachers form these communities of practice, whether in their buildings, across their districts and states, or all over the country through social media. Unions have a unique capacity, even as some lose their collective bargaining power, to bring teachers together to address the issues of professional ethics. We have a great deal to learn from teachers, and they from each other, in making the education system stronger and better able to meet the educational needs of students.

The historical chapters here help us to see that transformations are rarely instantaneous, nor are they linear. What might have first been seen as little more than Marjorie Rowland's loss of employment in "Staking a Claim in Mad River" now is recognized as a pivotal moment in the legal history of advancing LGBT rights. Emma Long's account of the two United Teachers of New Orleans strikes was followed by the story of the virtual destruction of the union as post-Katrina New Orleans became the first 100 percent charter district. As teachers continue to raise their voices on behalf of their principles, some charter schools in New Orleans have become incubators for new unionizing efforts. "Dedicated, Beloved, and Dismissed" offers a grim reminder of the potential outcomes of measures such as the "extreme vetting" proposed by the Trump administration. Then as now, thinly veiled political maneuvers can have deep and lasting effects on less powerful individuals and those they would serve if they were allowed to do so. Moreover, these threats have the potential to muzzle those who would express moral and ethical concerns. Democracy demands that we hear dissenting voices, including in cases when we disagree with the concerns being raised.

The education system of the United States comprises many voices, and many of us are in agreement with one another. As teacher educators and as academics, we have a twofold responsibility that is also a contradiction. It is the contradiction borne out in James Baldwin's "A Talk to Teachers."[6] We need to enable teachers to successfully make their way in the world of schools, to navigate and adapt to the bureaucratic reality that is part of every large system, but as these chapters show, many teachers will also need the tools to question the practices and policies of schools when they must.

Notes

INTRODUCTION

1. Betty Achinstein and Rodney T. Ogawa, "(In)Fidelity: What the Resistance of New Teachers Reveals About Professional Principles and Prescriptive Educational Policies," *Harvard Educational Review* 76, no. 1 (2006): 30–63.

2. Henry A. Giroux, *Theory and Resistance in Education: A Pedagogy for the Opposition* (South Hadley, MA: Bergin & Garvey, 1983); Angela McRobbie, *Feminism and Youth Culture: From Jackie to Just Seventeen* (New York: Routledge, 1990); Paul Willis, *Learning to Labor: How Working-Class Kids Get Working-Class Jobs* (New York: Columbia University Press, 1981). A notable exception is Bree Picower and Edwin Mayorga's *What's Race Got to Do with It? How Current School Reform Policy Maintains Racial and Economic Inequality* (New York: Peter Lang, 2015).

3. Jim Knight, "What Can We Do About Teacher Resistance?" *Phi Delta Kappan* 90, no. 7 (2009): 508–13; Kathryn Bell McKenzie and James Joseph Scheurich, "Teacher Resistance to Improvement of Schools with Diverse Students," *International Journal of Leadership in Education* 11, no. 2 (2008): 117–33.

4. Achinstein and Ogawa, "(In)Fidelity"; Annalisa Sannino, "Teachers' Talk of Experiencing: Conflict, Resistance and Agency," *Teaching and Teacher Education* 26, no. 4 (2010): 838–44.

5. Jamy Stillman, "Teacher Learning in an Era of High-Stakes Accountability: Productive Tension and Critical Professional Practice," *Teachers College Record* 113, no. 1 (2011): 133–80; Doris A. Santoro with Lisa Morehouse, "Teaching's Conscientious Objectors: Principled Leavers of High-Poverty Schools," *Teachers College Record* 113, no. 12 (2011):

2671–705; Doris A. Santoro, "I Was Becoming Increasingly Uneasy About the Profession and What Was Being Asked of Me: Preserving Integrity in Teaching," *Curriculum Inquiry* 43, no. 5 (2013): 563–87; Achinstein and Ogawa, "(In)Fidelity."

6. Leib Sutcher, Linda Darling-Hammond, and Desiree Carver-Thomas, *A Coming Crisis in Teaching? Teacher Supply, Demand, and Shortages in the U.S.* (Palo Alto, CA: Learning Policy Institute, 2016), https://learningpolicyinstitute.org/sites/default/files/product-files/A_Coming_Crisis_in_Teaching_REPORT.pdf.

7. Dana Markow and Andrea Pieters, *MetLife Survey of the American Teacher: Teachers, Parents and the Economy* (New York: MetLife, 2012), https://files.eric.ed.gov/fulltext/ED530021.pdf.

8. Alyssa Hadley Dunn, Matthew Deroo, and Jennifer VanDerHeide, "With Regret: The Genre of Teacher Resignation Letters," *Linguistics and Education* 38 (2017): 33–43; Doris A. Santoro, "Teachers' Expressions of Craft Conscience: Upholding the Integrity of a Profession," *Teachers and Teaching: Theory and Practice* 23, no. 6 (2017): 750–61.

9. Santoro with Morehouse, "Teaching's Conscientious Objectors"; Santoro, "Preserving Integrity in Teaching."

10. John Dewey, *Democracy and Education: An Introduction to the Philosophy of Education* (New York: Free Press, 1997; New York: The Macmillan Company, 1916), 356. Citations refer to the Free Press edition.

11. Achinstein and Ogawa, "(In)Fidelity," 32.

12. Thomas F. Green, "Formation of Conscience in an Age of Technology," *American Journal of Education* 94, no. 1 (1985): 1–32.

13. Linda Darling-Hammond quoted in Gunnel Colnerud, "Teacher Ethics as a Research Problem: Syntheses Achieved and New Issues," *Teachers and Teaching: Theory and Practice* 12, no. 3 (2006): 365–85.

14. Barbara S. Stengel and Mary E. Casey, "'Grow by Looking': From Moral Perception to Pedagogical Responsibility," *National Society for the Study of Education* 112, no. 1 (2013): 116–35.

15. Steven Fesmire, *Dewey* (New York: Routledge, 2014), 123.

16. John Dewey and J. H. Tufts, *Ethics* (New York: Henry Holt and Company, 1909), 333.

17. John Dewey, *Democracy and Education*, 353.

CHAPTER 1

1. US Department of Education, "Statement on National Governors Association and State Education Chiefs Common Core Standards,"

press release, June 10, 2010, https://www.ed.gov/news/press-releases
/statement-national-governors-association-and-state-education-chiefs
-common-core-.

2. Valerie Strauss, "6 Reasons to Reject Common Core K–3 Standards—
   and 6 Rules to Guide Policy," *Washington Post*, May 2, 2014, 2,
   https://www.washingtonpost.com/news/answer-sheet/wp/2014/05/02
   /6-reasons-to-reject-common-core-k-3-standards-and-6-axioms-to
   -guide-policy/; Defending the Early Years, "About," https://www.dey
   project.org/who-we-are.html.

3. Anthony Cody, "Common Core Standards: Ten Colossal Errors," *Living in Dialogue* (blog), *Education Week*, November 16, 2013, http://
   blogs.edweek.org/teachers/living-in-dialogue/2013/11/common_core
   _standards_ten_colo.html.

4. Diane Ravitch, *Reign of Error: The Hoax of the Privatization Movement
   and the Danger to America's Public Schools* (New York: Alfred A. Knopf,
   2013).

5. "Caucus of Rank and File Educators (CORE) By-Laws," *Caucus of
   Rank and File Educators*, last modified November 11, 2017, http://
   www.coreteachers.org/core_by_laws.

6. *Arguments Against the Common Core* (Chicago: Chicago Teachers
   Union, 2014), http://www.ctunet.com/quest-center/research/text
   /CTU-Common-Core-Position-Paper.pdf.

7. *Arguments Against*, 3. The resolution in its entirety can be found on
   Chicago Teachers Union blog ("Chicago Teachers Union Joins
   Growing National Opposition to Deeply Flawed Common Core
   Standards," May 7, 2014, http://www.ctunet.com/blog/chicago
   -teachers-union-joins-opposition-to-common-core).

8. MORE Caucus, "AFT14 Convention—Common Core Debate—
   UFT Leaders vs. Classroom Teachers," YouTube video, 3:00, filmed
   July 13, 2014, posted August 7, 2014, https://www.youtube.com
   /watch?v=ToNEs-C9HCU.

CHAPTER 2

We wish to thank the Social Sciences and Humanities Research Council of Canada for their generous support of this research.

1. Nel Noddings, *Caring: A Feminine Approach to Ethics and Moral
   Education* (Berkeley: University of California Press, 1984); *Happiness
   and Education* (Cambridge: Cambridge University Press, 2003); *The
   Challenge to Care in Schools: An Alternative Approach*, 2nd ed. (New

York: Teachers College Press, 2005); *Education and Democracy in the 21st Century* (New York: Teachers College Press, 2013), 11.

2. Clare Kosnik and Clive Beck, *Priorities in Teacher Education: The 7 Key Elements of Pre-service Preparation* (London and New York: Routledge, 2009); Clive Beck and Clare Kosnik, *Growing as a Teacher: Goals and Pathways of Ongoing Teacher Learning* (Rotterdam: Sense Publishers, 2014).

3. Kenneth Zeichner, "Beyond the Divide of Teacher Research and Academic Research," *Teachers and Teaching: Theory and Practice* 1, no. 2 (1995): 153–72.

4. Marilyn Cochran-Smith and Susan L. Lytle, *Inside/Outside: Teacher Research and Knowledge* (New York: TC Press, 1993), 1.

5. Jodi O'Meara, *Beyond Differentiated Instruction* (Thousand Oaks, CA: Corwin, 2010); Evangeline Harris Stefanakis, *Differentiated Assessment: How to Assess the Learning Potential of Every Student* (San Francisco, CA: Jossey-Bass, 2011).

6. Noddings, *Education and Democracy*; Diane Ravitch, *The Death and Life of the Great American School System* (San Francisco: Jossey-Bass, 2010); Diane Ravitch, *Reign of Error: The Hoax of the Privatization Movement and the Danger to America's Public Schools* (New York: Alfred A. Knopf, 2013).

7. Noddings, *Education and Democracy*, 11.

8. Deborah Meier, *The Power of Their Ideas* (Boston: Beacon Press, 1995), 167–68.

9. S. G. Grant and Jill Gradwell, eds., *Teaching History with Big Ideas: Cases of Ambitious Teachers* (New York: Rowman & Littlefield, 2010); Bruce VanSledright, *The Challenge of Rethinking History Education: On Practices, Theories, and Policy* (New York and London: Routledge, 2011).

10. Christopher Day and Qing Gu, *Resilient Teachers, Resilient Schools: Building and Sustaining Quality in Testing Times* (London and New York: Routledge, 2014); Viv Ellis, "What Happened to Teachers' Knowledge When They Played 'The Literacy Game'?," in *The Great Literacy Debate: A Critical Response to the Literacy Strategy and the Framework for English*, ed. Andrew Goodwin and Carol Fuller (London and New York: Routledge, 2011), 27–44; Dana Goldstein, *The Teacher Wars: A History of America's Most Embattled Profession* (New York: Doubleday, 2014).

11. John Bransford, Linda Darling-Hammond, and Pamela LePage, introduction to *Preparing Teachers for a Changing World: What Teachers*

Should Learn and Be Able to Do, ed. Linda Darling-Hammond and John Bransford (San Francisco: Jossey-Bass, 2005), 2–3.

12. Laura Chapman and John West-Burnham, *Education for Social Justice: Achieving Wellbeing for All* (London and New York: Continuum, 2010); Brent Davies, *Leading the Strategically Focused School*, 2nd ed. (Los Angeles: Sage, 2011); Daniel Goleman and Peter Senge, *The Triple Focus: A New Approach to Education* (Florence, MA: More Than Sound, 2014); Noddings, *Happiness and Education*; Noddings, *The Challenge to Care*; Noddings, *Education and Democracy*; Jeffrey Wilhelm and Bruce Novak, *Teaching Literacy for Love and Wisdom: Being the Book and Being the Change* (New York: Teachers College Press, 2011).

13. Hazel Hagger and Donald McIntyre, *Learning Teaching from Teachers: Realizing the Potential of School-Based Teacher Education* (Maidenhead: Open University Press, 2006), 55.

14. Rose Ylimaki, *Critical Curriculum Leadership: A Framework for Progressive Education* (New York and London: Routledge, 2011), 122–23.

15. Deborah Ball, "Bridging Practices: Intertwining Content and Pedagogy in Teaching and Learning to Teach," *Journal of Teacher Education* 51, no. 3 (2000), 241–47; Lee Shulman, "Those Who Understand: Knowledge Growth in Teaching," *Educational Researcher* 15, no. 2 (1986), 4–14; VanSledright, *Rethinking History Education*.

16. Sharan Merriam, *Qualitative Research: A Guide to Design and Implementation* (San Francisco: Jossey-Bass, 2009); Keith Punch, *Introduction to Social Research: Quantitative and Qualitative Approaches*, 3rd ed. (Los Angeles and London: Sage, 2014); Maggi Savin-Baden and Claire Howell Major, *Qualitative Research: The Essential Guide to Theory and Practice* (London and New York: Routledge, 2013).

17. Kathy Charmaz, *Constructing Grounded Theory*, 2nd ed. (Los Angeles and London: Sage, 2014); Punch, *Introduction to Social Research*.

CHAPTER 3

1. Richard Ingersoll and Henry May, *Recruitment, Retention and the Minority Teacher Shortage*, CPRE Research Report RR-69 (Philadelphia: University of Pennsylvania, Consortium for Policy Research in Education, and University of California Santa Cruz, Center for Educational Research in the Interest of Underserved Students, 2011); Yolanda Sealey-Ruiz and Chance W. Lewis, "Transforming the Field of Education to Serve the Needs of the Black Community: Implications

for Critical Stakeholders," *Journal of Negro Education* 80, no. 3 (2011): 187–93; Ivory A. Toldson, "How Race Matters in the Classroom," *The Root*, October 22, 2012, https://www.theroot.com/how-race-matters -in-the-classroom-1790893823.

2. Ashley Griffin and Hilary Tackie, *Through Our Eyes: Perspectives and Reflections from Black Teachers* (Washington, DC: Education Trust, 2016).

CHAPTER 4

1. Christine E. Murray and Gerald Grant, *Teaching in America: The Slow Revolution* (Harvard University Press, 2009); Richard M. Ingersoll, *Who Controls Teachers' Work? Accountability, Power, and the Structure of Educational Organizations* (Harvard University Press, 2003); David Labaree, "Power, Knowledge, and the Rationalization of Teaching: A Genealogy of the Movement to Professionalize Teaching," *Harvard Educational Review* 62, no. 2 (1992): 123–55.

2. Betty Achinstein and Rodney Ogawa, "(In)fidelity: What the Resistance of New Teachers Reveals About Professional Principles and Prescriptive Educational Policies," *Harvard Educational Review* 76, no. 1 (2006): 30–63; Laura Alvarez and Jennifer Corn, "Exchanging Assessment for Accountability: The Implications of High-Stakes Reading Assessments for English Learners," *Language Arts* 85, no. 5 (2008): 354–65; Lucinda Pease-Alvarez and Katharine Davies Samway, "Negotiating a Top-Down Reading Program Mandate: The Experiences of One School," *Language Arts* 86, no. 1 (2008): 32–41.

3. For a discussion of structuration, see Chris Shilling, "Reconceptualising Structure and Agency in the Sociology of Education: Structuration Theory and Schooling," *British Journal of Sociology of Education* 13, no. 1 (1992): 69–87. For a through account of agency, see Mustafa Emirbayer and Ann Mische, "What is Agency?" *American Journal of Sociology* 103, no. 4 (1998): 962–1023.

4. Dorothy Holland, William S. Lachicotte Jr., Debra Skinner, and Carole Cain, *Identity and Agency in Cultural Worlds* (Harvard University Press, 2001), 13.

5. For a chronological account of projects to professionalize teaching, see David Labaree, "Power, Knowledge, and the Rationalization of Teaching: A Genealogy of the Movement to Professionalize Teaching," *Harvard Educational Review* 62, no. 2 (1992): 123–55. Labaree argues for gender as a primary reason why these efforts have not been more successful.

6. Peter Munro, *Subject to Fiction: Women Teachers' Life History Narratives and the Cultural Politics of Resistance* (Buckingham, UK and Philadelphia: McGraw-Hill Education, 1998); Bettina Aptheker, *Tapestries of Life: Women's Work, Women's Consciousness, and the Meaning of Daily Experience* (Amherst, MA: University of Massachusetts Press, 1989).
7. James C. Scott, *Weapons of the Weak: Everyday Forms of Peasant Resistance* (New Haven: Yale University Press, 1985), 95.
8. *Cooperating teacher* refers to the classroom teacher that a preservice teacher works with for her student teaching placement.
9. EAS was invited to submit a chapter on the group's work for an edited volume by Christine Sleeter and Catherine Cornbleth. Members of EAS worked collaboratively on the chapter with input from the larger group.
10. Nicole Mirra and Ernest Morrell, "Teachers as Civic Agents: Toward a Critical Democratic Theory of Urban Teacher Development," *Journal of Teacher Education* 62, no. 4 (2011): 408–20; Judyth Sachs, *The Activist Teaching Profession (Professional Learning)* (Buckingham, UK, and Philadelphia, PA: Open University Press, 2003).

CHAPTER 5

1. Donald E. DeVore and Joseph Logsdon, *Crescent City Schools: Public Education in New Orleans, 1841–1991* (Lafayette: Center for Louisiana Studies, 1991), 271–91.
2. Ava Roussell, "4 Schools to Close in Settlement," *Louisiana Weekly,* September 16, 1978.
3. Nat LaCour, interview by Emma Long, New Orleans, March 11, 2016.
4. Melanie Boulet, interview by Emma Long, New Orleans, July 16, 2015.
5. Rhonda Nabonne, "Strike to Last to Bitter End, Teachers Vow," *Times-Picayune,* September 18, 1990.
6. Rhonda Nabonne, "Strike Won't Shut Schools, Board Vows," *Times-Picayune,* September 17, 1990.
7. Dr. Raphael Cassimere Jr., interview by Emma Long, New Orleans, February 4, 2016.
8. LaCour, interview.
9. LaCour, interview.
10. Boulet, interview.
11. Carmen James, interview by Emma Long, Harahan, March 15, 2016.

12. Rhonda Nabonne, "Teachers Turn Down $13 Million Offer," *Times-Picayune*, October 1, 1990.

13. James, interview.

14. Rhonda Nabonne, "Teachers Offered 3% Raise This Year," *Times-Picayune*, October 6, 1990.

15. Mike Stone, interview by Emma Long, New Orleans, July 17, 2015.

16. Connie Goodly, interview by Emma Long, New Orleans, March 14, 2016.

17. Patti Reynolds, interview by Emma Long, New Orleans, July 14, 2015.

18. Rhonda Nabonne, "School's in as Teachers Accept Pact," *Times-Picayune*, October 8, 1990.

19. Nabonne, "School's in."

20. Boulet, interview.

21. Goodly, interview.

22. Jessica Williams and Della Hasselle, "Morris Jeff Charter School Board Embraces New Teachers Union," *Lens*, May 17, 2013, http://the lensnola.org/2013/05/17/morris-jeff-charter-school-board -embraces-new-teachers-union/.

23. Danielle Dreilinger, "Louisiana's 1st Charter School Union Contract Up for Vote at Ben Franklin," *Times-Picayune*, March 18, 2015, http:// www.nola.com/education/index.ssf/2015/03/ben_franklin_charter _union.html.

24. Danielle Dreilinger, "Morris Jeff Teachers, Board Ratify Union Contract," *Times-Picayune*, June 21, 2016, http://www.nola.com /education/index.ssf/2016/06/morris_jeff_union_contract_rat.html.

25. Danielle Dreilinger, "Lusher Teachers Reject Union for Collective Bargaining," *Times-Picayune*, May 24, 2016, http://www.nola.com /education/index.ssf/2016/05/lusher_votes_no_to_union.html.

26. Marta Jewson, "National Labor Board Rules That Two Charter Schools in New Orleans Can Be Unionized," *Lens*, February 1, 2017, http:// thelensnola.org/2017/02/01/national-labor-board-rules-that-two -charter-schools-in-new-orleans-can-be-unionized/.

27. Jessica Williams, "Teachers at a Fifth New Orleans Charter School Seeking a Union," *New Orleans Advocate*, March 28, 2017, http:// www.theadvocate.com/new_orleans/news/education/article_68ab90ee -133e-11e7-ac66-8bb7ef1c2377.html.

28. Marta Jewson, "Coghill Teachers End the School Year by Voting for Union Representation," *Lens*, May 22, 2017, http://thelensnola.org

/2017/05/22coghill-teachers-end-the-school-year-by-voting-for-union
-representation/.

CHAPTER 6

1. National Commission on Excellence in Education, *A Nation at Risk: The Imperative for Educational Reform* (Washington, DC: US Department of Education, 1983).
2. Jack Schneider, *Excellence for All: How a New Breed of Reformers is Transforming America's Public Schools* (Nashville, TN: Vanderbilt University Press, 2011).
3. David K. Cohen and Jal Mehta, "Why Reform Sometimes Succeeds: Understanding the Conditions That Produce Reforms That Last," *American Educational Research Journal* 54, no. 4 (2017): 644–90, doi:10.3102/0002831217700078.
4. National Council on Teacher Quality, www.nctq.org.
5. Doris A. Santoro, "Good Teaching in Difficult Times: Demoralization in the Pursuit of Good Work," *American Journal of Education* 118, no. 1 (2011): 1–23, doi:10.1086/662010.
6. Henry Levin, *Privatizing Education* (Boulder, CO: Westview Press, 2001).
7. Sam Abrams, *Education and the Commercial Mindset* (Cambridge, MA: Harvard University Press, 2016).
8. David C. Berliner and Gene V. Glass, *50 Myths & Lies That Threaten America's Public Schools* (New York, NY: Teachers College Press, 2014).
9. Diane Ravitch, *Reign of Error: The Hoax of the Privatization Movement and the Danger to America's Public Schools* (New York: Knopf, 2013).
10. Ben Jensen et al., (Washington DC: National Center on Education and the Economy, 2016), http://ncee.org/wp-content/uploads/2016/05/169726_Not_So_Elementary_Report_FINAL.pdf.
11. Kenneth Zeichner and Hilary G. Conklin, "Beyond Knowledge Ventriloquism and Echo Chambers: Raising the Quality of the Debate on Teacher Education," *Teachers College Record* 118, no. 12 (2016): 1–38, doi:10.1017/CBO9781107415324.004; Kenneth Zeichner and César Pena-Sandoval, "Venture Philanthropy and Teacher Education Policy in the U.S.: The Role of the New Schools Venture Fund," *Teachers College Record* 117, no. 5 (2015): 1–44.
12. *Los Angeles Times* Editorial Board, "Gates Foundation Failures Show Philanthropists Shouldn't Be Setting America's Public-School Agenda," *Los Angeles Times*, June 1, 2016, http://www.latimes.com/opinion/editorials/la-ed-gates-education-20160601-snap-story.html.

13. Matthew N. Sanger and Richard D. Osguthorpe, "Teacher Education, Preservice Teacher Beliefs, and the Moral Work of Teaching," *Teaching and Teacher Education* 27, no. 3 (2011): 569–78, doi:10.1016/j.tate .2010.10.011

14. Catherine Gewertz, "Interest in Teaching Continues to Drop Among High School Students," *Education Week,* July 6, 2016, http://blogs .edweek.org/edweek/high_school_and_beyond/2016/07/interest_in _teaching_continues_to_drop_among_high_school_students.html.

15. Cynthia E. Coburn, Heather Hill, and James P. Spillane, "Alignment and Accountability in Policy Design and Implementation: The Common Core State Standards and Implementation Research," *Educational Researcher* 45, no. 4 (2016): 243–51, doi:10.3102/0013189X16651080c; Lorraine M. McDonnell and Michael S. Weatherford, "Recognizing the Political in Implementation Research," *Educational Researcher* 45, no. 4 (2016): 233–42, doi:10.3102/0013189X16649945.

16. Jal Mehta, *The Allure of Order* (New York: Oxford University Press, 2013).

17. Stephen Sawchuk, "Steep Drops Seen in Teacher-Prep Enrollment Numbers," *Education Week*, October 21, 2014, http://www.edweek .org/ew/articles/2014/10/22/09enroll.h34.html.

18. Emma Brown, "Teach for America Applications Fall Again, Diving 35 Percent in Three Years," *Washington Post*, April 12, 2016, https://www .washingtonpost.com/news/education/wp/2016/04/12/teach-for -america-applications-fall-again-diving-35-percent-in-three-years/.

19. Katie Ledwell and Celia Oyler, "Unstandardized Responses to a 'Standardized' Test: The edTPA as Gatekeeper and Curriculum Change," *Journal of Teacher Education* 67, no. 3 (2016): 120–34.

20. Dan Goldhaber, James Cowan, and Roddy Theobald, "Evaluating Prospective Teachers: Testing the Predictive Validity of edTPA," *Journal of Teacher Education* 68, no. 4 (2017): 377–93.

21. Alan J. Singer, "Hacking Away at the Corporate Octopus," *Cultural Logic: Marxist Theory & Practice* (2013): 209–223.

22. Celia Oyler, https://celiaoyler.wordpress.com/2016/05/.

23. Joey Aguirre, "Teachers, Supporters Rally at Capitol to Stop Collective Bargaining Changes," *Des Moines Register*, February 12, 2017, http:// www.desmoinesregister.com/story/news/education/2017/02/12 /teachers-supporters-rally-capitol-stop-collective-bargaining-changes /97827606/.

24. Ron French, "Study: Schools of Choice Don't Improve Test Scores," *Bridge Magazine*, April 7, 2016, http://www.bridgemi.com/talent -education/study-schools-choice-dont-improve-test-scores.

25. Kate Zernike, "A Sea of Charter Schools in Detroit Leaves Students Adrift," *New York Times*, June 28, 2016, http://www.nytimes.com /2016/06/29/us/for-detroits-children-more-school-choice-but-not -better-schools.html?emc=eta1&_r=0.

26. Bruce Baker and Gary Miron, *The Business of Charter Schooling: Understanding the Policies That Charter Operators Use for Financial Benefit* (Boulder, CO: National Education Policy Center, 2015), http://nepc .colorado.edu/files/rb_baker-miron_charter_revenue_0.pdf.

27. Valerie Strauss, "How Charter Schools in Michigan Have Hurt Traditional Public Schools, New Research Finds," *Washington Post,* July 15, 2016, https://www.washingtonpost.com/news/answer-sheet/wp /2016/07/15/how-charter-schools-in-michigan-have-hurt-traditional -public-schools-new-research-finds/.

28. Amber Arellano and Suneet Bedi, *Michigan's Talent Crisis: The Economic Case for Rebuilding Michigan's Broken Public Education System* (Royal Oaks, MI: The Education Trust–Midwest 2016), https:// midwest.edtrust.org/resource/michigans-talent-crisis-the-economic -case-for-rebuilding-michigans-broken-public-education-system/.

29. Michigan Teacher Corps website, http://michiganteachercorps.org /become-a-teacher. This program has been closed down, so the website is no longer functional.

30. Dorinda Carter Andrews, Tonya Bartell, and Gail Richmond, "Teaching in Dehumanizing Times: The Professionalization Imperative," *Journal of Teacher Education* 67, no. 3 (2016): 170–172, doi:10.1177/0022487116640480.

31. Jennifer Berkshire, "I Quit!," *Have You Heard Blog*, July 11, 2017, http://haveyouheardblog.com/tag/alyssa-hadley-dunn/.

32. Andy Henion, "Teacher Resignation Letters Paint Bleak Picture of U.S. Education," Michigan State University College of Education, April 7, 2017, https://msutoday.msu.edu/news/2017/teacher -resignation-letters-paint-bleak-picture-of-us-education/; Alyssa Hadley Dunn, Matthew Deroo, and Jennifer VanDerHeide, "With Regret: The Genre of Teachers' Public Resignation Letters," *Linguistics and Education* 38 (2017): 33–43.

33. Goldhaber, Cowan, and Theobald, "Evaluating Prospective Teachers," 377.

CHAPTER 7

1. James Moffett, *Teaching in the Universe of Discourse* (Portsmouth, NH: Heinemann Educational Books, 1968).
2. There is an ongoing conversation about the role of writing as a form of inquiry and professional development. For an overview, see Troy Hicks et al., *Coaching Teacher-Writers: Practical Steps to Nurture Professional Writing* (New York: Teachers College Press, 2017).
3. Betty Achinstein and Rodney T. Ogawa, "(In)Fidelity: What the Resistance of New Teachers Reveals About Professional Principles and Prescriptive Educational Policies," *Harvard Educational Review* 76, no. 1 (2006); Ann Lieberman and Linda Friedrich, *How Teachers Become Leaders: Learning from Practice and Research* (New York: Teachers College Press, 2010).
4. Dan Lortie, *Schoolteacher: A Sociological Study* (Chicago: University of Chicago Press, 1975).
5. Henry Giroux, "Teachers, Public Life, and Curricular Reform," *Peabody Journal of Education* 69, no. 3 (1994): 236.
6. Debra Meyerson, *Tempered Radicals: How People Use Difference to Inspire Change at Work* (Boston: Harvard Business School Press, 2001).
7. Ibid., 8.
8. Moffett, *Discourse*.
9. Christine Dawson, *The Teacher-Writer: Creating Writing Groups for Personal and Professional Growth* (New York: Teachers College Press, 2017).
10. Moffett's original framework did not take into account social media, which affords writers many opportunities to share their thinking with a mixture of trusted and unknown others.
11. For a valuable guide offering generative strategies for *how* to support teacher-writers, we suggest reading Hicks et al., *Coaching Teacher-Writers.*
12. Kenneth Burke, *The Philosophy of Literary Form: Studies in Symbolic Action* (Baton Rouge: Louisiana State University Press, 1941), 110.
13. Donald Murray, "All Writing Is Autobiography," *College Composition and Communication* 42, no. 1 (February 1991): 71.
14. Robert Yagelski, "Writing as Praxis," *English Education* 44, no. 2 (January 2012): 193.
15. Emma X, unpublished letter of reflection, 2016. Emma, like all names assigned to participants in this paper, is a pseudonym.
16. Peter Elbow, *Writing with Power: Techniques for Mastering the Writing Process*, 2nd ed. (New York: Oxford University Press, 1998), 59.

17. Renee X, unpublished loop writing exercise, 2015

18. Yagelski, "Writing as Praxis," 192.

19. Tammy X, unpublished letter of reflection, 2016.

20. Anne Elrod Whitney and Linda Friedrich, "Orientations: The Legacy of the National Writing Project for the Teaching of Writing," *Teachers College Record* 115, no. 7 (2013): 11.

21. Anne Elrod Whitney, "Teacher Transformation in the National Writing Project," *Research in the Teaching of English* 43, no. 2 (2008): 144–87.

22. Paulo Freire, *Pedagogy of the Oppressed* (New York: Continuum, 2005).

23. Emma X, unpublished professional fingerprints exercise, 2015.

24. Kyle X, unpublished letter of reflection, 2015.

25. Peter Johnston, *Choice Words: How Our Language Affects Children's Learning* (Portland, ME: Stenhouse Publishers, 2004), 11.

26. Henry Giroux, "Teachers, Public Life, and Curricular Reform," *Peabody Journal of Education* 69, no. 3 (1994), 35–47.

27. Sophie X, unpublished letter of reflection, 2015.

28. Sophie X, unpublished leadership narrative, 2016.

29. Johanna X, unpublished inquiry page, 2016.

30. Giroux, "Teachers."

31. Laila X, unpublished inquiry page, 2015.

32. Carol S. Dweck, *Mindset: The New Psychology of Success* (New York: Random House, 2006).

33. Laila, in classroom observation and informal interview by author, 2015.

34. Dawson, *The Teacher-Writer*, 4.

35. Emma X, unpublished professional fingerprints page, 2015.

36. Hicks et al., *Coaching Teacher-Writers*, 6–8.

37. Laila X, unpublished letter of reflection, 2015.

38. Achinstein and Ogawa, "(In)Fidelity."

39. Liza, unpublished "writing out of the day" exercise, 2016.

40. Marilyn Cochran-Smith and Susan L. Lytle, *Inquiry as Stance: Practitioner Research for the Next Generation* (New York: Teachers College Press, 2009); Jonas Soltis, "The New Teacher," in *Teacher Research and Educational Reform: Ninety-Third Yearbook of the National Society for the Study of Education,* ed. Sandra Hollingsworth and Hugh Sockett (Chicago: University of Chicago Press, 1994).

CHAPTER 8

1. Jocelyn Weeda, "An Open Letter to Ohio's Board of Education, Department of Education, Legislators, and Parents," *Buckeye Bats Heart of*

Education Blog Board, February 2015, https://buckeyebats.wordpress
.com/optout/.

2. James A. McLellan and John Dewey, *The Psychology of Number and Its
Applications to Methods of Teaching Arithmetic* (New York: D. Appleton
and Co., 1895), 14–15.

3. These macro discourses I am speaking of are the words, texts, and
effects that follow from the public and media discussions of education
and teachers—discussions about the teachers themselves, the teacher
unions, and the public education system as one that must be held
accountable for failing students.

4. John Dewey, *Democracy and Education* (New York: Dover Publications,
2004; repr., New York: Macmillan Company, 1916), 6.

5. Under the No Child Left Behind Act, each state is required to test
public school children in grades 3–10. FCAT is Florida's version of this
required testing.

6. Parker Palmer, *The Courage to Teach* (San Francisco: Jossey-Bass, 1998),
3.

7. Dan C. Lortie, *Schoolteacher: A Sociological Study* (Chicago: University
of Chicago Press, 1975).

8. Matt Ratto and Megan Boler, *DIY Citizenship: Critical Making and
Social Media* (Cambridge, MA: MIT Press, 2014).

9. Megan Boler, *Feeling Power: Emotions and Education* (New York: Routledge, 1999), 3–4.

10. Boler, *Feeling Power,* 6.

11. Doris A. Santoro, "Teaching's Conscientious Objectors: Principled
Leavers of High-Poverty Schools," *Teachers College Record* 113 (2011):
2670–704.

12. Jessica B. Kindred, "Bite Me: Resistance in Learning and Work,"
Mind, Culture and Activity 6 (1999), 218.

13. Kindred, "Bite Me," 198–99.

CHAPTER 9

Please note that following H. A. McKee and J. E. Porter ("The Ethics
of Archival Research," *College Composition and Communication* 64, no.
1 [2012], 75), I have chosen not to list archival sources by author's last
name. To protect the identity of the principals and department heads who
wrote observation reports, I have listed all papers pertaining to a teacher's
work by the teacher's name.

1. Principal to Mildred Flacks, January 3, 1952, box 8, folder 10, Teachers Union of the City of New York Records, 1916–1964, Kheel Center Archives, Industrial and Labor Relations Library, Cornell University.
2. Mildred Flacks, open protest letter, May 8, 1951, box 8, folder 10, Teachers Union of the City of New York Records, 1916–1964, Kheel Center Archives, Industrial and Labor Relations Library, Cornell University.
3. Clarence Taylor, *Reds at the Blackboard: Communism, Civil Rights, and the New York City Teachers Union* (New York: Columbia University Press, 2011).
4. Taylor, *Reds*.
5. Marjorie Heins, *Priests of Our Democracy: The Supreme Court, Academic Freedom, and the Anti-Communist Purge* (New York: NYU Press, 2013).
6. Sam Wallach to colleagues, 1952, TAM 241, box 1, folder 24, Robert F. Wagner Labor Archives, Tamiment Library, New York University.
7. Ibid.
8. Ibid.
9. Samuel Wallach papers, TAM 241, box 2, folder 25, Robert F. Wagner Labor Archives, Tamiment Library, New York University.
10. Principal to Stella Eliashow, April 11, 1945, box 8, folder 1, Teachers Union of the City of New York Records, 1916–1964, Kheel Center Archives, Industrial and Labor Relations Library, Cornell University.
11. Department chairman to Stella Eliashow, June 9, 1932, box 8, folder 1, Teachers Union of the City of New York Records, 1916–1964, Kheel Center Archives, Industrial and Labor Relations Library, Cornell University.
12. Alice Citron to Editor, *Christian Science Monitor*, January 5, 1974, Alice Citron papers, American Jewish Archives, Cincinnati, OH.
13. Alice Citron to Editor, *Newsday*, May 9, 1979, Alice Citron papers, American Jewish Archives, Cincinnati, OH.
14. Dorothy Rand, protest letter, November 27, 1951, box 15, folder 10, Teachers Union of the City of New York Records, 1916–1964, Kheel Center Archives, Industrial and Labor Relations Library, Cornell University.
15. Stella Eliashow to the Board of Education, April 9, 1953, box 8, folder 1, Teachers Union of the City of New York Records, 1916–1964, Kheel Center Archives, Industrial and Labor Relations Library, Cornell University.

16. Ibid.

17. Stella Eliashow to colleagues, April 21, 1953, box 8, folder 1, Teachers Union of the City of New York Records, 1916–1964, Kheel Center Archives, Industrial and Labor Relations Library, Cornell University.

18. Stella Eliashow to the Board of Education, April 9, 1953, Kheel Center Archives.

19. Mildred Flacks to superintendent, May 8, 1952, box 8, folder 10, Teachers Union of the City of New York Records, 1916–1964, Kheel Center Archives, Industrial and Labor Relations Library, Cornell University.

CHAPTER 10

1. "Marriage Equality: A Moment 65 Years in the Making," *Equality*, Late Spring/Early Summer 2015, 1.

2. Jackie M. Blount, *Fit to Teach: Same-Sex Desire, Gender, and School Work in the Twentieth Century* (Albany: State University of New York Press, 2005); Karen L. Graves, *And They Were Wonderful Teachers: Florida's Purge of Gay and Lesbian Teachers* (Urbana: University of Illinois Press, 2009); Karen M. Harbeck, *Gay and Lesbian Educators: Personal Freedoms, Public Constraints* (Malden, MA: Amethyst Press, 1997); Joyce Murdoch and Deb Price, *Courting Justice: Gay Men and Lesbians v. the Supreme Court* (New York: Basic Books, 2001).

3. Kate Rousmaniere, *City Teachers: Teaching and School Reform in Historical Perspective* (New York: Teachers College Press, 1997), 28–29.

4. Blount, *Fit to Teach*, 60–78; Katharine Bement Davis, *Factors in the Sex Life of Twenty-Two Hundred Women* (1929; repr., New York: Arno Press and New York Times, 1972); Willard Waller, *The Sociology of Teaching* (New York: John Wiley & Sons, 1932).

5. See James A. Schnur, "Closet Crusaders: The Johns Committee and Homophobia, 1956–1965," in *Carryin' On in the Lesbian and Gay South*, ed. John Howard (New York: New York University Press, 1997), 132–63; Graves, *And They Were Wonderful Teachers*; Stacy Braukman, *Communists and Perverts Under the Palms: The Johns Committee in Florida, 1956–1965* (Gainesville: University Press of Florida, 2012); Lisa Mills and Robert Cassanello, *The Committee*, produced and directed by Lisa Mills and Robert Cassanello (Orlando: University of Central Florida, 2015), DVD; Judith Poucher, *State of Defiance: Challenging the Johns Committee's Assault on Civil Liberties* (Gainesville: University Press of Florida, 2014).

6. Graves, *And They Were Wonderful Teachers*, 10–12.

7. Braukman, *Communists and Perverts Under the Palms*; see also Stacy L. Braukman, "Anticommunism and the Politics of Sex and Race in Florida, 1954–1965" (PhD diss., University of North Carolina at Chapel Hill, 1999).

8. Blount, *Fit to Teach*, 108–55; Fred Fejes, *Gay Rights and Moral Panic: The Origins of America's Debate on Homosexuality* (New York: Palgrave Macmillan, 2008); Karen Graves, "Political Pawns in an Educational Endgame: Reflections on Bryant, Briggs, and Some Twentieth-Century School Questions," *History of Education Quarterly* 53, no. 1 (February 2013): 1–20, doi:10.1111/hoeq.12000; Harbeck, *Gay and Lesbian Educators*, 39–81.

9. Richard Steele and Holly Camp, "A 'No' to the Gays," *Newsweek*, June 20, 1977, 27.

10. Cited in Murdoch and Price, *Courting Justice*, 252; see also Karen Graves, "Sexuality," in *Miseducation: A History of Ignorance-Making in America and Abroad*, ed. A. J. Angulo (Baltimore, MD: Johns Hopkins University Press, 2016), 53–72; Harbeck, *Gay and Lesbian Educators*, 83–98.

11. Cited in Murdoch and Price, *Courting Justice*, 255.

12. Blount, *Fit to Teach*, 108–34.

13. Murdoch and Price, *Courting Justice*, 176–80; Blount, *Fit to Teach*, 116–18; Harbeck, *Gay and Lesbian Educators*, 248–57.

14. Murdoch and Price, *Courting Justice*, 196–98; Blount, *Fit to Teach*, 118–20; Harbeck, *Gay and Lesbian Educators*, 258–63.

15. Cited in Harbeck, *Gay and Lesbian Educators*, 266.

16. Murdoch and Price, *Courting Justice*, 241–46.

17. Marjorie Rowland, in discussion with the Karen Graves, July 28, 2016.

18. Rowland, discussion, July 28, 2016.

19. Murdoch and Price, *Courting Justice*, 237–40; Linda Greenhouse, "Supreme Court Roundup; Case Refused for Bisexual in Loss of Job," *New York Times*, February 26, 1985, http://www.nytimes.com/1985/02/26/us/supreme-court-roundup-case-refused-for-bisexual-in-loss-of-job.html; Glen Elsasser, "Supreme Court Keeping Silent in Cases Involving Gay Rights," *Chicago Tribune*, March 4, 1985, http://articles.chicagotribune.com/1985-03-04/news/8501120683_1_supreme-court-justices-william-brennan-highest-court.

20. Marjorie Rowland, in discussion with authors, June 20–21, 2017.

21. Rowland, discussion, June 20–21, 2017.

22. Rowland, discussion, July 28, 2016.

23. Cited in Murdoch and Price, *Courting Justice*, 239.

24. Murdoch and Price, *Courting Justice*, 239.

25. Elsasser, "Supreme Court Keeping Silent." The Supreme Court took up its first gay rights case involving education, *Board of Education of Oklahoma City v. National Gay Task Force*, the next month. The difference: had they denied certiorari in that case, a pro-gay ruling would stand.

26. Rowland v. Mad River Local School Dist., Montgomery County, Ohio, 470 U.S. 1009, 1011, (1985).

27. *Rowland v. Mad River*, 470 U.S. at 1012.

28. *Rowland v. Mad River*, 470 U.S. at 1013.

29. *Rowland v. Mad River*, 470 U.S. at 1013.

30. *Rowland v. Mad River*, 470 U.S. at 1012.

31. *Rowland v. Mad River*, 470 U.S. at 1014.

32. *Rowland v. Mad River*, 470 U.S. at 1015–1017.

33. Rowland, discussion, July 28, 2016.

34. Graves, *And They Were Wonderful Teachers*, 20–49.

35. Kevin M. Cathcart, "Fast Forward," *Impact* 32, no. 3 (2015): 2; "Equality for All," *Impact* 32, no. 3 (2015): 3–5.

36. Rowland, discussion, June 20–21, 2017.

37. *"Marjorie H. Rowland v. Mad River Local School District, Montgomery County, Ohio*, 470 U.S. 1009 (1985)," *Court Listener*, accessed April 17, 2018, https://www.courtlistener.com/opinion/111388/marjorie-h -rowland-v-mad-river-local-school-district-montgomery-county/.

38. Stephen L. Sepinuck and Mary Pat Treuthart, eds., *The Conscience of the Court: Selected Opinions of Justice William J. Brennan, Jr. on Freedom and Equality* (Carbondale: Southern Illinois University Press, 1999), 126.

39. Rowland, discussion, June 20–21, 2017.

40. *Wiemann v. Updegraff*, 344 U.S. 183, 196, (1952).

CHAPTER 11

1. Adah Ward Randolph, "It Is Better to Light a Candle Than to Curse the Darkness: Ethel Thompson Overby and Democratic Schooling in Richmond, Virginia, 1910–1958," *Educational Studies* 48, no. 3 (2012): 220–43.

2. V. P. Franklin, "They Rose or Fell Together: African American Educators and Community Leadership, 1795–1954," in *The Sage Handbook*

of African American Education, ed. Linda C. Tillman (Thousand Oaks, CA: Sage Publishers, 2009), 35–54; Karen A. Johnson, *Lifting the Women and Their Race: The Educational Philosophies and Social Activism of Anna Julia Cooper and Nannie Helen Burroughs* (New York: Garland, 2003); Cynthia Nverton-Morton, *Afro-American Women of the South and the Advancement of the Race, 1895–1925* (Knoxville: University of Tennessee Press, 1989).

3. June Purcell Guild, *Black Laws of Virginia: A Summary of Legislative Acts Concerning Negroes from Earliest Times to the Present* (New York: Negro Universities Press, 1936), 12.

4. Lewis A. Randolph, "The Civil Rights Movement in Richmond, 1940–1977: Race, Class and Gender in the Structuring of Protest Activity," *Proteus* (1998): 15, 63–72.

5. James D. Anderson, *The Education of Blacks in the South, 1860–1935* (Chapel Hill, NC: University of North Carolina Press, 1988); V. P. Franklin and Carter Julian Savage, *Cultural Capital and Black Education: African American Communities and the Funding of Black Schooling, 1865 to the Present* (Scottsdale, AZ: Information Age Publishing, 2004); Heather A. Williams, *Self-Taught: African American Education in Slavery and Freedom* (Chapel Hill, NC: University of North Carolina Press, 2007).

6. Michael W. Homel, "Two Worlds of Race? Urban Blacks and the Public Schools, North and South, 1865–1940," in *Southern Cities, Southern Schools: Public Education in the Urban South,* ed. David H. Plank and Rick Ginsberg (Westport, CT: Greenwood Press, 1990), 239.

7. David R. Goldfield, *Black, White and Southern: Race Relations and Southern Culture, 1940 to the Present* (Baton Rouge: Louisiana State University Press, 1991).

8. Richmond Board of Education Minutes, Richmond Board of Education, Richmond, VA, June 1883, 101.

9. Ward Randolph, "It Is Better," 229.

10. Khaula Murtadha and Daud Malik Watts, "Linking the Struggle for Education and Social Justice: Historical Perspectives of African American Leadership in Schools," *Educational Administration Quarterly* 41, no. 4 (2005): 591–608.

11. Franklin, "They Rose or Fell Together."

12. Ward Randolph, "It Is Better," 229; Ethel T. Overby, *It Is Better to Light a Candle Than to Curse the Darkness: The Autobiographical Notes of Ethel T. Overby* (1975), 10.

13. Ward Randolph, "It Is Better," 210.
14. Adah Ward Randolph and Stephanie S. Sanders, "In Search of Excellence in Education: The Political, Academic and Curricular Leadership of Ethel T. Overby," *Journal of School Leadership* 21, no. 4 (2011): 521–47.
15. Ward Randolph, "It Is Better."
16. Ethel T. Overby, *It Is Better to Light a Candle Than to Curse the Darkness: The Autobiographical Notes of Ethel T. Overby* (1975), 5.
17. Eliza Valeria Atkins Gleason, *The Government and Administration of Public Library Service to Negroes in the South* (Chicago: University of Chicago Press, 1943); Louis Shores, "Library Service and the Negro," *Journal of Negro Education* (1932): 374–80.
18. Urban League Papers, Richmond Public Library Clipping File, 1943, 20.
19. Urban League Papers, 3.
20. Urban League Papers, 3.
21. Urban League Papers, 20.
22. *The Baltimore Afro-American,* June 8, 1947, 20.
23. *Norfolk Journal and Guide,* August 5, 1933, 1.
24. Michael Fultz, "African American Teachers in the South, 1890–1940: Powerlessness and the Ironies of Expectations and Protests," *History of Education Quarterly* 33, no. 4 (1995): 401–22; Hilton K. Kelly, "What Jim Crow's Teachers Could Do: Educational Capital and Teachers Work in Under-Resourced Schools," *Urban Review* 42 (2009): 329–50; Daniel Perlstein, "Mins Stayed on Freedom: Politics and Pedagogy in the African-American Freedom Struggle," *American Educational Research Journal* 39, no. 2: 249–77.
25. *Norfolk Journal and Guide,* December 1933, 1.
26. Ward Randolph, "It Is Better."
27. Ward Randolph, "It Is Better," 237.
28. Naomi Morse, interview by Adah Ward Randolph, Richmond, VA, June 14, 2001.
29. Overby, *It Is Better*, 11.
30. Overby, *It Is Better*, 21.
31. Nancy Robertson, *Christian Sisterhood, Race Relations, and the YWCA, 1906–1946* (Chicago: University of Illinois Press, 2007), 3
32. Ibid., p. 18.
33. YWCA Papers, Virginia Commonwealth University, M177, box 29, Richmond, VA.
34. Ward Randolph, "It Is Better."

35. Robertson, *Christian Sisterhood*, 30.
36. YWCA Papers, M177, box 9.
37. John Mitchell Brooks Collection, NAACP Archives, Virginia Commonwealth University, M296, box 2, Richmond, VA.
38. Overby, *It Is Better*, 11.
39. YWCA Papers, box 14, green scrapbook.
40. YWCA Papers, box 29.
41. YWCA Papers, box 14, 5.
42. YWCA Papers, box 27.
43. Richmond Crusade for Voters (RCV) Papers, Virginia Commonwealth University, box 1, Richmond, VA.
44. V. P. Franklin, *Black Self-Determination: A Cultural History of African-American Resistance* (Chicago, IL: Lawrence Hill Books, 1992).
45. RCV Papers, box 1.
46. RCV Papers, box 1.
47. RCV Papers, box 1.
48. Overby, *It Is Better*.
49. RCV Papers, box 1.
50. See Lewis A. Randolph and Gayle T. Tate, *Rights for a Season: The Politics of Race, Class and Gender in Richmond, Virginia* (Tennessee: University of Tennessee Press, 2003), 154–58.
51. RCV Papers, box 1; Randolph and Tate, *Rights for a Season.*
52. Virginia Union University Archives, Urban League Papers, Urban League Scrapbook; R. T. Bryant, *Black Women and Richmond: Sketches for Heritage I, Upsilon Omega Chapter, Alpha Kappa Alpha* (Richmond, VA: Virginia Historical Society Archives, 1983).
53. Ward Randolph, "It Is Better," 228.
54. Murtadha and Watts, "Linking the Struggle," 593.
55. Overby, *It Is Better*, 1.

CHAPTER 12

1. Kate Taylor, "Teachers Are Warned About Criticizing New York State Tests," *New York Times*, March 24, 2016, https://www.nytimes.com/2016/03/25/nyregion/opt-out-pressuresopen-rift-between-new-york-education-officials.html.
2. Betty Achinstein and Rodney Ogawa, "(In)Fidelity: What the Resistance of New Teachers Reveals About Professional Principles and Prescriptive Educational Policies," *Harvard Educational Review* 76, no. 1 (2006): 30–63.

3. Achinstein and Ogawa, "(In)Fidelity"; Doris Santoro, "Good Teaching in Difficult Times: Demoralization in the Pursuit of Good Work," *American Journal of Education* 188, no. 1 (2011): 1–23; Andrew Gitlin and Frank Margonis, "The Political Aspect of Reform: Teacher Resistance as Good Sense," *American Journal of Education* 103, no. 4 (1995): 377–405.

4. Paulo Freire, *Pedagogy of the Oppressed*, 30th anniversary ed. (New York: Continuum, 2000).

5. The tweeter's use of @[username] indicates that they are addressing others on Twitter directly. In turn, the author of the tweet may hope that the recipients extend the dialogue by retweeting the message to their followers.

6. See, for example, Malcolm Gladwell, "Small Change: Why the Revolution Will Not Be Tweeted," *New Yorker*, October 4, 2010; Evgeny Morozov, *The Net Delusion*, 1st ed. (New York: PublicAffairs, 2011).

7. Christopher Lutz, Christian Pieter Hoffmann, and Miriam Meckel, "Beyond Just Politics: A Systematic Literature Review of Online Participation," *First Monday* 19, no. 7 (July 7, 2014), http://firstmonday .org/ojs/index.php/fm/article/view/5260.

8. Jessica Vitak et al., "It's Complicated: Facebook Users' Political Participation in the 2008 Election," *Cyberpsychology, Behavior & Social Networking* 14, no. 3 (2011): 107–14, doi:10.1089/cyber.2009.0226.

9. On Twitter as a site of resistance and organizing, see, for example, Alexandra Segerberg and W. Lance Bennett, "Social Media and the Organization of Collective Action: Using Twitter to Explore the Ecologies of Two Climate Change Protests," *The Communication Review* 14, no. 3 (2011): 197–215, doi:10.1080/10714421.2011.597250; Zizi Papacharissi and Maria De Fatima Oliveira, "Affective News and Networked Publics: The Rhythms of News Storytelling on #Egypt," *Journal of Communication* 62, no. 2 (2012): 266–82, doi:10.1111 /j.1460-2466.2012.01630.x. On teachers' use of social media in their classrooms, see, for example, Dan Krutka, "Democratic Twittering: Microblogging for a More Participatory Social Studies," *Social Education* 78, no. 2 (2014): 86–89; Susan Meabon Bartow, "Teaching with Social Media: Disrupting Present Day Public Education," *Educational Studies* 50, no. 1 (2014): 36–64; Shanedra D. Nowell, "Using Disruptive Technologies To Make Digital Connections: Stories of Media Use and Digital Literacy in Secondary Classrooms," *Educational Media International* 51, no. 2 (2014): 109–23.

10. Kjerstin Thorson et al., "YouTube, Twitter and the Occupy Movement," *Information, Communication & Society* 16, no. 3 (2013): 421–51.

11. boyd, danah, "Why Youth (Heart) Social Network Sites: The Role of Networked Publics in Teenage Social Life," *Youth, Identity, and Digital Media: David Buckingham*, 1st ed. (Cambridge, MA: MIT Press, 2008).

12. danah, "Why Youth (Heart) Social Network Sites"; Sonia Livingstone, "Taking Risky Opportunities in Youthful Content Creation: Teenagers' Use of Social Networking Sites for Intimacy, Privacy and Self-Expression," *New Media & Society* 10, no. 3 (2008): 393–411; Dhiraj Murthy, "Twitter: Microphone For The Masses?" *Media, Culture & Society* 33, no. 5 (2011): 779–89.

13. Mizuku Ito et al., *Hanging Out, Messing Around, and Geeking Out* (Cambridge, MA: MIT Press, 2013).

14. Stephen Houser et al., "Using Clustering to Investigate Teacher Communication on Twitter" (paper presented at the International Workshop on Social Media Mining and Analysis, Exeter UK, June 2017).

15. We used two open source programs, Gephi and Tableau, to create our network visualizations.

CHAPTER 13

1. Geraldine J. Clifford, *Those Good Gertrudes: A Social History of Women Teachers in America* (Baltimore, MD: Johns Hopkins University Press, 2014).

2. James D. Anderson, *The Education of Blacks in the South, 1860–1935* (Chapel Hill, University of North Carolina Press, 1988).

3. Heather Lewis, *New York City Public Schools from Brownsville to Bloomberg* (New York, Teachers College Press, 2013).

4. Doris A. Santoro, "We're Not Going to Do That Because It's Not Right: Using Pedagogical Responsibility to Reframe the Doublespeak of Fidelity," *Educational Theory* 66, no. 1–2 (2016): 263–77; Terrenda White, "Philanthrocapitalism: Race, Political Spectacle, and the Marketplace of Beneficence in a New York City School," in *What's Race Got to Do With It? How Current School Reform Policy Maintains Racial and Economic Inequality*, eds. Bree Picower and Edwin Mayorga (New York: Peter Lang, 2015).

5. Allison Steele, "'Castle on the Hill' to Be Torn Down, New Camden School Coming in 2021," *Philadelphia Inquirer*, October 5, 2016,

http://www.philly.com/philly/education/20161006__Castle_on_the
_Hill__to_be_torn_down__new_Camden_school_coming_in_2021
.html.

6. James Baldwin, *Collected Essays*, ed. Toni Morrison (New York: Library of America, 1998), 678–86.

About the Editors

Doris A. Santoro is associate professor of education and chair of the Education Department at Bowdoin College. A philosopher of education and teacher educator, she studies professional and pedagogical ethics. She is senior associate editor for the *American Journal of Education* and has served on the board of directors of the John Dewey Society. She is the author of *Demoralized: Why Teachers Leave the Profession They Love and How They Can Stay* (Harvard Education Press, 2018).

Lizabeth Cain is an assistant professor at the State University of New York at New Paltz, where she teaches methods for teaching elementary social studies. Her research emphasizes teacher perspectives about good teaching and the cultivation of democratic and constructivist classrooms.

About the Contributors

Clive Beck is a professor in the Department of Curriculum, Teaching and Learning at the Ontario Institute for Studies in Education, University of Toronto (OISE/UT). He has held leadership positions including chair of the Chairs Council at OISE/UT, and president of the American Philosophy of Education Society.

Judy Caulfield has been a researcher in the Beck/Kosnik longitudinal study of teachers for over ten years. She brings to her research her experiences as a language arts instructor in OISE/UT's Initial Teacher Education Program, her time as a school teacher, and her activities as a storyteller.

Yiola Cleovoulou is an assistant professor in the Teaching Stream at OISE/UT, and coordinator of the MA in Education and Society Preservice Program at the Jackman Institute of Child Study. Her research interests are in the areas of critical literacy, classroom pedagogy, teacher development, and teacher education.

Margaret Smith Crocco is a professor in and chair of the Department of Teacher Education in the College of Education at Michigan State University. Her research has focused on issues of diversity, both national and international, within a social studies education context.

Karen Graves is a professor and chair of the Department of Education at Denison University. She has held leadership positions including president of the History of Education Society (USA) and vice-president of Division F: History and Historiography, American Educational Research Association.

Michelle Strater Gunderson is a twenty-nine-year teaching veteran who currently teaches first grade in the Chicago Public Schools. She is a vice-president for elementary schools for the Chicago Teachers Union, chair of the union's Education Committee, and a doctoral candidate at Loyola University in Chicago, where she studies the influence of social justice unionism on teachers' classroom practice.

Jacqueline Hesse is the founding English language arts teacher at Excelsior Academy, a New York State Pathways in Technology school in Newburgh, New York, and she serves as a teacher consultant with the Hudson Valley Writing Project. With Christine McCartney, she cofounded Global to Local, an international service-learning program for high school students, and she has volunteered extensively alongside her students in Ecuador, Cambodia, and the Hudson Valley.

Jessica Hochman is an associate professor at Pratt Institute School of Information. Her teaching and research focus on the nexus of youth culture and technology, informal literacy practices, discourses of teaching and teachers, and feminist theory and practice.

Stephen Houser is the director for academic technology and consulting at Bowdoin College and adjunct professor of computer science at the University of Southern Maine. As a technology professional and educator, he works at the intersection of computer science, technology, and the humanities.

Clare Kosnik is a professor at OISE/UT and director of the Jackman Institute of Child Study. She has been involved in many large-scale funded research projects on teaching and teacher education, including Key Components of Learning to Teach Literacy (2006–2010), Teacher Change and Growth (2010–2016), and Literacy Teacher Educators (2011–2016).

Emma Long is a recent history MA graduate from the University of New Orleans. She received her BA in English and history from Texas State University in 2013. She is employed by the San Marcos Consolidated Independent School District as a guest teacher and is currently working toward her teacher certification.

Christine McCartney started her teaching career by volunteering to tutor writing in an all-male maximum-security prison in New York through the Bard Prison Initiative. She has now been a high school English teacher for over a decade, a Fulbright alumna, and a codirector of the Hudson Valley Writing Project.

Tom Meyer is a founding director of the Hudson Valley Writing Project and an associate professor at the State University of New York at New Paltz, where he teaches curriculum and assessment, qualitative research, and literacy. Meyer has presented at the conferences of the American Educational Research Association, the National Council of Teachers of English, and the National Reading Council, and at the Penn Ethnography Conference in Education.

Randy R. Miller, Sr. is a director of a federally funded afterschool program in a school district in southern New Jersey. He was a social studies teacher for six years in charter schools in Camden, New Jersey, and is the author of the official *Urban Education Mixtape* blog. He is completing his doctoral studies at Rutgers, the State University of New Jersey, in public affairs and community development.

Margaret A. Nash is a professor at the University of California, Riverside. Her research focuses on the history of women's education in the United States, and the relationships between education and citizenship and between education and policy. Her first book, *Women's Education in the United States, 1780–1840* (Palgrave, 2005), won a Critics' Choice Award from the American Educational Studies Association. Her newest book is *Women's Higher Education in the United States: New Historical Perspectives* (Palgrave, 2018).

Lucinda Pease-Alvarez is professor emerita of education at the University of California, Santa Cruz, where she directed the teacher education program. Her scholarship has focused on the development of bilingualism and biliteracy among Latino students in home, school, and community settings. In addition, she has focused on the processes implicated in the way teachers implement educational policies, with an emphasis on how they are required to teach and assess English language learners.

Adah Ward Randolph is a professor of educational research and evaluation at Ohio University in the Patton College of Education, where she specializes in qualitative methodology. Her research has focused on African American teachers and principals in urban communities. She is a member of many professional organizations and has served in several leadership roles including the presidency of the History of Education Society.

Dwan V. Robinson is an associate professor in educational administration at Ohio University, and she holds a BA in government from Oberlin College, an MA in public policy from the University of Chicago, and a PhD in educational administration from the Ohio State University. Her research interests include educational leadership, education policy, school and community relations, the experiences of marginalized groups in education, and social justice in education.

Alisun Thompson is an assistant professor at Lewis and Clark College in Portland, Oregon. Her research focuses on the contours of the teacher workforce and the organizational conditions that attract, support, and retain teachers in schools.

Jocelyn Weeda earned her doctorate from Miami University in Oxford, Ohio. As a teacher and student advocate, she is currently working as a middle school science teacher in Ohio. She is a leader of the Ohio opt-out movement and focuses her time as a research participant with multiple teacher activist groups.

Index